THE *Ultimate* STUDENT TEACHING GUIDE

Ultimate
THE ^STUDENT
TEACHING GUIDE

Kisha N. Daniels
North Carolina Central University

Gerrelyn C. Patterson
North Carolina Central University

Yolanda L. Dunston
North Carolina Central University

SAGE

Los Angeles | London | New Delhi
Singapore | Washington DC

For information:

SAGE Publications, Inc.
2455 Teller Road
Thousand Oaks, California 91320
E-mail: order@sagepub.com

SAGE Publications Ltd.
1 Oliver's Yard
55 City Road
London EC1Y 1SP
United Kingdom

SAGE Publications India Pvt. Ltd.
B 1/I 1 Mohan Cooperative Industrial Area
Mathura Road, New Delhi 110 044
India

SAGE Publications Asia-Pacific Pte. Ltd.
33 Pekin Street #02-01
Far East Square
Singapore 048763

Printed in the United States of America

Library of Congress Cataloging-in-Publication Data

Daniels, Kisha N.
 The ultimate student teacher guide / Kisha N. Daniels, Gerrelyn C. Patterson, Yolanda L. Dunston.
   p. cm.
 Includes bibliographical references and index.
 ISBN 978-1-4129-7300-7 (pbk.)

 1. Student teaching—United States—Handbooks, manuals, etc. 2. Student teachers—Training of—United States—Handbooks, manuals, etc. I. Patterson, Gerrelyn C. II. Dunston, Yolanda Lyght III. Title.

LB2157.U5D36 2011
370.71′1—dc22   2010037772

This book is printed on acid-free paper.

10 11 12 13 14   10 9 8 7 6 5 4 3 2 1

Acquisitions Editor:	Diane McDaniel
Editorial Assistant:	Terri Accomazzo
Production Editor:	Belinda Thresher
Typesetter:	C&M Digitals (P) Ltd.
Proofreader:	Theresa Kay
Indexer:	Kathleen Paparchontis
Cover Designer:	Janet Kiesel
Permissions Editor:	Adele Hutchinson
Marketing Manager:	Erica DeLuca

Brief Contents

Detailed Contents

Preface

The need for effective teachers to prepare students for global citizenship is more urgent now than ever. Consequently, initial training for novice teachers has become even more critical to the success of teacher effectiveness. Thus, the mission of this text is to offer a guide complete with practical, yet research-based, field-tested strategies to assist novice teachers during the most pivotal experience in their teacher education or licensure program—the student teaching internship.

As veteran educators with over 30 years of combined experience teaching and supervising pre-service teachers in schools and universities, we have continuously searched for resources that will assist our students currently in the field. Although we have used several excellent texts, we have been unable to secure one with the appropriate blend of theory, practical strategies, and supplemental activities specifically designed for the student teaching internship. Also, our students expressed dissatisfaction with assignments and readings from texts during the internship. They chose, instead, to focus on completing tasks directly related to their responsibilities in the field (e.g., lesson planning, creating portfolios, studying for Praxis examinations, and applying for teaching positions). We needed a text with supplemental activities that didn't feel like "busy work;" it needed to speak directly to their current experiences in the field.

In addition, the types of pre-service teachers we were preparing began to change dramatically. A text for the traditional undergraduate student was insufficient. We needed a text appropriate for the diverse population of students we served: traditional undergraduate students, second-degree students, second-career students, lateral entry teachers seeking certification, and teacher assistants transitioning into lead teaching roles. No text seemed to address directly the unique circumstances and experiences these varying types of students brought to the internship. Plus, because these students were entering the internship with varying levels of experience in schools, we needed a text that was not only inclusive of current best practices in teaching (e.g., differentiation, technology integration, and brain-friendly teaching strategies) but also readable and accessible to diverse types of pre-service teachers.

Finally, as university supervisors of student teachers in the field, we realized we were spending an inordinate amount of time explaining issues neglected in the textbooks (legal and ethical issues, cooperating teacher conflicts, school politics, classroom management without "real" power, and more). As a result, we ceased using a text altogether and allowed the themes of our student teaching classes to emerge. Several themes consistently emerged across disciplines and grade levels: professionalism, the cooperating or mentor teacher relationship, managing the workload, stress and organization, classroom management, teacher confidence, and life after the internship. Furthermore, there was a clear correspondence between the themes discussed and the trajectory of the student teaching internship. *The Ultimate Student Teaching Guide* is a compilation of those themes.

Teacher education and licensure programs do an excellent job of preparing pre-service teachers, and this text in no way disputes the quality of these programs. Additionally, there are many excellent texts that help to prepare novice teachers. *The Ultimate Student Teaching Guide,* however, serves as a fresh approach to support a broad range of students dealing with issues and events likely to occur during the internship. Using a light-hearted tone, it candidly addresses the totality of the student teaching internship: its complexities, joys, frustrations, and challenges.

USES OF THE TEXT

This is an excellent textbook for pre-service teachers about to enter a student teaching internship or currently in an internship. It also will be useful to novice teachers in developing fundamental skills such as lesson planning, instructional strategies, classroom management, and understanding school culture. Students enrolled in alternative licensure programs will find this text useful as well. Additionally, those in nontraditional programs for preparing teachers (e.g., complete distance education instruction or distance education combined with face-to-face classes) will find *The Ultimate Student Teaching Guide* an invaluable resource that clearly explicates the universal experiences of the internship.

ORGANIZATION OF THE TEXT

The Ultimate Student Teaching Guide is divided into four parts: Part I: People, Part II: Politics, Part III: Planning, and Part IV: Performance. Part I provides readers with an overview of the *people* they will encounter during the internship, such as school personnel and the cooperating teacher (CT). School culture, legal and ethical issues, and general professionalism are addressed in Chapter 1 ("The Open House: Welcome to Student Teaching"). The relationship with the cooperating teacher is addressed in Chapter 2 ("The Teacher Conference: Meeting Your Cooperating Teacher"), which examines different types of leadership models and how they change over the course of the internship.

Part II focuses on *politics*—or the activities involved in managing the internship—including matters involving relationships, workload, and student behavior. An overview of the relationship between personality theory, strategic problem solving, and the development of a positive relationship with the cooperating teacher is presented in Chapter 3 ("The Rules: Understanding Your Cooperating Teacher"). Stress management and strategies for handling the various responsibilities that run concurrently with the internship are addressed in Chapter 4 ("The Late Bell: Managing the Workload"). A review of well-known classroom management plans and strategies for responding to management issues that arise during the internship are provided in Chapter 5 ("The Principal's Office: Classroom Management During Student Teaching").

In Part III, which focuses on *planning,* special attention is given to effective instruction. A review of assessment-based instruction, brain-friendly teaching, and technology infusion is provided in Chapter 6 ("The Planning Period: Strategies for Effective Teaching"), and fundamentals for developing sound instructional plans that meet the needs of all learners are discussed in Chapter 7 ("The Lesson Plan: Preparation and Performance").

Part IV concludes the book with an emphasis on *performance.* Readers are challenged to view student teaching as a process, to think about how that process affects self-confidence and impacts teaching assignments, and to use reflection as a tool for professional growth in Chapter 8 ("The Evaluation: Developing Confidence in Your Teaching Ability"). Finally,

guidelines for developing portfolios and resumés, studying for specialty area exams, applying for licensure, and applying for jobs are provided in Chapter 9 ("The Last STEP: Student Teacher Exit Plan").

_____ **FEATURES OF THE TEXT**

We have taken great care to write this book with the reader in mind. Over the years, we've received comments from many students about textbooks, and the feedback is always the same: "They are so boring." As a result of their feedback, we've chosen to incorporate two special features to make the text reader-friendly: a conversational tone and a visual presentation.

The reader will find that the tone of this book is less technical and more conversational than that of other textbooks. However, ample theory is interwoven into the content. There are references to the many significant educational, psychological, and social learning theories that collaborate to support and extend the objectives listed in the chapters. Furthermore, many chapter titles and headings refer to a specific school experience and/or phase.

The text is also supported by a variety of visuals (figures, checklists, pictures, diagrams, etc.) that encourage differentiated learning styles. It incorporates a glossary of professional terms that students will need to know and use, as well as an appendix of templates to help take the guesswork out of creating documents such as lesson plans and resumés.

Additionally, _The Ultimate Student Teaching Guide_ maintains the spirit of the tone by incorporating the following additional features that are similar to those in other texts, but are presented in a new format.

Letter to the Student Teacher: The reader will find these friendly letters at the beginning of every chapter. They are informal yet provide useful information about the context and contents of the chapter.

Special Feature Section: This section speaks directly to the special populations that are often overlooked (lateral entry, licensure only, teacher assistants, paraprofessionals, men, etc.). It provides specific information for these candidates whose experiences may be different from those of traditional audiences.

Bulletin Board: Bulletin boards are used to convey and present important information. Similarly, in this text, the Bulletin Board references all of the information that you need to know about a chapter. Essentially, it is the chapter summary presented to look like a bulletin board.

Extra Credit: The text is extended by suggested activities that allow the reader to further examine, reflect on, and activate content themes. Each chapter has an "Extra Credit" section; however, the activities vary. Within each section you will find these features:

Read About It. This section includes a list of web-based and traditional resources that provide additional information about methods, strategies, or research.

Think About It. By utilizing a variety of strategies that offer opportunities to reflect on the content themes and how they affect experiences, this section provides systematic methods to communicate successes, problems, and challenges.

Try It. Students will find activities, from the basic to the specific, that encourage the direct application of methodology and/or theories. The section may include worksheets or reference resources from the "Read About It" section.

Acknowledgments

This textbook would not have been possible without our student teachers. We've experienced such joy watching you develop into effective, passionate educators. Without you, we would not have stories to share. We sincerely thank you because you provide us with constant reminders of why we love teaching and learning.

Many thanks go to the cooperating teachers and university supervisors who have worked so diligently to provide nurturing and support for our student teachers. Without you, the internship would not be possible.

We also extend deep and sincere gratitude to the never-ending support of our families and friends. No one could ask for better parents, siblings, in-laws, neighbors, co-workers (the list could go on and on). We are eternally grateful for the many ways you pitched in so that we could have uninterrupted time to work on this project. Your support and encouragement are invaluable. But above all else, special thanks go to our children and husbands. While writing this book, we've received over 100,000 kisses and hugs, 5,000 caffeinated drinks, 1,000 pieces of chocolate, and 500 "I Love Mommy" pictures from our children. Priceless! And finally, to our husbands, Shan, Brandon, and Phil, thank you for being our number one fans, for believing in us, and for making it possible for us to follow our dreams.

Thank you also to the following prospectus and draft chapter reviewers:

Patrice Boyles, Chicago State University

Donna J. Cole, Wright State University

Lyman Goding, Bridgewater (MA) State College

Richard T. Scarpaci, St. John's University

Thomas J. Troisi, Hofstra University

Cindy Wilson, University of Illinois at Springfield

Jeffrey Winter, National-Louis University

PART I

People

The Open House

Welcome to Student Teaching

Dear Student Teacher,

Congratulations! You have worked really hard, and all of the late nights, presentations, papers, exams, and endless studying—not to mention the fights with your computer and hours of field experience—have finally paid off. You are ready for student teaching. It's an exciting experience filled with many unknowns. Most of you will spend at least 600 hours meeting your new "family," learning new rules, and navigating new experiences. If you aren't familiar with your placement site or your cooperating teacher, you may have asked a million questions in preparation for your first day, such as What should I wear? What will my school be like? Will I get along with my cooperating teacher? Does the cafeteria serve good food?

While these questions are all relevant, you may not have thought to ask yourself additional questions: What is the school culture? Who is the principal? What is the role of parent involvement at the school?

Every school has its own unique spoken and unspoken way of doing things. These rules can present themselves as specific policies in the teacher handbook or as vague guidelines for workplace etiquette. We've observed student teachers in many diverse schools, and some of the best student teachers struggle with this transition. So trust us when we say that you'll want to read this chapter thoroughly (we wouldn't waste your time with useless information). In our experience, understanding these politics (or at least knowing the questions to ask) can help you realize how you fit into the system and give you the steps toward a successful experience.

Sincerely,

Your School Culture Coaches

SCHOOL CULTURE

WHAT IS SCHOOL CULTURE?

The concept of *culture* refers to a group's shared beliefs, customs, and behaviors. A **school's culture** includes the obvious elements of curriculum and policies, as well as the social interactions that occur within those structures and give a school its look and feel. This look and feel might lend itself to school labels such as "friendly," "elite," "competitive," "inclusive," and so on. Some have also noted that school culture is the unwritten rules about interactions, problem solving, and decision making that give schools a "unique character," and almost everything in a school can have a set of unwritten rules about how to behave. These unwritten rules often reflect what the school and staff members care about (think mission and/or philosophy), what they are willing to spend time doing (what goes on in the classroom and parent involvement), how and what they celebrate (career accomplishments, birthdays, weddings, births, etc.), and what they talk about (the all-important school newsletter and teachers' lounge conversations).

Get on Board!

School culture is not about:

- **Race:** The categorization of humans into populations or ancestral groups on the basis of various sets of heritable characteristics
- **Socioeconomic status (SES):** A basis or measure of a person's work experience and of an individual's or family's economic and social position relative to others, based on income, education, and occupation
- **Size of the school:** The population and whether it is considered large or small
- **Religion:** A set of beliefs concerning the cause, nature, and purpose of the universe

Let's make this conversation a little more tangible. Think about your family and all of the habits, relationships, celebrations, and kitchen table conversations that make it unique. Would you dare say that your family is like every other family? Absolutely not. It may seem difficult to understand why someone's family would extend the Christmas season throughout the year (really—365 days, Christmas tree and all), or why a family would enjoy going ice fishing as a tradition on birthdays, not to mention a particular family who hurls dinner rolls instead of calmly passing around the breadbasket. Try not to judge, as it might be easy to do since their experiences might be vastly different from yours. Is this considered bad manners or just common courtesy? Would a visitor from another family instantly understand your unwritten rules? Probably not at first, but over time the family choices would become quite clear to visitors because:

1. They stay for an extended time because they agree with and appreciate your family's ideas and practices, or

2. They thank you for the evening and sneak out the back door, never to be seen again.

In either case, you would probably agree that knowing some basic elements of culture would help others understand how your family "does the things that they do."

We hope that no one will be throwing dinner rolls at you as you walk into the school cafeteria, but what they will be doing is an open question. How will you know what is valued and expected of you in the school where you will be spending the majority of your waking hours for the next 10,000 weeks? (Just kidding; the length will vary by program.) And if you find out, why does it matter?

WHY IS SCHOOL CULTURE IMPORTANT?

Have you ever heard the saying, "What you don't know might hurt you?" Well, you may want to replay this phrase as you think about the "unwritten and unspoken rules" of the school where you will complete your student teaching internship. This will be helpful as you understand and find your place in this new family. By focusing on the importance of school culture, it is our intention to give you some points to think about as you prepare for and establish yourself in the student teaching experience. Throughout this guide, you will hear us refer to the uniqueness of the student teaching experience. There is no place where the uniqueness of this experience is more apparent than in understanding how it is connected to the culture of your placement school. This sentiment is echoed by Cherubini (2008), who found that the student teaching experience is often marked by tensions relating to the difference between teacher candidates' expectations of school culture and their observed realities. He further noted that this is due mostly in part to the unique and distinctive circumstances of the student teaching practicum.

For a moment, let's discuss these unique circumstances:

- Student teachers are not paid employees of the school system,
- Student teachers are expected to fulfill the vast majority of the same responsibilities as teachers (within legal parameters),
- Student teachers are acknowledged as part of the staff, but may not be afforded the same luxuries as others,
- Student teachers are students, and
- Student teachers are also viewed as professionals (and expected to act as such).

SCHOOL CULTURE AND SCHOOL ROLES WORK TOGETHER

The student teaching experience typically puts you in a problematic spot in which you often straddle the fence (live in the two worlds) of student and teacher. In order to get over the fence, you must teach for a predetermined amount of time under the supervision of a certified teacher; thus, we now have your new title of **student teacher (ST)**. You don't have the same privileges as your **cooperating teacher (CT)** who is an experienced teacher selected to be a mentor, model, and guide, or the other teachers in the building, but you are expected to live by the same rules—whether they are spoken or unspoken. Some would say that you may be held to a higher standard since you are in a position to prove yourself, whereas the other teachers and staff have already gotten the seal of approval. They already have a signed contract for employment, and you don't. (Although, if you are a lateral entry teacher, you may have other unique circumstances that we take care to address throughout the book, so keep reading.) Since you probably didn't have the luxury of selecting the school (or the culture) of your student teaching experience, you will have to take the steps to ascertain information about the school culture and get some immediate on-the-job training as to how to fit in. Specifically, you will want to think about the ways in which the school culture dictates the following:

- The school's **mission statement**, which is a formal, short, written statement of the purpose of a company or organization (What are the academic goals? How does the school involve families?)
- The school's roles (What are the various school roles? Who does what job?)
- The school's relationships (What type of decision making is valued? How are conflicts handled?)
- The school's workplace **professionalism**, which refers to adhering to a set of values comprised of standards, obligations, formally agreed upon codes of conduct, and informal expectations (What can I wear? What is not appropriate to say in the hall?)

Consequently, how you respond to the culture will most often set the tone for how you are received and viewed as a student professional (and possibly a new hire). Of course, you won't be a student teacher forever; thus, it is also important to have a holistic perspective of school culture and take note of the impressive evidence researchers have compiled that strongly correlates positive school cultures with:

- Increased **student achievement** (an evaluation of performance based on a measurable standard),
- Increased student **motivation** (the intrinsic or extrinsic activation of goal-oriented behavior),
- Teacher productivity, and
- Teacher satisfaction.

This is important to think about as you search for schools where you would like to work in the future (we will discuss this further in Chapter 9).

ORGANIZATIONAL STRUCTURE

WHO ARE THE PEOPLE IN YOUR NEIGHBORHOOD?

School cultures may differ, but one thing that all schools have in common is an **organizational structure**. This structure is defined as the form of an organization or entities that collaborate and contribute to serve one common goal and devised to clearly define various roles and the day-to-day job responsibilities of everyone inside and outside of the school building. But if we refer back to our original discussion, you will remember that you may need to look deeper and examine the culture of your school in order to discover the unspoken roles and day-to-day tasks of each of its members. Table 1.1 provides you with a basic chart that defines the most common school roles and their corresponding tasks. Additionally, we've given you some top-secret information to help give you a complete picture of what it takes to make the school run smoothly. You'll be surprised at how much goes on behind the scenes.

Table 1.1 The School Directory

Title	Role	Additional Responsibilities (These are generalizations based on our years of experience. Specific roles and responsibilities differ at every school.)
Principal	The leader who provides guidance to teachers, students, staff, and community members (when appropriate)	• Fortune teller: Predicts the future • Juggler: Juggles many things at one time • Conflict mediator: Has to be able to resolve conflicts and counsel • Magician: Makes things appear out of nowhere • Politician: Makes sure everyone's needs are being voiced
Assistant Principal	Assists the principal in the general governance and leadership of a school	• Educational researcher: Conducts classroom observations • Detective: Solves "Whodunits" • Creative director: Supports and manages curriculum and instruction • Transportation supervisor: Facilitates and organizes the smooth transportation of precious cargo (the students)

(Continued)

(Continued)

Title	Role	Additional Responsibilities (These are generalizations based on our years of experience. Specific roles and responsibilities differ at every school.)
Secretary (VIP = Very Important Person. Secretaries tend to be in the know about everything in the school building.)	Answers telephone to provide information, take messages, and transfer calls. May order and dispense school supplies.	• Nurse: Takes care of basic medical needs • Mind-reader: Remembers everyone's names and needs • Activities director: Schedules and organizes the school calendar
Bookkeeper	Inputs, classifies, and records numerical data to keep financial records complete	• Auditor: Makes sure the financial records are in line and well organized
Counselor	Counsels individuals to help them understand and overcome personal, social, and/or behavioral problems affecting their educational or vocational situations Maintains accurate and complete student records as required by laws, district policies, and administrative regulations Confers with parents or guardians, teachers, other counselors, and administrators to resolve students' behavioral, academic, and other problems Meets with parents and guardians to discuss their children's progress and to determine their priorities for their children and their resource needs	• Social worker: Helps children or families who are experiencing a crisis (especially if the school does not have a full-time social worker) • Testing consultant: Organizes, coordinates, and supports the myriad assessments that kids have to take; makes sure that teachers are trained in new test administrations • Tour guide: Gives tours to prospective families
Teacher (includes teaching assistants)	Establishes and enforces rules for behavior and procedures for maintaining order among the students for whom they are responsible Observes and evaluates students' performance, behavior, social development, and physical health Prepares materials and classrooms for class activities Adapts teaching methods and instructional materials to meet students' varying needs and interests Plans and conducts activities to create a balanced program of instruction, demonstration, and work time that provides students with opportunities to observe, question, and investigate	• Nurse: Takes care of basic medical needs • Social worker: May be called on to help children or families who are experiencing a crisis • Event planner: Plans special projects, birthdays, coordinates assemblies, etc. • Editor: Checks lots of homework; helps students revise and edit their work • Lobbyist: Lobbies for the needs of the students, the school, and themselves • Sociologist: Carefully studies the behaviors of kids and how they form relationships (this helps teachers understand cooperative learning and playground behavior)

Title	Role	**Additional Responsibilities** (These are generalizations based on our years of experience. Specific roles and responsibilities differ at every school.)
	Instructs students individually and in groups using various teaching methods, such as lectures, discussions, and demonstrations Establishes clear objectives for all lessons, units, and projects, and communicates those objectives to students Assigns and grades classwork and homework Reads books to entire classes or small groups Prepares, administers, and grades tests and assignments in order to evaluate students' progress Confers with parents or guardians, teachers, counselors, and administrators in order to resolve students' behavioral and academic problems	• Judge: Has to hand down consequences
Cafeteria manager (VIP—if you are really nice to the cafeteria manager, you might be able to get the cookies that come right out of the oven.)	Determines production schedules and staff requirements necessary to ensure timely delivery of services Estimates amounts and costs of required supplies such as food Inspects supplies, equipment, and work areas to ensure compliance to established standards	• Event planner: Coordinates lunches for special occasions, and may need to rearrange the entire lunch schedule to accommodate special school functions • Health inspector: Serves healthy meals and ensures that the workspace is in top shape
Custodial staff (VIP—never overlook the knowledge of a well-informed custodian; plus, a custodian probably has the keys to the supply closet where the extra paper is kept.)	Keep the school building clean and in orderly working condition Inspect supplies, equipment, and work areas to ensure compliance to established standards	• Inspector: Makes recommendations to the administration for new products, designs, and other ways of making the building more efficient, and ensures that the facilities are in working order • Security specialist: Secures and protects the building
Community While not on the payroll, no one can dispute the fact that neighboring communities are a part of a school's organizational structure	Community members and activists work in the community to create positive social change in the school and surrounding the school, helping communities come together to solve problems	• Fundraiser: Helps to raise money for school needs • Writer: Writes countless letters, articles, and speeches for causes that he or she believes in • Visionary: Works for the vision of equal justice and social change

So, perhaps it really does take a village (or maybe a small army) of dedicated professionals to run a school. Now where do you fit in? The decision is totally up to you. It has often been said that student teaching is like a long job interview. Even if you do not want to be employed in that school, you will eventually want a job teaching in somebody's school and you'll need a reference. You can jump in and work for the greater good, or you can choose to stand on the sidelines and watch from afar (we do not recommend the latter). Set your sights on being a part of the team, not just in your cooperating teacher's classroom but in other aspects of the school as well. As you work toward being a team player, it is equally important to understand the legal and ethical issues that impact your profession.

LEGAL AND ETHICAL ISSUES

The impact of laws in many aspects of education has intensified since the landmark *Brown v. Board of Education* decision of 1954. It is clear that laws have carried substantial implications for teacher preparation and practice. You have spent several years in school working toward your teaching certification based on state teaching qualifications and regulations. Directly and indirectly, laws influence the learning environment for children and the adults who teach them. Moreover, whether you agree or disagree with the current educational laws (and policies), as a teacher, realize that they shape what you can and cannot do within the educational environment.

DEFINITIONS OF IMPORTANT TERMS

Interestingly, we found that although there have been a few (relatively minor) laws dealing with student teachers, overall, the majority of the legal problems that student teachers might face are the same ones that affect the entire profession. So our conversations in this section will largely pertain to general **legal** (concerning the protections that laws or regulations provide) and **ethical** (concerning what is moral or right) issues in teaching. Any good lawyer would tell you that you can't begin until everyone has all of the facts, so let's get on the same page with the terms and definitions that we will be using.

- *Legal* (lee-guhl), adjective: Permitted by law; of or pertaining to law; connected with the law or its administration; appointed, established, or authorized by law; deriving authority from law.
- *Law* (l-au), noun: A system of rules enforced through a set of institutions. It shapes politics, economics, and society in numerous ways and serves as a primary social mediator of relations between people. Also, any written rule or collection of rules prescribed under the authority of the state or nation, as by the people in its constitution.
- *Ethics* (e-th-iks), noun: The rules or standards governing the conduct of a person or the members of a profession.
- *Ethical* (e-th-ik-ul), adjective: Concerning a set of principles of conduct or a theory or system of moral values.
- *Issue* (ish-oow), noun: Any matter of dispute in a legal controversy or lawsuit.

LEGAL VS. ETHICAL

Now that we've presented the definitions of the terms that are most commonly used, we'd like to spend a moment discussing the distinct differences. It is most often the case that people tend to use words such as *legal* (or *the law*) and *ethical* (or *ethics*) interchangeably, but they are in fact quite different. They are separate concepts and are not dependent upon each other. Laws are enacted by an authority, whereas ethics attempt to determine morals. Ethical issues have no force of law to uphold them, but they can affect the society around you. However, depending upon the law, what is legal may also be construed as unethical (e.g., slavery).

Most licensing, professional institutions have enacted ethics to which their members must adhere. This is most often a direct result of the culture of the professional community. Violations of the ethical culture are not criminally actionable, but you can be penalized according to the contract you have signed and/or even expelled from the organization. Simply put, don't break the law and don't act in an unethical manner. A violation of either the law or ethics will more than likely result in losing your job. We will address some of the most common ethical violations in the Workplace Professionalism section below, but first let's review some legal history in the field of education.

A History Lesson

Here are some landmark decisions that have affected teaching. It is important to take this brief journey, as the decisions of these cases have shaped the teaching profession. In an effort not to bore you with legal jargon, we have provided this information for you in a handy reference chart. Table 1.2 summarizes some of these historic cases and explains how they may affect your day-to-day teaching experiences. Of course, this list is not inclusive of every major decision, but we felt that it was important to highlight the big ones.

Table 1.2   Landmark Education Cases

Landmark Education Case/Legislation	Why It Matters to You	What You Should Do
Brown v. Board of Education (1954) Issue: Should Blacks and Whites receive an education integrated with or separate from each other? The U.S. Supreme Court declared that state laws establishing separate public schools for Black and White students and denying Black children equal educational opportunities are unconstitutional. Chief Justice Warren said the Court concluded that in the United States "the doctrine of 'separate but equal' has no place. Separate educational facilities are inherently unequal."	While some critics have argued that the Brown decision did more to help other institutions and left the schools largely where they were in 1954, others would say that the spirit of the law has moved people to be catalysts for social justice and change. It helped to shed light on the things that you can change within your own classroom, school system, and state.	The issues surrounding equity in the schools are very large (achievement gaps, disproportionate funding that relies on property taxation, teacher quality, etc.), and many are out of the hands of teachers, but you can make a difference. Make a pledge to be an advocate for the students in your class. Work through your local teacher associations to say the things that some of your students and their families cannot. Do the hard work of making high-quality education nonnegotiable for all students, regardless of race, gender, or creed.
Florence County School District Four v. Carter (1993) IDEA (Individuals with Disabilities Education Act) (1990) Issue: Should public schools be held accountable for teaching children with exceptionalities and disabilities?	Children who have disabilities and/or exceptionalities in your classroom are your responsibility, regardless of any additional staff working to support and facilitate their education. If they are in your class, you must work to design instructional strategies to meet their needs.	What you should do if you suspect that a child has an exceptionality: Talk to your CT. Ask about the process for identification.

(Continued)

(Continued)

Landmark Education Case/Legislation	Why It Matters to You	What You Should Do
Shannon Carter had dyslexia, which compromised her school performance. In desperation, her parents placed her in a private school for disabled children, where she jumped several grade levels within a few years and graduated reading on grade level. The Carters then sued the school system for the private school tuition they'd paid. At the time, the law limited the school choice of parents with disabled children to state-approved schools. In this case, however, the court ruled that the school system failed to provide an "appropriate public education." IDEA governs how states and public agencies provide early intervention, special education, and related services to more than 6.5 million eligible infants, toddlers, children, and youth with disabilities. The act has been reauthorized and amended a number of times, most recently in December of 2004. Other documents often associated with this law include Americans with Disabilities Act (ADA, especially Section 504); Education for All Handicapped Children Act (EAHCA) (PL 94-142); Free Appropriate Public Education (FAPE); Individualized Education Program (IEP) (PL 99-142); Least Restrictive Environment (LRE)	Every local education agency (LEA) has a method for identifying and supporting children with exceptionalities.	Observe the child. Take detailed and objective notes. Revisit your textbooks (or consult new books) that focus on strategies for working with children with special needs.
Norwalk Teachers' Association v. Board of Education (1951) Issue: Do teachers have the right to organize and/or strike? Should the Board of Education recognize the Teachers' Association as the bargaining agent? Are arbitration or mediation acceptable methods? Dispute over salaries involving stalwart negotiations between the Teachers' Association and the Board of Education led to a legal decision that prohibited public employees' method of conflict resolution. (It's important not to confuse striking with protesting. Striking is leaving work or stopping work as a coercive	It is a given that during your long, happy career as a teacher, you might have a dispute with someone else in the organization. If and when this happens, be glad that you can go to your local or national teacher association. This law helped to support the creation of local, state, and national teacher organizations as well as solidify their place in aiding teachers through myriad issues.	Teacher associations work hard on your behalf. Their roles include (but are not limited to) grassroots efforts involving collective bargaining for better pay, workloads, and working conditions; and they use negotiations, arbitrations, and mediation to achieve their purposes. But in order to take advantage of all that these organizations have to offer, there are some things that you have to do:

Landmark Education Case/Legislation	Why It Matters to You	What You Should Do
measure, whereas protesting is making a formal declaration of disapproval or objection; both can involve a concerned person, group, or organization.) The court held that since government is established by and run for all people (not for the benefit of any one person or group), to strike is a contradiction. A strike by public employees is in effect a strike against the government and hence goes against public policy.		Find out more about teacher organizations, associations, and unions. Locate your local, state, and national representatives. Decide which organization is best for you.
New Jersey v. T.L.O. (1985) Issue: Can schools search students' possessions? T.L.O. was 14 years old at the time that she was caught smoking cigarettes in a public school bathroom. When she denied the accusation, the assistant principal demanded to see the contents of her purse. Inside he found not only a pack of cigarettes but rolling papers, marijuana, and a list of names of students who owed her money. T.L.O. was later charged with drug dealing. Her family argued that the school was unlawful in their search of T.L.O.'s property. However, the U.S. Supreme Court stated that searches and seizures may be conducted by school officials based upon "reasonable suspicion."	The assistant principal probably looks back on that search and seizure and is thankful that there was enough evidence to make a case, because without it, he would have lost his job. The moral to this story is, make sure that you have a good reason to search a student's locker, person, book bag, clothes, etc. Your suspicion of "Well, she just looked guilty" will not cut it.	If you have a suspicion that a student has done something or has something harmful, take the following precautions: Notify the school building administration immediately. If it is not an emergency, make sure to document and date everything that you notice.
Tinker v. Des Moines (1969) Issue: Do students have First Amendment protection at school? To protest the Vietnam War, Mary Beth Tinker and her brother wore black armbands to school. Fearing a disruption, the administration prohibited wearing such armbands. The Tinkers were removed from school when they failed to comply, but the Supreme Court ruled that their actions were protected by the First Amendment. The court's 7-to-2 decision held that the First Amendment applied to public schools, and that administrators have to demonstrate constitutionally	Yes, students do have rights that are protected under the Constitution! They have a right not only to think differently than you but to voice their opinions as well. Moreover, it is your responsibility as a teacher to encourage your students to engage in conversation that is supportive of diverse viewpoints.	How can you support this decision in your classroom? Get to know your students and find out what makes them special. Offer multiple ways for students to share their thoughts and ideas (suggestion box, community meeting, webcast, etc.). Incorporate debate techniques as a regular part of your instruction.

(Continued)

(Continued)

Landmark Education Case/Legislation	Why It Matters to You	What You Should Do
valid reasons for any specific regulation of speech in the classroom. As Justice Fortas put it, "In order for school officials to justify censoring speech, they must be able to show that [their] action was caused by something more than a mere desire to avoid the discomfort and unpleasantness that always accompanies an unpopular viewpoint."		
Title IX of the Education Amendments (1972) Issue: Should institutions that limit gender equality receive federal funds? Although Title IX is best known for its impact on high school and collegiate athletics, the original statute made no explicit mention of sports. Title IX of the Civil Rights Act of 1964 says that any institution receiving federal funding may not discriminate against anyone based on gender. The legislation covers all educational activities and complaints under Title IX alleging discrimination in fields such as science and math education and in other aspects of academic life such as access to health care and dormitory facilities. It also applies to other extracurricular activities, including school band and clubs; however, social fraternities and sororities, sex-specific youth clubs (Girl Scouts and Boy Scouts) are specifically exempt from Title IX requirements.	If nothing else, this law should make you think twice about how you work toward gender equality in your classroom (and school).	Ask yourself these questions: Do I have any gender biases that I need to face and change in order to be a better teacher? Do I equally call on all of my students? Do my class and school offer academic opportunities for underrepresented populations?
The Child Abuse Prevention and Treatment Act (PL 93-247) (1974) Issue: Should states be mandated to provide funding for the prevention of the welfare of children? This key federal legislation addressing child abuse and neglect provides federal funding to states in support of prevention, assessment, investigation, prosecution, and treatment activities; it also provides grants to public agencies and nonprofit organizations for demonstration programs and projects. All 50 states have passed some type of mandatory legislation that requires certain professionals and institutions to report suspected child abuse. These include (but are not limited to) health care providers, mental health care providers, teachers and other school personnel, social workers, day care providers, and law enforcement personnel. The act, originally passed in 1974, has been amended several times and was most recently amended and reauthorized on June 25, 2003, by the Keeping Children and Families Safe Act of 2003 (P.L.108-36).	This one is a no-brainer—it is your legal and ethical responsibility as a teacher to report any suspected abuse of a child. This extends not only to children who are in your classroom but also to others who attend the school.	If you have a suspicion it is best to do the following: Take your concerns to your CT, administrator, school counselor, or school social worker. Document and date everything that you notice.

SOURCE: United States Courts, http://www.uscourts.gov/EducationalResources/ConstitutionResources/LegalLandmarks/LandmarkSupremeCourtCasesAboutStudents.aspx

_____ **WORKPLACE PROFESSIONALISM**

So far in this chapter, we have walked you through an overview of school culture and its importance to your role as a student teacher, unmasked the hidden roles of school professionals, and given you an overview (or maybe a review) of the major legal and ethical issues involved in teaching. Never is an understanding of these concepts more important than when it comes to professionalism. This term is defined as the ability to adhere to a set of values that are comprised of standards, obligations, formally agreed upon codes of conduct, and informal expectations. Think about your attire, how you carry yourself, your attitude, and how you interact with others. Typically, these issues revolve around a common understanding (sometimes unspoken but, if you're lucky, spoken) about expectations. Remember, culture in the workplace may have less to do with art, music, and literature than with shared belief systems, expected effort, and behavior expectations. This definitely includes such things as dress codes, socialization expectations, how the group feels about attendance, work output, problem solving, and so on.

Additionally, these expectations are also closely linked to _principles of professional ethics,_ which are defined as "the norms, values and principles that should govern the professional conduct of a teacher" (Strike & Ternasky, 1993, p. 3). Now, before you begin the internship, we have to make sure that you don't overlook some obvious details that, if not observed, might jeopardize the first impressions you make. We want to ensure that you're not at risk of making a negative impression that can hurt your career, but we certainly don't want this to turn into a boring review section of dos and don'ts; so, as your school culture coaches, we'd like to offer a fresh perspective on the tried-and-true rules.

𝕹𝖊𝖜𝖘 𝖸𝖔𝖚 𝕮𝖆𝖓 𝖀𝖘𝖊
WHAT TO WEAR

It has been a long time since teachers dressed in their Sunday best to teach in a school. Nowadays, most schools are pretty casual, which can sometimes present a problem. With the freedom of being able to dress casually comes the responsibility of being able to maintain a professional work environment. Everything is not for everybody (even if it is the latest fad) and certain things are best left in your closet (even if your friend or mother tells you that you look fabulous in it). Let's be honest. Do your co-workers really need to see you in tight pants (yes, guys, this is also for you, too), a miniskirt, or plunging neckline? Come on! Not only does it look unprofessional, it is inappropriate. On the other hand, sweats or overly baggy pants and a T-shirt that says, "Where's the Party?" or "I Love Beer" shouldn't be worn at your job. What you wear to work makes an individual statement about you that communicates your professionalism to others. Wearing something to work that you would wear to a nightclub on Friday night or for a weekend stroll at the beach says that your free time is more important than or indiscernible from your job.

Be mindful of the dress code that the school culture dictates in the building. If one hasn't been presented to you, take clues from the teachers you work with (or just ask). If your CT wears a suit every day, that doesn't necessarily mean you have to, but it most likely means that you should dress nicely. Now we're not saying that you need to go out and spend a lot of money on a new wardrobe. Some simple understated pieces can carry you through the semester. Add flair with your personality, not with your wardrobe. You always hear "Dress for success" and "Dress for the job you want, not the job you have." As cheesy as those may sound, they couldn't be truer. Save your casual dress for when you've got the job. Until that time—dress like you want someone to offer you a job.

TOP 10 RULES OF CONDUCT

These are things you should *never* hear during your student teaching experience:

1. "You left your Facebook page up for the kids to read."

   Don't use the school day to advance your personal activities.

2. "Can you please take that cell phone call outside?"

   Put your phone on silent or vibrate when you come into the building.

3. "Are you dating my mom?"

   Keep your relationships with your students and their families on a professional level.

4. "Where is your lesson plan?"

5. "You overslept again?"

   Always be prepared and punctual.

6. "Did you forget to proofread this before you sent it home?"

   Go beyond spell check when using written communication (proofread it yourself or ask your CT for help).

7. "Did you hear about Mr. Jones and Mrs. Kelly?"

   Don't feed into the rumor mill. This extends to verbalizing generalizations about children based on prior experiences with their siblings or family members.

8. "My husband heard your name on the police scanner on Saturday."

   Don't break any laws.

9. "My 10-year-old daughter has that shirt."

   Dress professionally.

10. "I'm sorry, I thought that you were the custodian."

    Know all of the players.

THE DOCTOR IS IN . . .

Dear Doc,

My CT's team member is so rude. It's gotten to the point that I just have stopped trying to be nice. My CT just seems to know how to deal. They plan and teach a lot together so it's not like I can stay away from him. I don't want to blow my top, but I am on the edge.

Sincerely,
HELP!

Dear HELP,

I'm glad you sought out my advice before you lost your temper. It seems as though you need to take a page from your CT's book of cool. He obviously has had some practice when it comes to working with lots of different people. While I can't tell you what to say, I can offer some tips to help you focus on what matters most.

Look for the positive

Strive to understand and value other people's opinions and differences

Listen carefully

Try not to interrupt

Don't overreact (much harder to say than to do)

Know your boundaries/limits

When in doubt. . . . Smile

Sincerely,

Doc

According to a Yahoo! Hot Jobs and Banana Republic survey (2007), 82% of HR managers and directors agree that the way you dress directly affects the prospect of getting hired, retaining your position, and/or getting a promotion.

TRANSITIONING INTO YOUR NEW ENVIRONMENT

We know that you have a lot on your plate right now, but forgetting to **transition** (moving from one thing to another) into the school culture could be detrimental to your success as a student professional. Transitions are important. You would never ask your students to move from one activity to another without planning for a transition, so why should you be any different? You can make a successful transition by better understanding how everything works together; this will help connect you to the school community. The alternative to this adaptation is to stick out like a sore thumb, or give the impression that you really don't want to get to know (or care about) your new community. When you find a way to link transitioning ideas into the phase-in schedule dictated by your teacher licensing and/or certification program, also referred to as your **teacher education program (TEP)**, the ideas will support your student teaching experience. We give you additional activities on this topic in the "Extra Credit" section below (you will find these to be most helpful if your internship site is unfamiliar or if you've had limited experience at your placement site).

FINAL THOUGHTS

You are now armed with important information to help you get started on your student teaching journey. As you begin your internship, consider how school culture and organizational structure work together. They really go hand in hand to make your placement unique. The outcome of the relationship between the school culture and the organization will determine many spoken and unspoken rules regarding workplace professionalism. Yet, some rules are the direct result of legal policies. Now that you understand the concepts, it's time to put your best foot forward. In the next chapter, we'll be introducing you to your CT, so go out, take what you've learned, and make your first impression the best.

BULLETIN BOARD

The Open House: Welcome to Student Teaching

School Culture

School culture refers to a school's shared beliefs, customs, and behaviors. School cultures are typically exemplified by unspoken or unwritten rules. These unwritten rules often reflect what the school and its members care about. The student teaching experience is unique, and it is important for you to understand a school's culture in order to be able to transition into a successful experience.

Legal and Ethical Issues

Many landmark, historic cases helped to shape the way that we teach and interact with students, staff, and administration in schools. As a teacher, it is important for you to know the difference between the legal and ethical responsibilities of the profession.

Organizational Structure

Every school has an organizational structure. Often the employees do much more than their job title leads us to believe. It is important to understand the different school roles, how they work together, and how you fit in. Take the time in the beginning of your internship to transition into your new surroundings.

Workplace Professionalism

Always remember that professionalism is determined by the school's culture. Take this into account as you make appropriate etiquette choices, as the right decisions will make a great first (and last) impression.

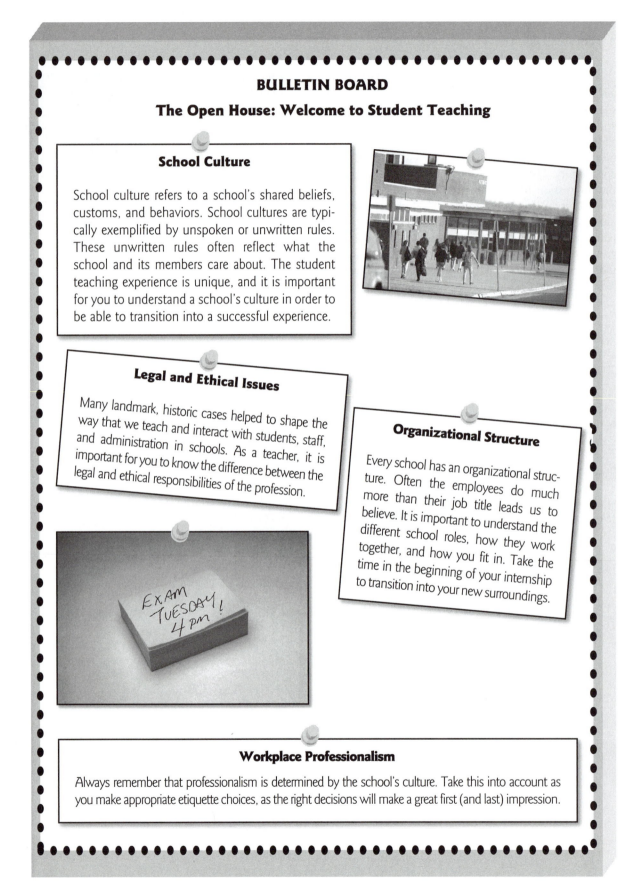

EXTRA CREDIT

READ ABOUT IT

School Culture

> The Center for Improving School Culture
> www.smallschoolsproject.org/PDFS/culture.pdf

Legal and Ethical Issues

> http://www.streetlaw.org/en/landmark.aspx
> http://www.uscourts.gov/outreach/resources/landmark_studentcases.htm
> http://everything2.com/title/Important+Landmark+Cases+in+Educational+Law
> National Education Association's (NEA) Code of Ethics of the Education Profession: http://www.nea.org

Workplace Professionalism

Are You Primed for a Promotion? Check Your Wardrobe First: http://yhoo.client.shareholder.com/releasedetail.cfm?

THINK ABOUT IT

Understanding School Culture

The following section includes artifacts from two schools that have taken great strides to connect their school culture and mission statements to their school activities. Artifact 1 is from the Met and Artifact 2 is from the Academy of the Pacific Rim. Review the following school profiles and/or artifacts and ask yourself the following questions:

- What values and expectations are respected at this school?
- How has the school attempted to communicate these values and expectations to the community (students, staff, faculty, parents, etc.)?

1. The MET: http://www.bigpicture.org

2. Academy of the Pacific Rim: http://pacrim.org

   A middle school begins each day by publicly honoring a student who has demonstrated a *gambatte* spirit. This word, taken from Japanese education, indicates that opportunity is not due to luck or happenstance, but to effort, diligence, and perseverance. Students participate in daily community meetings, wear student uniforms, and enroll in Mandarin Chinese language classes beginning in the seventh grade. Students also participate in cleaning the school and their classrooms. Students and staff clean desks, sweep floors, take out the trash, sweep stairs, clean bathrooms, and pick up trash around the grounds of the school. In addition to the progress report, a journal is sent home with each student at the end of each week outlining major events that have gone on at the school. It also contains information about student achievement and reminders to parents of upcoming events. Parents/guardians must sign the Reply Form every week to indicate that they have read the journal and have seen their child's progress report. The Reply Form also provides space for comments or questions for teachers and/or advisors. Families are encouraged to call or e-mail teachers or staff when questions or concerns arise.

3. Now focus on your student teaching placement site and answer the following question: How does the school use expectations, traditions, celebrations, scheduling, and physical space to support and reinforce the culture?

School Culture Element	Evidence
Ex. Traditions and celebrations	My school recognizes each child's birthday by announcing his or her name over the PA system and giving the child a pencil. The birthdays of teachers and staff are posted on the school calendar and are celebrated with a cake in the teachers' lounge at the end of the month. This shows that the school really values and sets aside time to recognize the kids and people who work in the building.

Legal and Ethical Issues

Read this case study and answer the questions that follow it.

CASE STUDY

Gail is very excited about beginning her student teaching placement. She is hoping she will receive a job offer in the district (or school) where she is completing her student teaching internship. This also happens to be the same town that she grew up in, as well as the same district where she received her education. In fact, she knows most of the teachers and students in the building. She has even worked out a transportation schedule with a couple of the teachers in the building who are friends of her older sister. They will bring her to school, and her boyfriend will pick her up. Because she is saving money for a car, Gail has decided that in spite of the long hours during the day, she will keep her job at a restaurant and just switch her shifts to the evenings. Her boss has already agreed to it, and she is confident that she has thought of everything.

As the semester gets under way, Gail's cooperating teacher, Mr. Jones, notices that she doesn't seem to be available to meet as often as he would like. He would like to meet after school in order to plan for the following day or week, but Gail is always rushing out of the school to get to work. Additionally, Gail is observed yawning throughout the day and is constantly sending a student to the lounge to refill her coffee mug. Her lesson planning has dropped off considerably as well, and she just doesn't seem to be prepared to teach.

To add to these issues, Mr. Jones has noticed other behaviors that concern him. For example, Gail is typically seen talking to her friends (other teachers at the school) while the children are on the playground during recess, rather than interacting with the children. When she takes the students to the computer lab, instead of instructing them, she surfs the web. She also has been overheard telling the children that if they don't complete their work, they will not have snack or recess, and she has been caught gossiping about students' families and other teachers at the school. Mr. Jones is very disappointed in her performance thus far. He sees that she has a lot of potential, but he is concerned by her lack of professional ethics.

Questions

1. List some possible reasons to explain Gail's behavior.

2. After reading the National Education Association's Code of Ethics of the Education Profession listed in the "Read About It" section, answer the following question: Does Gail's behavior violate any of the principles? If so, which one/s?

3. What would you say to Gail if you were Mr. Jones?

SOURCE: Adapted from (bigpicture.org). Reprinted article by Ron Wolk. Wolk, R. "Education: The Case for Making It Personal." *Educational Leadership.* 67, 7 (April 2010): 16–17.

TRY IT

What Are the Expectations?

Use this worksheet as a planning tool to outline and understand your CT's expectations and to develop strategies for addressing them during your student teaching internship. The worksheet provides you with one as an example, and there are additional spaces for you and your CT to design expectations that may not be on the worksheet. This activity is particularly helpful to complete during the first week of the internship.

Expectation	My CT expects me to . . .	I will do the following . . .
Dress attire	Dress in comfortable clothes that are not too tight or revealing and do not have suggestive language. And follow her recommendation that I not wear very high heels, as I will be responsible for taking the kids outside during recess and participating in games with them.	Make sure that I have the appropriate attire that also looks good with low-heeled shoes or sneakers.
	Fridays are school spirit days and everyone wears the school colors or school T-shirts.	If necessary, purchase a school T-shirt or see what clothes I have that have the school colors.
Time management		
Planning		
Instructional strategies		
Classroom management		
Technology integration		
Exceptional children		
Family involvement		
Professional development		
Extra school duties (staff meetings, curriculum nights, PTA meetings, etc.)		

Transition Checklist

Sunday: Get ready for a walk around the block.

Spend some time before your first day of work thinking about how you will transition into your new surroundings. Start by making a great first impression.

Write a brief narrative about yourself. It should be four or five sentences. Include information about your interests outside of school, where you are from, your family, your pets, and so on. Make sure to end with how excited you are about being a part of the school community.

(Continued)

(Continued)

Monday: Meet the neighbors (school and clerical staff).

This is no time to be shy. Begin your first week with a smile and a firm handshake.

Make a special trip to the front office and introduce yourself to all of the office staff.

Deliver your narrative (via mailboxes) to every staff, faculty, and PTA member.

Stop by the office of the principal or assistant principal to set up an appointment for Friday.

Tuesday: Meet the neighbors (teachers).

Find out more about the school's mission and professionalism policies and what is valued at the school.

Ask your CT how the school engages the community, families, and businesses in the goals and objectives of the school.

Ask a teacher at your grade level the following question: "If testing were not an issue, what would you spend most of your time teaching?"

Talk to your CT about the school's dress policy. Ask specifically about any dos and don'ts.

Wednesday: Meet the neighbors (custodial and cafeteria staff).

Take the time to celebrate and show your new neighbors that you value their daily contributions.

Buy a few cards or have your class make a special card or picture for the custodial and cafeteria staff to show your appreciation for all that they do (clear this with your CT first). Present it to them personally (you may have to re-introduce yourself).

Thursday: Meet the neighbors (the community).

With the support of your CT, prepare a letter of introduction to send home with your new students. Don't forget to proofread it before you send it home—better yet, let someone else read it.

Friday: Meet the neighbors (administrator/s).

Ask the following questions during your meeting with the school building administrator/s. This will help you to gain a more substantive understanding about the school culture.

What is the mission of the school/district?

What type of decision-making structure is valued at the school?

How does the school recognize celebrations and traditions?

What advice can they offer you?

Saturday: R&R (rest and reflect).

Think about all of the new information that you have learned. How will it support your student teaching experience? Are there additional questions that you would like to ask? Who would have the answers?

The Teacher Conference

Meeting Your Cooperating Teacher

Dear Student Teacher,

We know how excited you are about meeting and getting to know your CT. This could potentially be a long-lasting mentoring relationship and friendship. By this point you have had a lot of time to visualize the student internship from where you stand. But have you ever stopped to think about this experience from your CT's position? We are lucky to have had experiences on both sides of the fence, and it is really true what they say—you never know someone until you've walked a mile in their shoes. As student teachers, we had experiences that made us want to laugh and cry. However, we had many "aha" moments after we became supervisors. The opportunities to mentor, coach, and facilitate learning for new student teachers were never ending. We haven't yet decided unanimously on which role is more difficult—being a student teacher or a cooperating teacher.

Understanding your CT's role in this process will help you to gain a better perspective on the time and effort that goes into the job (and don't forget—your CT will still have to teach).

Your cooperating teacher is one of the most important participants in your internship. In order to start things off right, there must be mutual understanding and respect. Get ready to thank your CT in advance for the guidance and direction that he or she will unselfishly offer you during your last phase of this incredible journey.

Sincerely,

Your Merry Matchmakers

IT'S NICE TO MEET YOU

Have you ever been on a blind date? Perhaps a friend or co-worker thought you might really hit it off with someone they knew. Or, perhaps your blind date was the result of an online dating service that matches people based on their personality profiles. Regardless of the method, once a date is agreed upon, you anxiously anticipate the meeting, hoping to make a love connection. If you recall this blind date scenario, you certainly remember those anxious feelings where you hoped the person would be funny and attractive—and would think you were the perfect date.

For many of you, meeting your cooperating teacher has sort of been like being fixed up on a blind date. The ideal situation is when someone who knows you, (preferably the person who is employed by the university to supervise you), a **university supervisor (US)**, thinks you would be a good match for someone he or she knows well. As you prepared for that first meeting, you hoped the person would be a great teacher, while also being kind, funny, and helpful. You also hoped he or she would like you and think you were a well-prepared, natural-born teacher.

However, just like a blind date, while the meeting can turn out to be the start of a wonderful, long relationship, it also has the potential to go awry (sometimes the match just isn't what you envisioned). It doesn't happen often, but when it does (and everyone survives the experiences with smiles), it is always worth sharing the funny tales. This was actually the case for us during our student teaching. As you read on, we'd like to note that no cooperating teacher's feelings were hurt during the writing of this chapter. All the names have been changed to protect the innocent. For the sake of anonymity, we'll refer to the STs as Larry, Curly, and Moe. Remember *The Three Stooges*, 1935–1959 (http://www .threestooges.com/)? You may be thinking that these names are odd choices, but the definition of a *stooge* is "one who plays a compliant role," so the names actually fit quite well. Larry had a cooperating teacher who handed over a class of first graders to him during the first week of the internship. The CT was present and supportive, but didn't hover; he encouraged Larry to think of and implement his own ideas for teaching and classroom management—quite a different approach for Larry, who typically preferred to be told exactly what he should be doing all of the time. Larry was in a split internship, in which midway through the semester he moved to a different class in a different grade level with a different CT—who also "allowed" him to figure out what to do on his own.

Curly's cooperating teacher was the ultimate warm fuzzy teacher. Like a fairy godmother, she was always positive, in a perpetual good mood, and syrupy sweet. Even when Curly's efforts required constructive criticism, his CT kindly flipped the feedback into a positive (and from Curly's perspective, less than useful) comment. This CT was quite the overachiever, as well. She wouldn't allow Curly to use "store bought" resources—he had to create all of his supplemental material from scratch. He wasn't even allowed to show a video, unless of course he'd made it himself. This posed a bit of a problem for Curly, who would have happily stocked up on Carson-Dellosa materials in order to have a life outside of student teaching. (For those of you who are unfamiliar with Carson-Dellosa, they are one of the leading publishers of affordable supplemental educational materials in the United States [see www.Carson-Dellosa.com]).

Moe's cooperating teacher required him to wear a suit or dress coat and pants (and this was during his surfer phase), asked that he cut his hair super short, and required him to refer to all students by their last names. The CT said that Moe's youthful appearance (along with his California good looks) wouldn't allow the kids to take him seriously. Not wanting to make waves (no pun intended), Moe called his mom for money, went to the local department store, and bought three pairs of dress pants, two jackets, two shirts, and a couple of extra ties—which he rotated for 15 weeks. Once the semester was over, he tossed them to the back of his closet and pulled out his swim trunks and Vans.

Even though these relationships had their challenges, there were many valuable lessons that were learned from them. Larry discovered he had the content knowledge and pedagogical skills to be an effective teacher and that he *could* teach with minimal guidance. Curly learned how to create engaging materials and activities to address the needs of specific students rather than relying on purchased supplements that appeal to the mass market. Moe learned how appearance can hinder or help in creating a professional, authoritative demeanor in the classroom. (He eventually decided khakis and oxford shirts might be more appropriate than shorts and T-shirts in the classroom.)

We all learned something from our relationships with our CTs, even though they clearly were not perfect matches (we are your Merry Matchmakers, not your Perfect Matchmakers). Although we will offer you many tips throughout this chapter, two essentials that we all learned from our student teaching experiences were (1) it is important to stay focused, and (2) continue to look for the positives.

_____ DO I HAVE TO?

You're probably wondering why you even need a cooperating teacher. You know your content, you've taken all of your education classes, and you've spent a great deal of time observing, tutoring, and volunteering in the schools. You're ready to use what you know. But, let's be honest. Even though you're pretty confident that you have what it takes (you wouldn't have made it through your teacher education program if you didn't), you're probably a little nervous about tackling all of the responsibilities that come with teaching. The truth is, you should be nervous. These are real children you are working with. Would you want a pilot flying your plane that had never trained with an experienced pilot or flown a real plane? Would you want a doctor operating on you who hadn't practiced with an experienced surgeon? Would you want a hairstylist cutting your hair who had only cut doll's hair? Do you get the idea? Tackling the daily demands that come along with teaching is a daunting task for even the most seasoned of teachers. Educational policy makers and teacher education programs know this, so the **student teaching internship**, which is characterized by a specific number of weeks spent teaching under the supervision of a certified teacher and US, has a built-in checks and balances system to ensure that you have the proper guidance to help you successfully navigate the challenges that will arise. This checks and balances system is known to most as a **standard**. Standards are important as they serve as the basis for comparison against which other things can be evaluated.

In the world of education, standards and NCATE are synonymous. The **National Council for Accreditation of Teacher Education (NCATE)** is officially recognized by the U.S. Department of Education. It is a council made up of 34 educational organizations created to ensure and raise the quality of teacher preparation and teacher certification programs of U.S. colleges and universities.

Essentially, NCATE sets the standards for preparing "competent, caring, and qualified teachers and other professional school personnel who can help all students learn" (NCATE Professional Standards, www.ncate.org, 2008). We're not going to bore you with more information than you need about accreditation and standards (if you'd like the details on accreditation and NCATE's role in teacher education, visit www.ncate.org). Just know that reputable teacher education programs seek accreditation. This is just a fancy way of saying they provided multiple forms of evidence to document effective teacher preparation and now have public verification that they have a good program. In the short and long run, you will be very happy you attended a program that took the time to jump through all of the hoops. Most programs use NCATE's standards for measuring their effectiveness in preparing high-quality teachers. There are six standards:

- Standard 1: Candidate Knowledge, Skills, and Professional Dispositions
- Standard 2: Assessment System and Unit Evaluation
- Standard 3: Field Experiences and Clinical Practice
- Standard 4: Diversity
- Standard 5: Faculty Qualifications, Performance, and Development
- Standard 6: Unit Governance and Resources (NCATE Professional Standards, 2008)

While they all deal with the quality of your teacher education program, the one that explains why you have a cooperating teacher is Standard 3: Field Experience and Clinical Practice. The unit and its school partners design, implement, and evaluate field experiences and clinical practice so that teacher candidates and other school professionals develop and demonstrate the knowledge, skills, and professional **disposition** (a tendency or inclination to act or behave a certain way under given circumstances) necessary to help all students learn. Basically, this standard requires teacher education programs to create a student teaching internship that allows you to grow in the profession and show what you know. Part of what this means is that you have partners during student teaching—a university supervisor and a cooperating teacher. Remember that checks and balances system mentioned earlier? The university supervisor and cooperating teacher work together to ensure that you get exactly what you need from the student teaching internship. We'll discuss the university supervisor's role in depth in Chapter 8, but for now, let's explore cooperating teachers and what makes them tick.

YOUR CT ISN'T IN IT FOR THE MONEY (AND OTHER TIDBITS) _____

Here's some straight talk about finding cooperating teachers. The truth is that in some areas the pool of candidates is extremely small. In other areas, there are several universities within miles of each other, and they are all looking for qualified CTs. You need to realize that CTs are paid very little money (if any) to guide the student teacher through the internship. When you factor that in, along with asking them to relinquish control in their own classroom, turn over the students, model effective teaching, serve as your advocate in the building, yet still remain responsible for the final outcome—it is a tough job. In spite of those factors, teachers continue to agree to serve as CTs for a variety of reasons, including opportunities to give back to the teaching profession and the prospect of gaining new knowledge and teaching techniques (Kitchel & White, 2007).

For whatever reason, your CT has agreed to do the job. Now, her primary task is to help you develop professionally by hosting you in her classroom during your internship. She provides the environment for you to grow as a teacher, to demonstrate the content knowledge, pedagogical skills, and professional disposition necessary to assist students in learning. You teach the CT's students, typically cover the content she has scheduled, and usually incorporate her management strategies. That doesn't sound very difficult, does it? Keep reading.

To make this work, you must keep in mind that you are a *guest* in her room. She was there before you arrived, and she will be there after you leave. Similarly, the students in her classroom belong to her, and she is ultimately responsible for their academic, social, and emotional growth—even though you are borrowing them for several weeks. Try to imagine how this must feel by looking at a similar situation. Let's say you have been living on your own in an awesome apartment for a few years, and you have gotten things just the way you like them. You're used to a clean kitchen, your poodle or Labrador has been trained to stay off the couch, and you like to fall asleep around 10:00 p.m. in pure silence. Now, your younger brother has asked if he can stay with you for a few weeks, which you know will actually mean 3 months or more. Of course, you really want to help him, but in your mind you are picturing an all-out disaster area, a dog that's now encouraged to lounge on the couch, and the need for ear plugs after 10:00. You agree to allow him to stay, but you know it will get tense if you have to keep reminding him that he is a guest in your home. In an ideal world, he would realize he is a guest, pick up his dirty socks, and make sure he respected your need for peace and quiet. And he would bring you mocha lattes every evening to remind you what a wonderful host you are. Since we don't live in an ideal world, and because he's family, you probably spritz the couch with generic fabric freshener, kick his dirty socks out of the way, and grit your teeth when you can still hear the sound of a TV in the distance at 10:00 p.m.

Imagine how a CT feels with another *teacher* in the room—someone she is not even related to, whom she has to nurture, talk to, and physically share a space with. She has to entrust her students in your care—knowing that their end-of-year scores will reflect *her* rather than *you*. If there's a problem in the class, the principal is going to address *her* rather than *you*. It's no wonder this relationship has the potential to be a bit of a challenge for both of you. So, never forget that you are a guest in her room, and unless some other agreement has been reached, do your best to follow her example and instructions. She takes the heat, so she calls the shots. Although you may not have complete and total control during the internship, you and your CT will still need to work together to get you ready to teach in your own classroom. She is the instructional leader of the classroom, and she will use different leadership styles to guide you to success. The outcome will cause you to change and grow as a person and teacher. Before we cue you into the different leadership styles your CT may employ, we'd like to further discuss these ideas and share why they are important to a successful experience.

CHANGE vs. GROWTH

During the internship, you may hear references to **change** and **growth**. Examples include the following:

- "This is a growing experience."
- "How have you grown during this experience?"
- "You will go through many changes during student teaching."
- "Please reflect on the changes you made in this growing experience."

We could go on, but we think you get the point. Your college instructors or professors have spent a lot of time getting you to reflect on your early and clinical field experiences. For good reason too, as reflection is critical to professional *growth* and it encourages you to *change* things that aren't working (we'll talk more about the importance of reflection in Chapter 8). See, it just can't be avoided; teaching goes hand in hand with change and growth. Likewise, two major outcomes of your student teaching experience are for you to change and grow. It is very common for these two words to be used interchangeably, but they are in fact distinctly different terms.

What Is Change?

Take a moment to think about how many different phrases you can come up with that start, end, or have the word *change* in them. We'll start you off: *change* agent, have a *change* of heart, *change* of scenery, and *change* the channel. . . . Okay, now it's your turn. How many additional *change* idioms could you come up with? The idea of change has been around for too many centuries to count, but have you ever really stopped to think about what it means and, more important, what it means for you as you embark upon this journey? We've listed a few definitions for the word *change* as offered by *Webster's Dictionary*.

- To become different in some particular way;
- To switch, lay aside, abandon, or leave for another;
- The result of alteration or modification;
- To exchange or replace with another, usually of the same kind or category; and
- A thing that is different.

Additionally, *change* can be categorized as a one-time event or a series of one-time events that are either internally or externally imposed. For example, the internally imposed decision to start a family is a one-time event that changes a person's life for a long time after the decision is made. The one-time event of losing a job may have been externally imposed, prompting the person to follow her heart's desire and enroll in a teacher education program. This one event likely spiraled into a series of other changes (selecting a school, maybe moving, learning new skills, finding time to study, etc.). Whatever changes come your way, it's how you respond to them that will either encourage or stifle growth.

What Is Growth?

The spring season always ushers in massive growth spurts. Every time you turn around, it seems as though something new has sprouted in a place where there was nothing. In some cases there was something very small there (like a stem and a leaf), and by the end of the day there is a bloom. Or, you might already have a green lawn, but a week of showers turns it into a lush, dark green carpet. These scenarios paint a picture of growth. *Webster's* gives us the following definitions:

- A progression from simpler to more complex forms,
- An emergence, and
- An increase (whether planned or not).

While it is typically easy to see growth occurring, the process by which you get there is still a bit of a mystery. And although the process is different for everyone, the experts tell us that there are common themes involved.

1. *Growth takes time.* Teachers do not become great overnight. Neither do doctors, lawyers, singers, or athletes, for that matter. It takes time to understand the theories, become skilled in the methods and practice effective dispositions. You have to consistently work on growing.

2. *Growth is gradual.* Baby steps, baby steps. Set your course in the right direction and forge ahead. You may have setbacks, but knowing where you are trying to go makes it easier to get back on track. This might mean trying a new classroom management strategy, even when it seems as though none of the others have worked.

3. *Growth requires inspiration.* Teachers need to get rid of the fragment, inspiration and perseverance, enthusiasm, impetus, incentive, and encouragement. Are you up for the

challenge? Growth will not occur unless you really want it. You can take all of the exams, read all of the books, tutor all of the children, but if you haven't made the commitment to grow from your experiences, not only will student teaching be hard, but keeping up with the profession will be even harder.

Do You Need to Change or Just to Grow?

We think it is fair to say that most people need both change and growth. Honestly, entire theories have been built on this premise. Forced change (whether internal or external) imparts some type of growth. Or, is it that your growth causes you to make a radical change? Either way, the two are connected. This is important to acknowledge, especially since you have selected a profession that relies on your ability to change and grow at the drop of a hat. The good thing to remember is that there is no single prescription for *change* and *growth*. Your fellow classmate might need to grow in his understanding of algebraic content knowledge, and you might need to work on your instructional presentation. One person's baby step is another person's giant leap. Changes may come from the outside, but growth always comes from within. Ultimately, the decision to grow is a deliberate, personal choice.

Although we don't know you personally, we can assume that because you are reading this book and are getting ready to be (or are) a student teacher, you have done your fair share of changing and growing. It may have been easy for some and challenging for others, but you're here. You are ready and willing to put in the time and effort it takes to grow and change a little bit more, and luckily, you have a willing participant (your CT) who is going to help you every step of the way.

ON TIME SUPERVISION

Let's cut to the chase: Your CT has a real job to do—teach the students in her room—and you are to (somehow) learn to do that within her environment. That "somehow" is evidenced by the level of guidance and support she provides for you; it will vary with what she perceives her role to be, and how willing, ready, and able you appear to be for jumping in and doing the job.

First, cooperating teachers view themselves in a variety of roles, which impact the type of leadership they will provide (Weasmer & Woods, 2003). Your CT may see herself as one of the following:

- *Model.* This CT *shows the student teacher how the job is done* by demonstrating what she believes are effective practices. The student teacher's job is to *observe and replicate* the CT's instructional strategies and techniques for interacting with students and others in the school community.
- *Mentor.* This CT *allows the student teacher to try out strategies and techniques,* then later sets up conferences to discuss strengths and areas for growth. Additionally, the student teacher is encouraged to ask questions for clarity.
- *Guide.* This CT *promotes dialogue about activities or strategies the student teacher would like to implement.* This way, the student teacher gets an expert's opinion of whether a so-called great idea will work or not—before actually trying it. As an expert guide, this CT may also intervene mid-lesson when she believes the student teacher has gone off track (e.g., providing misinformation or using a blatantly ineffective management strategy).

It may help to think of these styles as cyclical processes. Figure 2.1 provides a visual of the process.

Figure 2.1 Three Types of Cooperating Teacher Roles

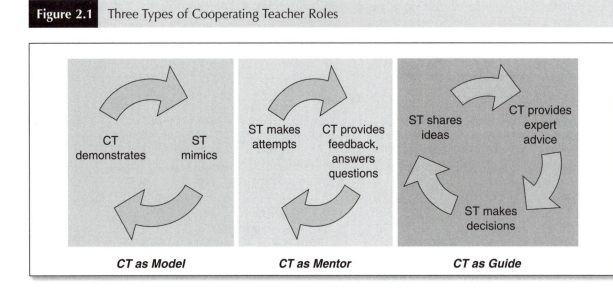

CT as Model

CT as Mentor

CT as Guide

Additionally, Weasmer and Woods (2003) found that cooperating teachers saw themselves in one, two, or all three of these roles at different points during the internship. Perhaps this fluctuation in perceived role is impacted by how prepared the student teacher appears to be for the job. Rando (2000) studied this connection between preparedness and level of supervision when observing participants in a counselor training program. In his model, Rando found that supervisors could consciously select the appropriate level of direction and support a particular supervisee needed in order to grow, based on the supervisee's readiness for the task at hand. Critical to the model is the concept of match and move—meaning supervisors *match* the support provided to the supervisee's readiness (defined in terms of willingness, ability, and self-confidence) for the task, and then *move* the supervisee to increased readiness for dealing with that task in the future. Another way to think of this is like a scaffold or a support system in a work-related environment. The supervisor (teacher) provides the supervisee (student) with the support needed to be able to do the task independently in the future.

SUPERVISORY LEADERSHIP ROLES

Rando developed a continuum for understanding how supervision varied with readiness. Supervisory style was viewed in terms of high/low direction, high/low support, and high/low supervisee readiness. Table 2.1 highlights the four different supervisory styles.

So, what can this possibly mean in the world of student teaching? Well, it means that your cooperating teacher may be quite deliberate, rather than haphazard or irrational, when it comes to her interactions with you. Her choices may be based on how she views her role (model, mentor, or guide), as well as her perception of your readiness for the job (willingness, ability, and confidence). But don't forget—just as your preparedness and confidence evolve during the course of the internship, your cooperating teacher's perceived role (and, consequently, level of direction and support provided) will change as well.

There is a great deal of literature documenting how important the cooperating teacher's role is in the professional development of student teachers. We offer additional resources at the end of the chapter, but if you just have to check right now, do an online search of Beck and Kosnik, 2000; Ganser, 2002; Weasmer and Woods, 2003. This will give you further reading about CTs helping student teachers prepare for the realities of teaching.

Your relationship with your cooperating teacher can make or break your internship. Remember, you will be spending on average 8 hours a day, 5 days a week, for 15 weeks with your CT. You want to make sure that you enjoy that time in the classroom. There will be

Table 2.1 Supervisory Leadership Styles				
Supervisory Style	**Degree of Supervisee Readiness**	**Degree of Supervisor Direction**	**Degree of Supervisor Support**	**What Does It Mean?**
Technical director	Low	High	Low	You are really new at this. You're unfamiliar with the fundamentals of the job. I can provide you with the basics, and in time, your readiness will improve.
Teaching mentor	Moderately low	High	High	You are still new to this job. I can provide you with resources, strategies, and support. As you learn more, your confidence in your abilities will grow.
Supportive mentor	Moderately high	Low	High	You know what to do, but you still need me to boost your confidence. Make some decisions on your own. I'll offer feedback for your choices.
Delegating colleague	High	Low	Low	You're ready for this task. I don't need to tell you what to do, how to do it, or to boost your confidence. I can stand back and let you handle this on your own.

SOURCE: Adapted from Rando, R. A. (2000). *Adaptive supervision in counselor training*. Retrieved from http://ccvillage.buffalo.edu/Village/ElecProj/Rando.htm

plenty of challenges that will come during the internship (and we'll help you with those throughout the text) without adding the challenge of managing a difficult relationship with your CT. Also, do not forget that you'll need your CT to verify through various forms of documentation that you have successfully completed the internship. She will also be the person that potential employers will most likely call for a detailed reference on your teaching performance, ability to work with others, and content knowledge. You need for this relationship to work, and we'll show you how.

GUIDELINES FOR THE RELATIONSHIP

There are some very basic guidelines that you can follow to create the makings of a great relationship with your CT. These guidelines apply to all student teachers, regardless of the specifics of your placement. The following chart offers a few helpful hints to get you started.

BASIC GUIDELINES FOR MAKING THE ST-CT RELATIONSHIP WORK

✓ *Make a good first impression.* We don't care what anyone tells you. . . . First impressions matter. You only get one shot at this, so make it a good one.

✓ *Be a respectful guest.* Observe how your CT manages her entire school day, and try to figure out how you fit in. If you want to make changes (e.g., to the schedule, the room layout, the classroom management system), ask first, and don't be offended if the answer is *no*. Relax. . . . You will have your own class before you know it.

✓ *Do your research.* If you discover you don't know enough about what you are expected to do (e.g., content, pedagogy, management, school policies), take the initiative to find the answers on your own. Revisit textbooks, talk to other student teachers or teachers, and/or try an Internet search.

✓ *Don't be afraid to ask questions.* This is no time to be timid. It helps to begin with, "I've already looked into this, but I am not finding the answers I need. Can you help me?" Your CT may be more willing to help you if she believes you have been trying to help yourself.

✓ *If you think you're ready, ask for more responsibilities.* CTs may not realize that you're up for a challenge. Be specific about what you want to do (e.g., write the weekly newsletter, lead a parent-teacher conference, or pick up third period) and the level of support you think you will need. Be realistic, and follow through.

✓ *If you think you're not ready yet, ask to scale back a bit.* Sometimes CTs give you too much too soon. Develop a plan for eventually moving forward in a timely manner. For example, you might say, "I don't think I'm ready to take on third period, but I would like to start by team teaching with you. Maybe by the end of the week, I'll be ready to teach it on my own."

✓ *Give it time.* The relationship with your CT may not be roses and rainbows from Day 1. You will have to allow time for you to figure out what each other's quirks are and how to work together in harmony. Even if you have a less-than-perfect beginning, you can use the strategies above to try to make positive changes in how your CT views you, which will consequently impact the types of interactions that you and your CT have.

✓ *If the relationship is exceptionally unpleasant, speak with your university supervisor.* At times, a case may arise when the student teacher–cooperating teacher relationship is not conducive to a positive student teaching experience. If this is your situation, you will need to make your supervisor aware of this. We recommend keeping a written (and dated) log of concerns that are *specific* and *factual*. We also recommend that you ask your supervisor to come in to purposefully observe what may be a tense or hostile relationship. If it is warranted, your supervisor may even schedule a meeting involving all three of you, in which your concerns can be shared with support from the university. What happens after this meeting varies by university, but options may include a plan for remaining in the classroom, moving to another classroom, or moving to a new school.

FINAL THOUGHTS

Cooperating teachers work diligently to guide you through the internship by serving as a resource and sounding board. CTs are an essential component of your experience, and they are mandated by NCATE. Additionally, a major role they fulfill is providing you with guidance to help you extend your knowledge, skills, and teaching dispositions (remember our discussion of *change* and *growth*). A CT's supervisory style is based on the CT's perceptions of his or her role and your readiness for teaching. This style may be one of the three styles of model, mentor, and guide, or it may be a combination of the three.

Your CT will help you avoid pitfalls, give you advice on creating relationships with students and parents, and serve as your advocate within the school. If this describes your cooperating teacher, great. Feel free to skim the next chapter and refer to it later if you need to remind yourself of all of the work that your CT does behind the scenes. We don't want to waste your valuable time when you could be planning a lesson, organizing your files, or just taking a much-needed break. If, however, you've had a few tense moments with your cooperating teacher, or if his or her style is not compatible with yours, Chapter 3 will be a great resource for you.

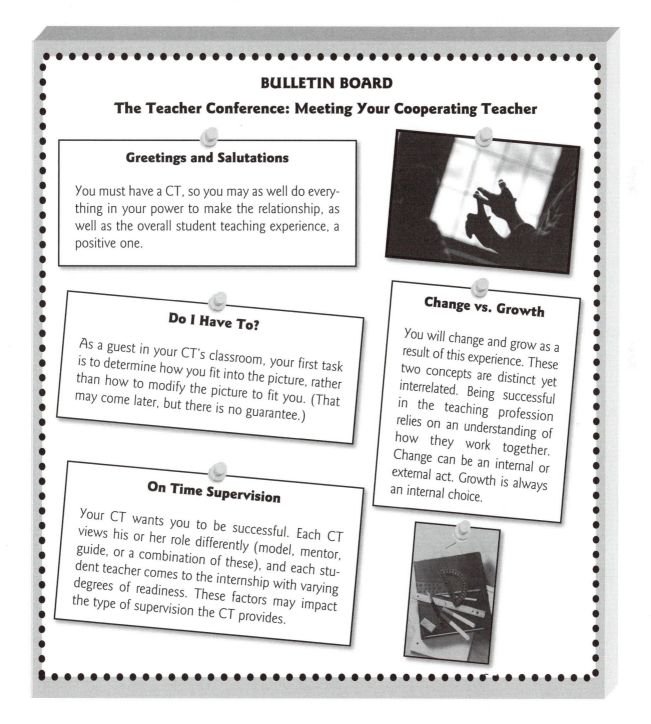

BULLETIN BOARD

The Teacher Conference: Meeting Your Cooperating Teacher

Greetings and Salutations

You must have a CT, so you may as well do everything in your power to make the relationship, as well as the overall student teaching experience, a positive one.

Do I Have To?

As a guest in your CT's classroom, your first task is to determine how you fit into the picture, rather than how to modify the picture to fit you. (That may come later, but there is no guarantee.)

On Time Supervision

Your CT wants you to be successful. Each CT views his or her role differently (model, mentor, guide, or a combination of these), and each student teacher comes to the internship with varying degrees of readiness. These factors may impact the type of supervision the CT provides.

Change vs. Growth

You will change and grow as a result of this experience. These two concepts are distinct yet interrelated. Being successful in the teaching profession relies on an understanding of how they work together. Change can be an internal or external act. Growth is always an internal choice.

EXTRA CREDIT

READ ABOUT IT

Working With Your Cooperating Teacher

> http://connected.waldenu.edu/index.php/blogs/34-teaching-experience/403-working-with-your-cooperating-teacher.html

National Council for Accreditation of Teacher Education (http://www.ncate.org) Leadership Styles

> http://www.buzzle.com/articles/types-of-leadership-styles-in-education.html
> http://psychology.about.com/od/leadership/a/leadstyles.htm

Understanding the Process of Change

> http://www.eric.ed.gov/ERICDocs/data/ericdocs2sql/content_storage_01/0000019b/80/33/fa/5c.pdf

Teacher Blogs

> http://www.gwu.edu/~cooptchr
> http://www.tooter4kids.com/classroom/tips_for_cooperating_teachers.htm

THINK ABOUT IT

Dealing With Unique Supervisory Issues

Read the case study and complete the activities that follow.

"Help! I'm Older Than My Cooperating Teacher"

Dear Merry Matchmakers,

I have just returned from meeting my cooperating teacher, and I'm not sure whether I want to laugh or cry. I walked into my CT's classroom and was greeted by a young woman who looked to be about 30 years old. Well, you could have knocked me over with a feather when I found out that she is actually 25. I mean, gosh—I have grandchildren who are older than she is. To add insult to injury, she is cute and perky and has an actual bounce in her step when she walks (rumor has it that she was captain of her college cheerleading team). I'm not sure that I am going to be able to take feedback from her, whether it's good or bad. Since I don't think it appropriate to share my age with the world, let's just say that I am a mature student. I've had a career and raised a family, and I didn't want to sit around the house all day. I love children and have done really well in all of my teacher education classes. I'm excited about student teaching, but this really feels like a setback. I don't want to ask for a change in placement so soon, but I know myself, and I don't think that I will be able to deal with this all semester. What should I do?

Sincerely,

Doomed From Day One

1. Write a response to Doomed From Day One. Be sure to include a discussion of change and growth in your letter. What will she need to hear about these concepts that might help her? We've also written a response, but don't take a look at it until you have completed your letter. Who knows, yours might just be better.

2. If you were in charge of making student teaching placements, what type of leadership style do you think would match well with Doomed From Day One? Explain your answer.

3. What type of leadership style do you prefer? Why? Explain your answer.

4. Write a one-page letter introducing yourself to your cooperating teacher. Make sure to highlight things that may not have to do with school (e.g., your hobbies, interests, family, etc.). You are one of a kind—make sure this comes out in your letter.

The Merry Matchmakers' Response

Dear Doomed From Day One,

We're going to have to be blunt here and just tell it like it is. We actually think that you are being too hard on yourself and on the Perky Princess. First of all, you sound like you are selling yourself short by not giving your CT a chance. If you opened yourself up to the experience, you might learn something from her as well as be able to offer her some of your infinite wisdom. She might be a teaching superstar, but we're sure that you've got something in your "Mom toolbox" to help in the classroom.

Before you try to jump ship, think about all of the hard work that you have put into getting here. It is unlikely that your university supervisor will give you a new placement without first assessing if there is an instructional issue with your current placement, so what's the harm in trying to make it work? We sense that the real issue may have more to do with your pride and ego than you're letting on. If she is an excellent teacher, it shouldn't matter that she's younger than you are. But if you're concerned with not being able to connect with her due to your age difference, then be up front about it and invite your US to sit down with both of you to see how you might be able to connect. Remember, the university matched you two together for a reason; it might be because of your calm temperament and her drill sergeant organizational skills. Or maybe you have strengths in math and science and her strengths are in language arts and social studies. Either way, you may make a winning team. We'd like to see you give it a try. Like Mom always says, "Try it; you just might like it."

Good luck, and keep us posted.

Sincerely,

Your Merry Matchmakers

TRY IT

Getting to Know You

You will spend a considerable amount of time with your CT during the student teaching internship. It might be helpful to connect with him or her on subjects other than teaching. Use these fun questions to get to know your CT better. Feel free to create other questions (just as long as they are not about work). Try asking your CT a couple of questions a week. Don't forget to offer some information about yourself as well. Here are some examples:

- If you knew could you try anything and not fail, what dream would you attempt?
- What superpower would you most like to have, and why?
- Would you rather take pictures or be in pictures?
- Are you a beach, country, or city person?
- Do you live in a house or an apartment?
- Have you ever lived in another country?
- Have you ever met a famous person?
- How do you spend your free time?
- Tell me about a favorite event of your adulthood.
- Tell me about a favorite event of your childhood.
- What are your hobbies?
- What countries have you visited?

- Which country are you from?
- What do you do on Sundays?
- What is your motto in life?
- What kind of food do you like?
- Which languages do you speak?
- What cartoon character best describes you?
- If you could live anywhere in the world for a year, where would it be?
- What are you best at?
- Who do you respect the most?
- Who has had the most influence in your life?
- Would you like to be famous?
- Be creative.

Write three new questions.

PART II

Politics

The Rules

Understanding Your Cooperating Teacher

3

Dear Student Teacher,

When it comes to cooperating teachers, we've seen it all. Whether through our own experiences as student teachers (back in the Stone Age), watching the experiences of student teachers in the schools where we worked, or serving as supervisors and liaisons for student teachers at the university level, we have observed a variety of different types of student teacher–cooperating teacher relationships. Based on our extensive experience in this area, we feel well qualified to give you the information you need to have a positive professional relationship with your cooperating teacher. In our experience, most cooperating teachers have excellent content knowledge (they know what to teach), are skilled in pedagogy (they know how to teach), and  *are kind, caring, understanding, and enthusiastic educational leaders (they know how to act). Most of them are great (really, they just want to help you), but if you happen to encounter conflicts based on differing personality traits, after reading this chapter, you'll walk away with practical strategies for turning lemons into lemonade (along with a few very funny stories).*

Aside from entertaining you with stories from our own experiences, our ultimate goal is to provide you with the secrets to a successful relationship with your cooperating teacher, no matter what.

Sincerely,

Your Relationship Therapists

CHAPTER OBJECTIVES

After reading this chapter, you will be able to:

- Provide an overview of personality theory,
- Understand the value of the many traits approach of personality theory and provide concrete examples of each trait,
- Explain why personality factors and descriptors are important to relationship building,
- Outline the process of strategic problem solving and appreciate the importance of this theory in creating a successful environment, and
- Identify the benefits of having a win-win attitude (especially in unique circumstances).

PERSONALITY THEORY

An important factor in any relationship is to understand the **traits** or characteristics that each person brings to the table. In short, what specific personality traits do you and your CT possess? The answers are important for three reasons:

- Understanding personality traits may give you insight into behavior—both yours and your CT's.
- Understanding the traits behind the behaviors will allow you to select appropriate strategies to handle most any situation (we will refer to this as *strategic problem solving*).
- Understanding the to keep parallelism art of practicing strategic problem solving (with a win-win attitude) often leads to a positive outcome (i.e., a better student teacher–cooperating teacher relationship).

Initially, you may feel as though you are back in Psych 101, but bear with us. There's a lot of information presented that you might even be able to use in other relationships. But if you're having trouble retaining all the valuable information in this chapter, then focus on the charts, which provide you with the same valuable information in an easy to read visual format. So, there you have it; now let's get started.

GETTING THE COLD SHOULDER

To set the scene for this section, we'll have to go back to the '70s (key the wacky music, and think cheesy sitcom flashback scenes).

Has this ever happened to you? You are in your favorite coffee shop and you see someone who you know (not a particularly good friend, but you know her nonetheless). You acknowledge her and say "Hi." Of course she is equally as happy to see you, and she responds by smiling and saying "Hi" back to you. You don't slow down to engage in trivial chit-chat, but go along on your merry ways. The act of saying "Hi" was enough to solidify the fact that there is mutual respect on both of your parts. Now, let's fast forward—different day, similar scenario with a much different outcome. You are in the same coffee shop and you see the same person you know. But this time when you smile and say "Hi," the person looks right through you, doesn't smile, doesn't say hello but just keeps on walking. "Wait," you say to yourself. "Did that just happen?" Clearly you were still being your ever-polite (dare you say charming) self. What could have happened to make this person not respond? Who would do something like that, and what should you do as a result of the person's actions?

By channeling your inner Oprah or Dr. Phil, you've probably come up with the following solutions:

- You decide that she has a major character flaw and the behavior will be a recurring interaction—in which case you decide to ignore it forever (or until she decides to speak again).
- You decide that she was just having a really bad day and was so preoccupied that she didn't even notice you—in which case you secretly forgive and forget (because we've all been there at least once in our lives—right?).
- You decide that even if the rude behavior continues, you are a better person and you will still continue to say hello every time—in spite of the apparent flaw in her disposition.

With either decision, you are inherently making judgments about a personality and basing your response on this opinion. In order to level the playing field, here is some basic information along with other interesting facts about personality traits. This information is not intended to fast track you to a psychology degree, but it should be used to gather additional information in understanding different behaviors.

PERSONALITY TRAITS

Gordon Allport (1897–1967) is considered by many the father of **personality theory**. This branch of psychology studies personality and individual differences. Among his various contributions to the field, he believed that people have consistent personalities, that individuals are unique, and that personality traits could be better understood through careful review of autobiographies, diaries, and letters. Needless to say, he did a lot of reading and writing in his lifetime. In one now-classic study, he read over 300 letters written by the same person (a girl named Jenny) and after it was all said and done, he was able to describe her in eight distinct personality traits (Cattell, 1990).

Many Traits Theory

Personality traits are distinguishing qualities or characteristics. Think back to the coffee shop cold shoulder incident. Is there a personality trait that can be used to describe what some would call "fickle" and others might call "snobbish"? The answer is a resounding yes. What is most important to note is that many personality traits work together to make you and your CT unique people. You have specific traits, and your CT also has specific traits. Basically, personality development is an ongoing process. How a trait is displayed (as behavior or action) is dependent on more than one factor. All of your traits work together in different situations to give you your unique personality. Figure 3.1 illustrates how seven important factors represent this complex idea of personality as an ongoing process.

Figure 3.1   Many Traits Approach

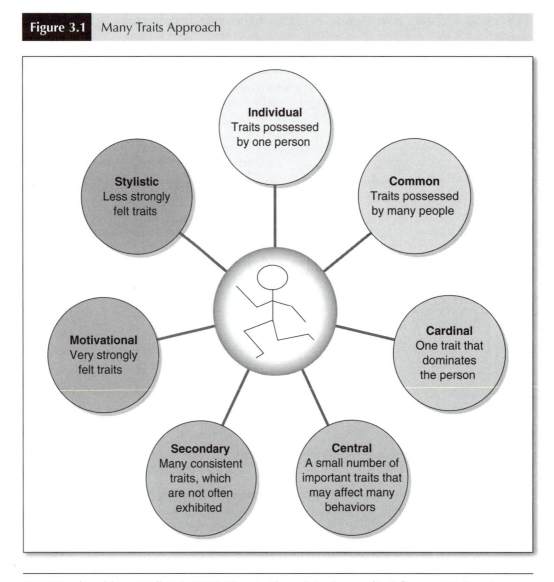

SOURCE: Adapted from Cattell, R. B. (1965). *The scientific analysis of personality.* Baltimore, MD: Penguin.

Think about it like this: You may be extremely outgoing (Common and Cardinal traits) with people you know well, but when you are in a new situation with strangers, you become shy, sensitive, and intimidated (Central traits). However, you feel strongly that it is rude not to converse (Motivational trait), so you force yourself to say hello to whoever looks your way. Some theorists find that looking at many personality traits at once can help determine which traits can be linked to certain behaviors. This is an interesting idea because it could provide a better understanding of what sustains certain conduct and actions and how they should be handled. Would you like to know which personality traits are linked to getting straight A's? What about a more serious issue such as which personality traits are linked to a person's propensity to take drugs? Believe it or not, there was actually a study done that found that four-year-olds rated as aggressive, fidgety, restless, and disobedient were more likely to use illegal drugs nearly a decade later (Carver & Scheier, 2000). But more important, let's go back to the reason you are reading this chapter. Would a better understanding of your unique personality traits and those of your cooperating teacher influence how you might handle **conflict** (an actual or perceived opposition of needs, values, and/or interests)?

PERSONALITY TRAITS AND THE STUDENT/ COOPERATING TEACHER RELATIONSHIP

There are an unlimited number of potential traits that could be used to describe personality. For the sake of time, we have condensed the work of Cattell (1965), who came up with 16 primary personality factors and their corresponding traits. Cattell was a smart man (he went to college at 16 and earned a doctorate at age 20) and his theory is useful, but his findings were criticized and were never replicated with similar results, which is frowned upon in research. His work was later revised by Conn and Rieke (1994). Table 3.1 presents a condensed version of Cattell's work. It introduces some factors and personality descriptors. If you'd like to see all of the factors, check the Further Readings section at the end of this book and/or do an online search of "Raymond Cattell" or "16 Personality Factors." Some important points to keep in mind as you are reading the table include the following:

- The primary factor (first column) represents the overall personality, and the traits (second column) represent the characteristics or behaviors that you might observe.
- Each factor is connected to a cluster of specific traits that typically go together, and Cattell labeled these low range (LR) traits and high range (HR) traits.
- The traits should be viewed as a range of behaviors that give you your individuality. For example, Warmth (in the high range) includes such related qualities as kind, easygoing, participatory, and friendly. But exceptions and situational influences exist (e.g., even the most easygoing among us may get their feathers ruffled at times).

Take a look and see if the characteristics in Table 3.1 describe you or your CT.

Table 3.1 Personality Factors and Descriptors

| Personality Factor | Personality Traits (i.e., observed behaviors) | |
	Low range (LR)	High range (HR)
Warmth	Reserved, distant, cool, impersonal, detached, formal, aloof	Outgoing, attentive to others, kind, easygoing, participating, likes people
Dominance	Cooperative, avoids conflict, submissive, humble, obedient, easily led, docile, accommodating	Dominant, forceful, assertive, aggressive, competitive, stubborn, bossy
Liveliness	Serious, restrained, prudent, taciturn, introspective, silent	Lively, animated, spontaneous, enthusiastic, happy go lucky, cheerful, expressive, impulsive
Rule-Consciousness	Expedient, nonconforming, disregards rules, self-indulgent	Rule-conscious, dutiful, conscientious, conforming, moralistic, staid, rule bound
Sensitivity	Utilitarian, objective, unsentimental, tough minded, self-reliant, no-nonsense, rough	Sensitive, aesthetic, sentimental, tender-minded, intuitive, refined

(Continued)

(Continued)

Personality Factor	Personality Traits (i.e., observed behaviors)	
	Low range (LR)	High range (HR)
Vigilance	Trusting, unsuspecting, accepting, unconditional, easy	Vigilant, suspicious, skeptical, distrustful, oppositional
Abstractedness	Grounded, practical, solution oriented, steady, conventional	Abstract, imaginative, absentminded, impractical, absorbed in ideas
Apprehension	Self-assured, unworried, complacent, secure, free of guilt, confident, self-satisfied (untroubled)	Apprehensive, self-doubting, worried, guilt prone, insecure, worrying, self-blaming
Openness to Change	Traditional, attached to familiar, conservative, respecting traditional ideas	Open to change, experimental, liberal, analytical, critical, free thinking, flexibility
Self-Reliance	Group-oriented, a joiner and follower dependent	Self-reliant, solitary, resourceful, individualistic, self-sufficient
Perfectionism	Disorder, flexible, undisciplined, lax, self-conflict, impulsive, careless of social rules uncontrolled	Perfectionist, organized, compulsive, self-disciplined, socially precise, exacting will power, control, self-sentimental
Tension	Relaxed, placid, tranquil, patient	Tense, high energy, impatient, driven, overwrought, time driven

SOURCE: Adapted from Cattell, R. B. (1970). Advances in Cattellian personality theory. In L. A. Pervin (Ed.), *Handbook of personality: Theory and research* (pp. 101–110). New York: Guilford Press.

Did you notice yourself in any of the descriptors? Better yet, did you notice your cooperating teacher? Of course you did. This list of characteristics is extensive, and personality is always an interesting topic. You and your CT (and the rest of the world) are individuals who bring unique personalities to every situation. So how does all of this information about personality traits help you? You want to work positively with your CT. Let's be honest, you wouldn't really be as interested in this chapter if you and your CT weren't butting heads on at least one important issue. Or, you might not disagree with your CT on anything and want to know how it is that you are so alike. You want to have a positive student teaching experience and understanding your CT's unique personality is important to this goal. The idea is to recognize how your traits and your CT's traits can work together to foster a positive relationship between you.

A Day in the Life

As we mentioned earlier, over the years we've helped a lot of student teachers and CTs. So you can imagine that we have a lot of stories to share. Fortunately for you, many of our former student teachers don't mind sharing. So, we are now going to give you an unprecedented opportunity to eavesdrop on the conversation of three student teachers who, during a small-group reflection session, discussed their relationships with their CTs (see "The Daily News" below). These are real experiences, and only the names have been changed.

THE DAILY NEWS

DAY 15

Luis: Is anybody out there? I really need to get something off of my chest or I might just quit.

Jane3: Hey I'm here. You must have been reading my mind. I'm not even going to the gym tonight, I'm so exhausted. What's up?

Latasha: Wait, I'm here too. Don't start without me. I know that I can contribute to this conversation. ☺

Luis: I don't think that I can take it another day. He is driving me crazy. . . . I have secretly renamed him "Lazy Larry." He has just given me all of his teaching manuals, pacing guides, courses of study for English. I mean, I haven't even learned all of the kid's names yet, not to mention that some of them really scare me>-).

He's never in the room. He gets here in the morning and posts the schedule and disappears to get coffee but there is no way that it takes four periods to get coffee. Where is he going—Starbucks?

Jane3: LOLH, can't respond right now.

Luis: But wait—he even wants me to take over his elective courses. I don't know a thing about editing the school newspaper. I don't even like to read the newspaper. . . . Okay, this is the last thing, and then I want someone to tell me why I should stay. Every time I ask him a question, guess what he says—"I'll let you figure that out. I'm sure that "Top Notch U" has totally prepared you for this, so I trust your judgment. If you have any questions, I'll be in the lounge." He's got no real advice, except what not to eat from the cafeteria—my all time favorite, "By the way, don't eat school lunch on Taco Day."

Latasha: ?4U. Why would you go back? It doesn't sound like you're learning anything except how to have a stressful senior year.

Luis: I have to graduate. I have about 50 people coming to see me walk ☺

Jane3: Tell me about it. Everyone in my family is a teacher. Ha! Ha!

Latasha: But you think you've got it bad, I call my CT the Kill Joy. I've learned all of this stuff in my classes, but she won't let me try any of it. She says teacher ed programs teach you how to teach in "perfect" schools, but that if I just follow her advice, I'll learn how to teach in a "real" school. So, do you know what that means for me? It means that she wants me to do everything she does. She wants me to plan my lessons exactly like hers, using only her resources and the activities she has used in the past. She has totally killed all of my ideas and taken the joy out of teaching.

(Continued)

(Continued)

Jane3:   Sounds good to me. You don't have to plan much.

Latasha: On my last lesson plan, she wrote down the exact words she wanted me to say and suggested that I model her clothing style because she thought mine was a distraction for the students.

Luis: Is she talking about your tongue ring?

Jane3:   OMG, you did take that thing out, didn't you?

Latasha: I have absolutely no room to be myself. I can't go to the teachers' lounge because she believes it will taint my enthusiasm. I think it's because she doesn't want me to get to know other teachers. I stand with her during cafeteria duty and bus duty, and if I leave the room I have to tell her where I'm going. I sit with her at every meeting and have lunch with her every day. She even suggested that we take our bathroom breaks together. I'm fed up, and I have no idea of how I'll make it through the internship.

Luis: Wow. I'm not sure which one is worse, yours or mine %-(.

Jane3:   Okay, just when I thought I got myself together from laughing myself silly from Luis's problems, you come along with another one. Geez.

Latasha: RU saying that things R GR8 with your CT?

Jane3:   No way! I just don't have much advice since I've got my own problems. Let me tell U what my CT did today. She is over the top. I've been trying to make a good impression by getting to school earlier than normal, I mean, I'm even coming before the other student teachers, and that is saying a lot. Anyway, I get to school at 7:15 and when I walk in she is already organizing the morning work (this is supposed to be my job), she has reshelved all of the take-home books (my job too), cutout all of the bulletin board shapes (my job—again) and written the parent newsletter (not my job, but she said that she would show me). And you know what's the worst part? I think she did it this morning before I got here. I know this woman slept in the classroom (LOL).

Latasha: LHO and picking my jaw up off the floor.

Jane3:   Wait, there's more. She is always telling me that she gets here early, but I stay pretty late (7:00 p.m.), and she is here when I leave and she is here when I come in. I really like her, but she is so impatient sometimes, like she can't take the time out to teach me or she thinks I won't do it exactly like she does it, so she just goes ahead and does it herself. I wonder if that is why she tends to work alone on a lot of projects? She is an awesome teacher—too bad I'm being left in the dust. Either she is treating me like an errand girl, or she is watching over my every move, so either way I feel like I don't have room to breathe. Do you know that she makes up songs for everything. She's written at least 25 since I've been here. She takes common melodies (think "Twinkle Twinkle") and changes the words to fit the theme (like spiders). She also did a unit on baskets and actually went out into the woods, gathered up sticks, put them in water (so that they'd get flexible) and made a basket from scratch.

Who does that kind of stuff? She is obviously the real deal, but I don't know how much I'm getting out of this experience because I am not like her at all. I didn't think ST was supposed to be like this. I think she is setting herself up to burn out, really fast. Are you guys still out there?

Latasha: Okay, that was worth every long-winded moment. I'm too tired to offer you any help.

Luis: I guess @TEOTD life is just going to have to get better to the end.

LEGEND:

LOLH = Laugh out loud hard	%-(= Puzzled Face
?4U = Question for you	*GR8 = Great
>-) = Scary face	LHO = Laughing my Head Off
OMG= Oh My Gosh, God, Goodness	@TEOTD = At The End Of The Day

Could you feel their pain (or find a similar pain with which to empathize)? We are by no means saying that all cooperating teachers fit into one or more of these categories. Remember, we've said that most cooperating teachers are awesome mentors. Schools of education take great care to avoid placing student teachers with cooperating teachers who are not prepared to mentor. However, even with all of the policies and systems in place to ensure that you are placed with an excellent cooperating teacher, there are times when conflicts arise in this very important relationship.

If you noticed, the behaviors of the CTs who participated in the conversation can be found in many of the descriptions of personality traits in Table 3.1, Personality Factors and Descriptors. The CT's personality traits come from both the low range and the high range in the table. This further solidifies the theory that personalities should be thought of as a range of behaviors with many possible combinations. Figure 3.2 shows you how the behaviors of each CT stack up.

The way a person (your CT) acts is fluid. It may change based on the situation, day of the week, or person with whom she is interacting. When you see your CT demonstrate a trait that conflicts with yours, remember she has many traits. The point is that even the traits that frustrate you can be viewed from a positive perspective. We will talk more about the steps that you can use to guide you through this process, but right now, take a moment to note the following example. Table 3.2 illustrates a few common experiences that when viewed in a positive light, don't really look so bad after all.

STRATEGIC PROBLEM SOLVING

So where are we now? Even though you have learned a lot about personality traits, you might still be frustrated and unsure as to how you're going to deal with your current conflict with your CT (or one that may be brewing). We'd like to suggest that the answer lies in looking at your situation through a different lens. This is the beginning of a three-step process that we referred to earlier as **strategic problem solving**. In essence, this higher-order,

Figure 3.2 Cooperating Teacher's Personality Traits

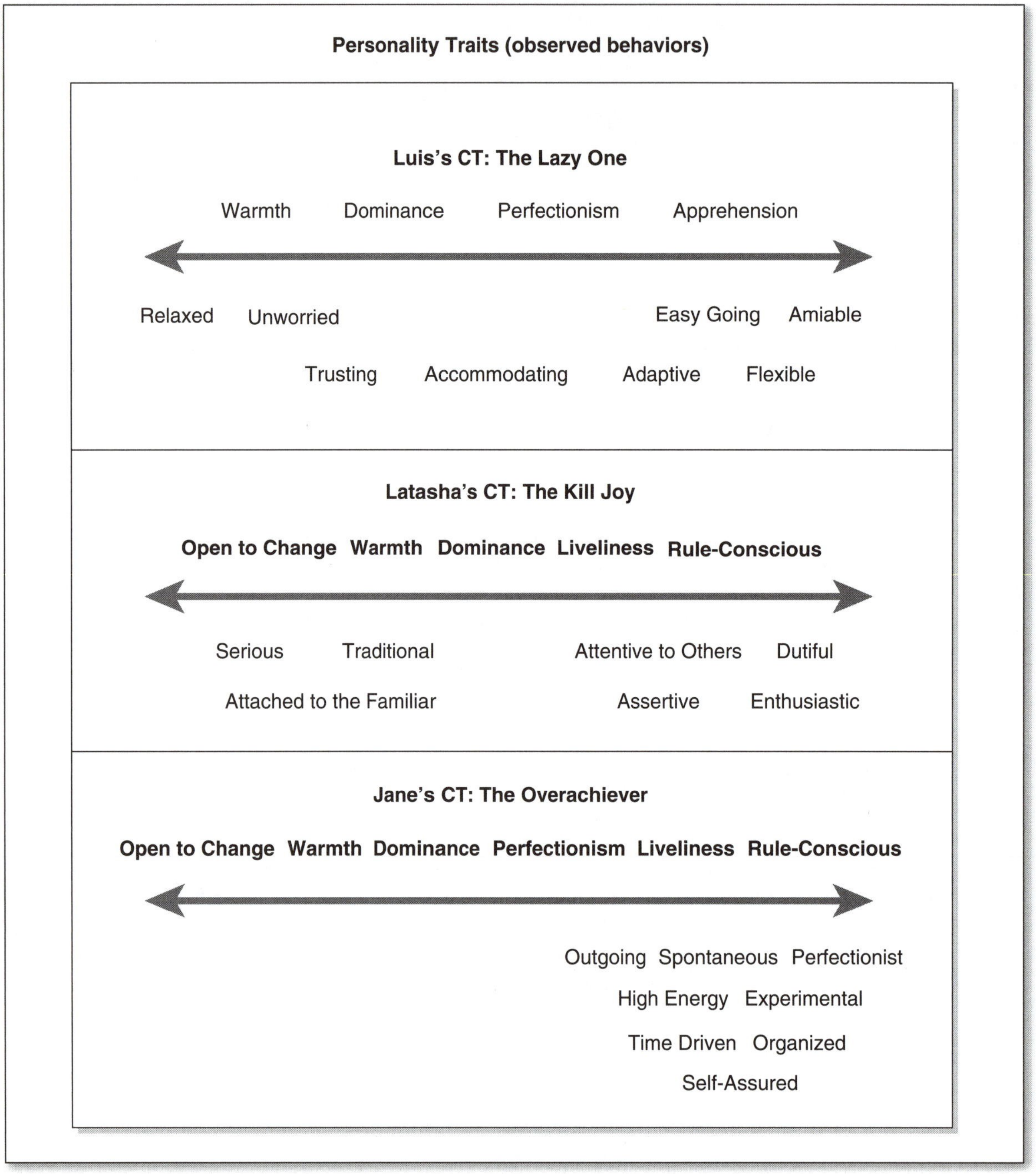

Personality Traits (observed behaviors)

Luis's CT: The Lazy One

Warmth   Dominance   Perfectionism   Apprehension

⟵————————————————————————⟶

Relaxed   Unworried   Easy Going   Amiable

Trusting   Accommodating   Adaptive   Flexible

Latasha's CT: The Kill Joy

Open to Change Warmth Dominance Liveliness Rule-Conscious

⟵————————————————————————⟶

Serious   Traditional   Attentive to Others   Dutiful

Attached to the Familiar   Assertive   Enthusiastic

Jane's CT: The Overachiever

Open to Change Warmth Dominance Perfectionism Liveliness Rule-Conscious

⟵————————————————————————⟶

Outgoing Spontaneous Perfectionist

High Energy Experimental

Time Driven Organized

Self-Assured

cognitive process facilitates progress toward a desired goal. It outlines the steps you can take to build a positive relationship with your cooperating teacher. Here's what you need to do:

1. Think about the traits that drive you the craziest and look at them in a positive light. You just might have to work a bit to see them as positives, so we'll help you. Personality traits influence your actions. If the interaction between your traits and actions and those of your CT leads to a conflict, you must select the appropriate lens for the conflict and a problem-solving strategy to solve it that will lead to a positive outcome.

Table 3.2   The Win-Win Attitude

Negative Trait	Transform	Positive Trait
Rule Conscious Kill Joy wanted to make sure that the ST followed all of the same rules she followed.	**Shine a New Light**	**Solution Oriented** Seen in a new light, this behavior will help you understand the importance of policies and procedures in the educational environment.
Overly Relaxed or Laid Back Lazy Gunther made his ST do all of the work while he chilled out. Nothing seemed to phase him.		**Imaginative** Seen in a new light, this behavior can give you the opportunity to get creative and design your own organizational system.
Perfectionist The Overacheiver had to have her ST complete everything to perfection.		**Conscientious** Seen in a new light, this behavior can help you learn how to pay attention to details.
Forceful, or Bossy This CT needs to be heard on every topic that is brought up at the faculty meeting, or in the hallway, or in the front office, or at carpool, or . . .		**Assertive** Seen in a new light, this behavior can teach you how to have confidence in your abilities and to speak out for strongly held beliefs.

2. Commit to having a win-win attitude (this is the strategic part). This is an effective form of problem solving where you pledge to work cooperatively so that all parties can win. In this case *win* doesn't have to mean making a friend for life, but it definitely means keeping the peace, learning from your experience, and completing your internship successfully. You must first be willing to set aside any attitudes that may undermine positive results, and resist your human urge to be right, look good, or teach a lesson. We've provided an activity in the "Try It" section at the end of the chapter to help you practice the art of turning lemons into lemonade or take a perceived negative and turn it into a positive. This is not always easy, but for the student teacher–coordinating teacher relationship to work, someone has to start the process of communicating effectively, and it might as well be you.

3. Select a strategy (this is the problem-solving part) and "Just Do It" (we know that Nike coined this phrase first, but it works well here). We offer you 10 tried-and-true strategies to get you started. You may need to try a couple (or many) before you find the one that works the best (this is why we gave you 10). Figure 3.3 gives you a visual depiction of how this should work.

STRATEGIES THAT WORK

One of the most important steps in using the strategic problem-solving model is the selection of a strategy. After you have viewed the once negative conflict into a positive, you are ready to select a strategy and solve the conflict. How you handle the situation and the outcome will

Figure 3.3 Strategic Problem Solving Flow Chart

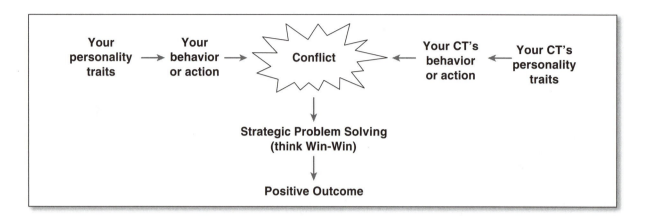

directly result from your strategy selection. Alan Fairweather is the author of four ebooks in the "How to Get More Sales" series. He describes many practical actions you can take to build your business and motivate your team. Here he outlines ways to deal with difficult people.

1. *Don't get hooked.* When people behave toward you in a manner that makes you feel angry, frustrated, or annoyed—this is known as a *hook*. We have a choice of whether we decide to get hooked or stay unhooked. We often allow another person's attitude to irritate or annoy us. This becomes obvious to the other person through our tone of voice and body language, which only fuel a difficult situation.

2. *Don't let them get to you.* We often allow the other person's attitude to irritate or annoy us. This becomes obvious to the other person through our tone of voice and our body language. This only fuels a difficult situation.

   When dealing with difficult people, stay out of it emotionally and concentrate on listening non-defensively and actively. People may make disparaging and emotional remarks—don't rise to the bait!

3. *Listen, listen, listen—and then listen some more.* Look and sound like you're listening. When face-to-face, you need to look interested. Nod your head, and keep good eye contact. If the other person senses that you care and that you're interested in the problem, then she is likely to become more reasonable.

4. *Get all the facts, and write them down.* Repeat (paraphrase) the problem to ensure your understanding and to let the other person know that you are listening. Keep a complete paper trail of things that have been discussed. This is not to be used as a "gotcha"—but so that you are sure of your next step.

5. *Use names.* A person's name is one of the warmest sounds they hear. It says that you have recognized them as an individual. It is important not to overdo it as it may come across as patronizing to the other person. Make sure they know your name and that you'll take ownership for the problem.

6. *Don't blame someone or something else.*

7. *Watch out for people's egos.* Here is a list of things for you to remember not to say or do:
   - Don't interrupt.
   - Don't argue.
   - Don't jump in with solutions.
   - Allow them to let off steam.
   - Don't say, "Calm down."

8. *See the situation from the other person's point of view.* Too often we think the "difficult" person is making too much fuss. We think, "What's the big deal? I'll fix it right away." When it's a big deal for others, they want you to acknowledge it.

9. *Be very aware of your body language and tone of voice.* We often make a situation worse without even realizing it. Our tone of voice and body language often contradict what we're saying. We may be saying, "I'm sorry" while our tone of voice and body language (rolling eyes, sighing, chewing gum, crossing arms, etc.) are communicating our frustration and annoyance. Thus people are actually listening with their eyes and will notice more *how* you say something than *what* you say. In addition, it's important to use a warm tone of voice when dealing with a difficult situation. This doesn't mean being disingenuous or fake.

10. *Words to avoid.* There are certain trigger words that can cause people to become more difficult especially in emotionally charged situations. These include the following:
    - "You have to"
    - "But"
    - "I want you to"
    - "I need you to"
    - "It's company policy"
    - "I can't" or "You can't"
    - "Jargon" or "Buzz" words
    - "Sorry"
    - "I'll try"

11. *Stop saying sorry.* "Sorry" is an overused word. Everyone says it when something goes wrong and it has lost its value.

    How often have you heard someone say, "Sorry about that. Give me the details and I'll sort this out for you." Far better to say, "I apologize for . . . " If you really need to use the words "I'm sorry" make sure to include it as part of a full sentence. "I'm sorry you haven't received that information as promised, Mr. Smith." (Again, it's good practice to use the person's name.)

    There are many other things you can say instead of "I'm sorry."

12. *Empathize.* The important thing to realize when dealing with a difficult person is to:
    - Deal with the person's feelings first and then deal with his or her problem.
    - Using empathy is an effective way to deal with a person's feelings. Empathy isn't about agreement, only acceptance of what the person is saying and feeling. Basically, the message is "I understand how you feel."

    Examples of an empathetic response would be to say, "I can understand that you're angry" or "I see what you mean." Again, these responses need to be genuine.

13. *Build rapport.* Sometimes, it's useful to add another phrase to the empathy response, including yourself in the picture. Try saying, "I can understand how you feel, I don't like it either when that happens to me." This has the effect of getting on the other person's side and helps build rapport.

    Some people get concerned when using this response, as they believe it'll lead to "Well, why don't you do something about it then?" The majority of people won't respond this way if they think you are a reasonable and caring person. If they do, then continue empathizing and tell the person what you'll do to try to resolve the situation.

14. *Under promise and over deliver.* Whatever you say to resolve a situation, don't make a rod for your own back. We are often tempted in a difficult situation to make promises that are difficult to keep. We say things like, "I'll get this sorted this afternoon and phone you back." It may be difficult to get it sorted "this afternoon."

Far better to say, "I'll get this sorted by tomorrow lunchtime." And then phone them back that afternoon or early the next morning and they'll think you've done a great job.

15. *You don't win them all.* Remember that everyone gets a little mad from time to time, and you won't always be able to placate everyone. There's no magic formula. However, the majority of people in this world are reasonable people and if you treat them as such, then they're more likely to respond in a positive manner.

16. *Some more thoughts to consider.* These notes are primarily designed to help deal with difficult people when we have made a mistake. We often have to deal with other people in a situation where we have not made a mistake. Occasionally, however, people will prove to be difficult and unwilling to accept what we say.

    Therefore, demonstrating assertive behavior helps to communicate clearly and confidently what our needs, wants, and feelings are to other people without abusing their human rights.

17. *Some books to read.*
    - *A Woman in Your Own Right* by Anne Dickson
    - *Feel the Fear and Do It Anyway* by Susan Jeffers
    - *Irresistibility* by Philippa Davis
    - *Why Men Don't Listen and Women Can't Read Maps* by Allan and Barbara Pease

SOURCE: Copyright ©Alan Fairweather 2010. Retrieved September 7, 2010, from http://EzineArticles.com/?expert =Alan_Fairweather

The strategic problem-solving model is an excellent tool, but we know that nothing is infallible. The method tends to work best when you allow yourself to be open to the process. If you go into a difficult situation armed with a constructive attitude and positive goals, you are more than likely to be pleased with the results. We also realize some of you may have student teacher placements that include special circumstances, and you may even be thinking that the strategic problem solving model will only work for your classmates who have those "perfect" placements. A word of caution (in case we haven't yet made it clear): Nothing is perfect. Let us take a moment to share with you some unique situations and how you might handle them.

Unique Situations

If you are a teacher's assistant or a lateral entry teacher, or if you think there is a factor (such as gender, race, or sexual orientation) that might pose a bit of a challenge for you in the internship, the following section is for you. Be forewarned: If you think we are going to tell you that you get a free pass on the "Let's Make This Relationship Work" train, you are sadly mistaken. We're going to require you to see things from a different perspective and to choose a strategy that brings about a positive outcome: a successful internship. Consistency is a wonderful thing. Table 3.3 explains a variety of responses that may typify unique situations.

The Win-Win Attitude

The art of achieving positive results through strategic problem solving is using all three steps together. We assure you, if you pick a strategy and try to implement it, but don't adopt a Win-Win attitude, you won't get the same results. You must engage in all of the steps:

1. Think about the trait,

2. Think about the win-win, and

3. Think about the strategy.

Table 3.3	Dealing With Unique Situations

If you are . . .	Keep this in mind
A lateral entry teacher completing your student teaching while teaching	*Your CT/mentor will not be around as much, or able to offer immediate and regular feedback.* It's up to you to make sure that the two of you are communicating and that you are being observed and provided with enough pointers and praise. Additionally, it might be a good idea to find a peer on your grade level or team whom you can go to for advice or to blow off some steam. *Because you're a full-time paid teacher, others around you may not always remember that you are involved in some serious on-the-job training.* It may be hard for others to relate to your newness, and you may sense that they are being less than supportive. In this case, our advice to you is to locate a first-year teacher who is probably going through some of the same experiences you are (minus the portfolio and reflection journal entries). This way, you'll be able to ask those questions you may be apprehensive about asking of the more seasoned teachers in your building.
A teaching assistant working as a student teacher in your own classroom or school	*It may be difficult for others around you to see you in your new role.* Be sure to emphasize your student teaching role by playing the part. That may mean dressing a little more professionally or spending time with student teachers and teachers. Remember that you are transitioning into the role of teacher, and it may be awkward (for you as well as others) as you discover how you fit in. *Your CT (and even the administration at your school) may continue to expect you to perform your TA duties in addition to your student teaching duties.* This issue must be addressed early in the internship. Your CT, supervisor, and possibly even the school principal need to be in on this important conversation, because even though the university expects you to be on campus for weekly seminar, your school still needs someone to handle bus duty. These issues have to be worked out. Once your responsibilities have been defined and an agreement for meeting them has been reached, put it in writing and sign it. But don't be surprised if situations arise where you must fulfill a duty that wasn't on the list. On occasion, this is okay; however, if it becomes a recurring request, it will begin to detract from your student teaching responsibilities. At that time, all involved parties will need to revisit the original agreement. *It may be a little uncomfortable as you assume full responsibility and provide directions for your CT (who was providing directions for you just a few weeks ago).* It is certainly normal for you to feel weird about asking your CT to make copies for you, manage a small group, or to take the kids to PE while you meet with your university supervisor. Sure, you could try to do it all, but let's be realistic: You are only expected to do on your own what a regular classroom teacher is expected to do on her own. In fact, one of your responsibilities as a student teacher is to use available resources—both material and human—effectively. The role reversal period is brief, and if your CT isn't okay with you giving her responsibilities, she will let you know. In that case, you will have to do it all. But, again, it will be brief.

(Continued)

(Continued)

If you are . . .	Keep this in mind
Considerably older or younger than your CT	*Don't make assumptions or generalizations about younger or older teachers.* Get to know your CT as an individual, and make a point of learning something from her every day. You might discover some refreshingly insightful ideas. You never know. Your task will be to absorb everything as data—information that will guide what you will and will not choose to do once you get your own classroom of students. Additionally, be willing to look at issues from your CT's perspective. You may find yourself mirroring a classroom management tactic or an instructional strategy that you never thought you would try. *Your CT may have expectations that are either too high or too low, entirely based on your age.* Present yourself as a professional who is well prepared for the internship, but who is also willing to learn and grow. Be teachable, but not needy. If you have great ideas, share them. If you have questions, ask them. But you will need to find a balance between the know-it-all and the doe-eyed newbie. Really, no one wants to work with either of those student teachers.
A different race, gender, or sexual orientation than your CT	*Don't rush to conclusions about the type of relationship you will have with your CT based on these factors.* Remember that teachers are individuals. Instead of assuming that you will have everything (or nothing) in common based on these characteristics, get to know your CT as a person. You'll have to do this without getting too personal, though. A little too much information (TMI) from either party can cross the boundaries of professionalism and negatively impact a relationship. Each day, try to discover something the two of you have in common. Start with an easy one—you both chose teaching as a career. *Refrain from attributing your CT's behavior to these factors.* You wouldn't want someone accusing you of "just being an irrational female" or "a typical insensitive male." We all know that rationality and sensitivity are not gender-specific. Our traits and behaviors are not bound by race, culture, religion, and/or sexual orientation. There are many other factors that impact how we act and respond. These factors change daily, if not hourly—or even more frequently. Try to think of what else might be causing your CT to behave in a particular way. Even if you're wrong, at least you will be functioning from a multiple perspectives point of view rather than stereotyping.
Contemplating a more personal relationship with your CT	*Keep it professional.* We've all heard of people finding love in the workplace. However, as long as you are functioning as a student teacher, it is not okay to develop a relationship with your CT (or for that matter, another person at your school) that involves or even resembles intimacy. Your CT is in a supervisory role, and while an intimate relationship is not illegal it could cause problems if your CT doesn't have the same feelings for you, or if the relationship goes sour before your internship ends. To prevent a catastrophic chain of events, we suggest that you refrain from doing or saying anything that could be misconstrued or possibly blur the lines of a professional working relationship.

The strategic problem solving steps are dependent on each other, but even then it is not an exact science. You may still have conflicts, still want to scream, still beg your university supervisor to change your placement, but inevitably this probably means that you need to select a different strategy.

_____ FINAL THOUGHTS

Understanding how personality theory and traits fits into the student teaching experience can be challenging. Keep in mind the basics. You and your CT have a wide range of personality characteristics, and these traits (behaviors) are fluid (they change often) and are dependent on the situation. These situations will vary, as not all internships are traditional, although we expect that they all will be successful. However, there may be a time when you have to deal with a conflict. If this happens, we advise that you use strategic problem solving as a means of resolution. This model encourages you to view conflict with a positive lens and then utilize a strategy to solve the conflict. Remember, in the end, you and your CT are both striving for success. In order to do this, you must be organized. Chapter 4 will give you the tools to manage your increasing workload.

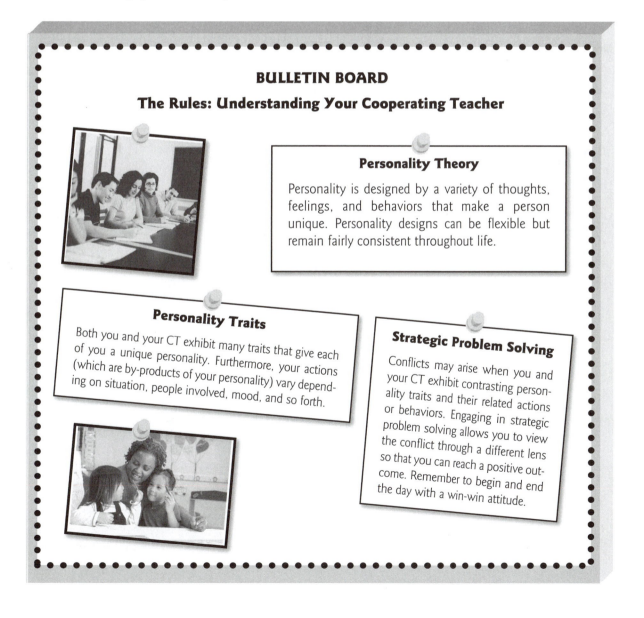

BULLETIN BOARD

The Rules: Understanding Your Cooperating Teacher

Personality Theory

Personality is designed by a variety of thoughts, feelings, and behaviors that make a person unique. Personality designs can be flexible but remain fairly consistent throughout life.

Personality Traits

Both you and your CT exhibit many traits that give each of you a unique personality. Furthermore, your actions (which are by-products of your personality) vary depending on situation, people involved, mood, and so forth.

Strategic Problem Solving

Conflicts may arise when you and your CT exhibit contrasting personality traits and their related actions or behaviors. Engaging in strategic problem solving allows you to view the conflict through a different lens so that you can reach a positive outcome. Remember to begin and end the day with a win-win attitude.

EXTRA CREDIT

READ ABOUT IT

Personality

What's Your Teacher Personality?

About.com. 22 Apr. 2008.
http://712educators.about.com/library/quizzes/blteacher_personality.htm
http://www.personalityquiz.net
http://www.gotoquiz.com/personality_quiz_1
http://www.outofservice.com/bigfive
http://www.humanmetrics.com/cgi-win/JTypes2.asp

The Student Teacher–Cooperating Teacher Relationship

Glenn, W. J. (2006, Winter). Model versus mentor: Defining the necessary qualities of the effective cooperating teacher. *Teacher Education Quarterly.* www.teqjournal.org/backvols/2006/33_1/12glenn.pdf

Montgomery, B. (2000). The student and cooperating teacher relationship. *Journal of Family and Consumer Sciences Education, 18*(2), 7–15.

Schauffele, R. (2008, April 22). A student-teacher's reflection on school relationships. Ezinearticles.com. http://ezinearti cles.com/?A-Student-Teachers-Reflection-on-School-Relationships&id=689753

THINK ABOUT IT

Understanding Personality Traits

Grab a highlighter and get ready to think. Using the information from Table 3.1, Personality Factors and Descriptors, complete the following exercises.

Select the top five traits that describe you best, and in a brief statement (or list) explain how you have effectively used each trait in the following situations (you may select the same or different traits for each situation, but only pick five):

I effectively use the following traits with my friends and family:

I effectively use the following traits in my university/college classes:

I effectively use the following traits in my student teaching internship:

The Student Teacher–Cooperating Teacher Relationship

This worksheet will help you plan for how you might handle those tough situations with your CT. Think about some experiences that you've had with your CT and consult the Personality Factors and Descriptors chart (Table 3.1) to complete this activity. Be honest.

Critical Incident Chart		
Your CT is . . .	You want to . . .	Instead, you should . . .
Forceful and asks you to begin teaching sooner that you are ready.	Say "Sure, no problem" to show him that you are well prepared for this job.	Say "Thank you for the vote of confidence, but I think I need some more time observing before I jump in. Would you work with me to develop a plan for gradually assuming responsibility?"
A risk-taker and expects you to teach but does not provide sufficient information about what or how to teach it.	Whine about the lack of support you are receiving. You might even suggest to others that your CT is trying to sabotage your grade in the internship.	See this as an opportunity to take on a true professional role—complete with mistakes and growth. Hey, this person actually trusts your judgment.
Lax and does not offer guidance for classroom management.	Say, "Well, if my CT doesn't do anything about it, why should I be expected to?"	Remember that management is your responsibility. Dig back into your notes from courses dealing with classroom management. Search websites. Talk to your peers. Find and try new ways to manage the class. Like every other teacher, you will have students who misbehave at some point. Your effectiveness depends on whether or not and how you address the behavior.

TRY IT

Strategic Problem Solving

Avoid trigger words. There are certain trigger words that can cause people to become more upset, especially in emotionally charged situations. Can you think of some trigger words and/or phrases that would cause you to shut down? These are probably the same words and phrases that other people would not like to hear.

List five words or phrases that you will vow not to use in conversations with your CT, students, friends, and others. And while you are at it, also list what you will say in place of that word or phrase. We've done the first one for you.

Trigger Word or Phrase	What You Can Try Instead
Ex. "You did it wrong."	"I see where you got confused. Can I help you fix it?"

SOURCE: Adapted from Fairweather, A. (2005, January 29). *Dealing With Difficult People.* Retrieved May 19, 2010, from http://ezinearticles.com/? Dealing-with-Difficult-People&id=12110

Personality Quiz

How well do you really know yourself? If someone stopped you on the street and asked you to identify your personality traits, could you do it? Could you answer with 100% accuracy? Why don't you test yourself just to be sure? You might actually find out something new about yourself. In the "Read About It" section above, we have provided you with links to a variety of different online personality quizzes in order to help you gain insight into the wonderful world of trait theory. Here are some helpful hints:

1. Take more than one quiz, if possible. This will help you to be able to compare and contrast the outcomes. Take all of them if you have the time.

2. Compare and contrast various aspects of the quizzes. Were the answers similar? Did you prefer one quiz over the other? Were you in the same mood when you took each quiz?

3. Think about the outcome. Do you agree or disagree with the traits? If not, why? If so, why? Can you think of specific examples that support or negate your explanations?

4. Share your results with a loved one or close friend and see if that person agrees or disagrees with the outcome.

5. Remember to have fun and try not to take the outcome too seriously, as we cannot guarantee the reliability or validity of the results.

The Late Bell

Managing the Workload

4

Dear Student Teacher,

By now, you've gotten a chance to figure out and understand who the key players are in this next stage of your quest to become a teacher. No doubt it will be challenging in the beginning, as you try to remember the names, roles, and personality traits of all of these new people. But it's not enough to learn titles, office or classroom locations, and personal quirks. There are many, many more balls you'll need to keep in the air to maintain this juggling act. For example, what do you do with all of the papers that continue to collect on your desk? Who do you talk to about filling out paperwork for licensure? How will you manage the internship along with a part-time job?

Year after year, student teachers tell us that no one ever prepared them for the number of new responsibilities—essentially, a three-ring circus of new duties—which must all be handled concurrently and (seemingly) effortlessly. In all honesty, it can be a bit overwhelming. This chapter serves as a warning—a "heads up" about the new mountain of work you'll be expected to handle. And we'll do our best to help your three-ring circus of student teaching run smoothly.

Sincerely,

Your Workload Warriors

STUDENT TEACHING IS A JUGGLING ACT

The student teaching internship is a tremendous undertaking. In order for it (and you) to be successful, you have to manage some very important responsibilities. Let's compare the experience to a juggling act, with the following instructions:

1. You must manage multiple things (keep track of several balls) while only being able to do one thing (toss one ball) at a time.

2. You must keep more items in the air than you can hold in your hands. (Two hands means at least 3 balls.)

3. You can't let any of the balls hit the ground. (This is the critical part.)

To relate this to student teaching, imagine your juggling act with these three balls—*classroom, university,* and *home.* You've got be in control—as much as possible—of all three responsibilities at all times. However, you can only focus on one of them at a time. In other words, you can't let issues from one area over-flow into another area, such as arriving habitually late to school because of child care issues, or opting out of writing lesson plans in order to put final touches on your teaching portfolio. Additionally, when there's a problem with any of the balls, it prevents you from successfully managing the remaining balls. In the internship, if you are having trouble with outside issues, this may affect your experience in many ways—you may be late or physically absent, unable to focus, and/or feeling rushed or stressed.

We know it's humanly impossible to fully compartmentalize all of your responsibilities, but we do want you to work toward maintaining your focus as much as possible—without letting any of your responsibilities fall by the wayside. Table 4.1 lists several of those responsibilities.

Once you have reviewed the table, you will see that we've made your responsibilities crystal clear, right here in Chapter 4, so there are no surprises down the road. After seeing such a transparent display of the balls you'll have to juggle, we hope that you will find it easier to wrap your mind around the real responsibilities ahead. Don't despair. You can do this. Students do it every semester, every year—and not only do they survive, they succeed. In the sections that follow, we'll provide you with an overview of stress (which is brought on by this juggling act) and guidelines for keeping each of the individual balls in the air so that you can decrease your stress and increase the likelihood of your survival and success.

Table 4.1	Your Responsibilities During the Internship

Classroom Responsibilities	University Responsibilities	Home Responsibilities
✓ Writing lesson plans and preparing materials ✓ Providing quality instruction ✓ Learning and using technology ✓ Managing the classroom ✓ Assessing and evaluating student progress ✓ Providing prompt feedback for students ✓ Participating in parent–teacher conferences and IEP meetings ✓ Writing weekly newsletters or updating your class webpage ✓ Attending team and faculty meetings and workshops ✓ Completing paperwork required by your school or district ✓ Participating in school events after school and on weekends	✓ Keeping up with two calendars—one for the university and one for your school placement ✓ Reflecting on your teaching through journals, blogs, and/or discussion boards ✓ Preparing for and attending scheduled seminars, workshops, and/or other meetings ✓ Completing required readings and submitting assignments on time ✓ Meeting with your supervisor to discuss your performance or ask questions ✓ Studying for and taking specialty area exams (if required) ✓ Submitting paperwork required for graduation and/or licensure ✓ Completing a portfolio or other culminating document	✓ Maintaining part-time jobs ✓ Dealing with personal health/medical issues ✓ Getting enough rest ✓ Organizing child care or care for your parents or other family members ✓ Managing transportation issues ✓ Maintaining relationships with friends and significant others ✓ Dealing with unexpected events ✓ Desiring to have a life

STRESS: IT'S HERE, EMBRACE IT

What is stress? **Stress** is your body's way of responding to different kinds of demands placed on it. Stress can affect both the body and mind, and at extreme levels, it can cause people to become tired, sick, and unable to focus. Sound familiar? Student teaching is such a new, big, and important task that a level of stress naturally comes with the job.

Most of the stress associated with student teaching is

environmental stress—including frustrations from everyday life, such as pressure from work or family,

and/or

stress from overwork and/or fatigue—including struggles with managing your time or balancing work and relaxation.

Everyone gets stressed, and everyone experiences stress differently. In fact, it is our ability to channel stress that determines whether and to what extent we are affected by it (Joseph, 2000). During periods of stress, chemicals are released into your bloodstream that in turn can give you more energy and strength. A little stress is good, in that the extra boost of energy allows you to perform at your best for short-term events. However, extreme stress drains you of energy and negatively affects your performance.

As stated previously, student teaching in particular is by no means exempt from stress. In fact, teachers have been stressed for decades. In the 1970s, the notion of teacher stress was just beginning to emerge; however, by 1980, a growing body of researchers were exploring the issue, and in the 1990s, teacher stress was recognized on an international level, prompting the rise of workshops and widespread public awareness regarding the issue (Dunham & Varna, 2002).

In the sections that follow, we will examine three types of demands (your "juggling balls") that can cause stress during the student teaching experience. We will also provide you with several useful strategies for dealing with those demands and the stress that they cause.

BALL #1: CLASSROOM DEMANDS

The list of classroom demands in the previous section probably looks a bit daunting, but we believe you can handle it if you plan ahead. To help meet your classroom demands, we recommend the following three basic strategies: getting and staying organized, managing time wisely, and dealing with deadlines.

CLASSROOM STRATEGY 1:
GET ORGANIZED AND STAY ORGANIZED

Organization may or may not be a strength for you. Regardless, it is a critical strategy for managing the huge responsibility of teaching—which becomes exponentially more difficult when the tools you need are scattered and in disarray. For those of you who know nothing about organizing for effective teaching, and for those of you who need a refresher, below are ideas for keeping track of materials, kids, and time.

1. *Give your stuff a home.* You probably recognize this phrase often used by moms: "A place for everything, and everything in its place." Well, they knew what they were talking about. Not only does this strategy keep a house neat and orderly, but it can also make your teaching job easier because you will always know where to find what you need. And for many teachers, finding their stuff is half the battle. One way to keep up with the many items you're responsible for is to make use of your personal workspace in the classroom. Some CTs may not realize the importance of providing a personal space for you. It is okay to ask for one. You may have to be creative due to the room arrangement or availability of supplies. There may even be surplus items that can be used temporarily, so ask around. This space may be a small teacher's desk or table, or a corner of the room set up just for you. Regardless of how this area is set up, you should work hard to begin your organization with your area— and be sure to keep your CT's items organized in the way that has already been established. However, if your CT isn't a role model for good organizational skills, do not follow suit. You still have to keep things in order. Maybe you can serve as the role model in this instance.

2. *Clean your desk.* As the saying goes, "a clean desk is a sign of genius"—or perhaps a sign of a respectful guest. When you were a teenager (after your mom finally gave up on the "everything in its place" rule), you could close the door to your messy room and no one would be the wiser. Not so with student teaching. Your chaos is in the middle of the room for all to see—your CT, the students, their parents, and the principal. So, keep it neat. This is, of course, easier said than done. It can be so tempting to just drop everything on your workspace with the honest intention of putting it away later. Resist the urge, and put it away now. If you wait until later, you'll have so many loose and unrelated items that the job will be more intimidating—and less likely to get cleaned up until it reaches critical mass. We know that many of you really believe you have a "system," but if your system looks like a tornado swept through your area, there's a problem. Our suggestion is to straighten your workspace every afternoon. This will get much easier over time, especially if you're putting most items where they belong throughout the day. This may also help you feel calmer when you return the next morning, because instead of cleaning and finding items, you'll be able to get started with tasks that are better uses of your precious time.

3. *Be your own secretary.* Getting organized isn't easy, but it can be less difficult if you have the right tools. For starters, you're going to need a three-ring binder to keep up with critical documents such as meeting agendas, memos from the principal, and handouts from workshops you attend. You may also wish to include information specific to your class or the internship, such as the class roster, the school handbook or conduct code, and contact information for your CT and supervisor. Use dividers and label them so you can further organize your paperwork and easily find what you need. (Note: Lesson plans should be kept in a separate notebook that is accessible to your CT and supervisor at all times.)

4. *Save time with class rosters.* One of the best organizational strategies we've found for keeping up with what's going on in your classroom is the basic class roster. We have used rosters to keep up with everyday information as well as student academic progress. This is a basic grid with all students' names in order on the far left column, and additional columns for keeping up with critical information such as attendance, who paid for the field trip, who has completed the Unit 12 History Test, and so on. Print several copies of the roster (with names only) and keep them on hand (or filed away) for easy access.

5. *Track your time.* Part of staying organized is having a good awareness of time. This includes making realistic estimates of how much time different tasks will take, as well as the awareness of time as it is actually passing. While a school day might have seemed torturously long when you were a student, you may notice that as a teacher, time passes in the blink of an eye. This makes it easy to get behind, both during teaching and planning periods. The obvious recommendation is to watch the clock—but this doesn't always work. Another suggestion is to use a timer, which may help you focus and stay on task—and prevent you from arriving late for lunch and dismissal every day.

> ✓ Keep a timer nearby, and set it for the amount of time you think you'll need to complete a task. When it rings, stop and reflect briefly on the following questions:
>
> ✓ Did I use my time the way I was supposed to?
> ✓ Did I allot enough time (or too much time) to get this job done?
> ✓ How can I make better use of my minutes in the future?

Remember, there are no rollover minutes in teaching. You can't use today's leftover minutes (what leftover minutes?) tomorrow, so use your minutes wisely while you have them.

CLASSROOM STRATEGY 2: MANAGE YOUR TIME

Time management was touched on briefly in the previous section, but it bears mentioning again. You must manage your time well, or it will be wasted. Having said that, we have four words for you: Plan during planning time. You really don't want to spend all of your nights and weekends creating materials, grading papers, and writing lesson plans, so try to protect this sacred few minutes. Sure, there will be team meetings on some days and other days when unexpected events arise, but for the most part, you should plan during your planning time. Resist the urge to hang out in the teachers' lounge—at least for more than 5 minutes or so—and get back to your classroom to deal with all the projects that need grading.

Most student teachers only get one block of planning time per day, and this is usually somewhere between 40 minutes and 1 hour. So, let's say you have 50 minutes. How easily will that time slip through your fingers? Very easily, if you're not focused. Figure 4.1 illustrates how 50 minutes of planning time are often wasted.

| Figure 4.1 | Fifty Minutes of Planning Time Wasted |

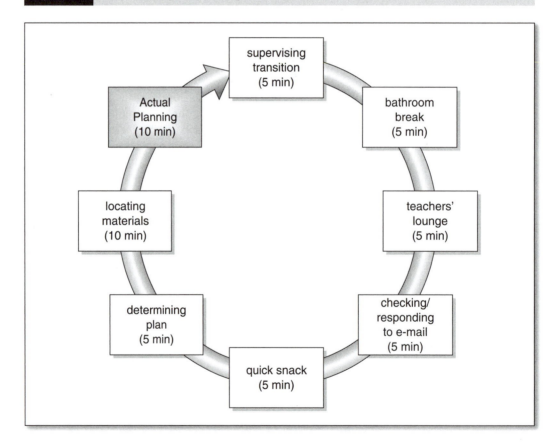

And now, here are a few tips to *maximize* your planning time:

1. *Multitask.* Pack a mess-free snack and drink that you can have while checking your e-mail or working.

2. *Plan to Plan.* So much of planning time is lost on trying to determine what to do and locating the right materials. To save time, create a planning folder that you keep on your desk at all times. Use sticky notes to remind yourself what you need to do, and toss them into your planning folder throughout the day and week.

3. *Prioritize.* As far as planning for instruction, you can prioritize by urgency or complexity—whichever makes the most sense. For e-mail, however, only respond during planning time to messages that are critical. Save the others for after school or at home.

4. *Chunk.* When jobs seem too large, break them up into manageable pieces and tackle one task at a time. You'll feel a sense of accomplishment as you tick items off your to-do list, even if they're small items.

5. *Collaborate.* Find someone else—either another student teacher or someone on your grade level or team—who is teaching the same unit as you. Work together and share ideas. If a lesson or activity emerges that both of you like, then one of you should prepare all of the materials for both of your classes. Be sure to share the load. Bring your own good ideas to the table so it doesn't appear that you are always taking, never giving.

6. *Delegate.* Set up and rotate student jobs so that all of the work doesn't fall on you. Let students pass out work and materials, file nonconfidential items, and help with maintaining some of your classroom areas. Have a kid who's a tech whiz? Let her update your class webpage (with your direction and approval, of course). If you have a teacher's assistant (TA), allow him or her to be responsible for some of your jobs. We know this may sound strange or wrong, but this is how TAs work in the real world—the TA assists you. Your TA can transport students, supervise transitions, make copies, distribute work, prepare instructional materials, and help with bulletin boards and displays. Also, a growing number of TAs are able to carry out instructional duties, especially when training has been provided. However, be sure you are not using your TA as your own personal assistant. Your TA needs to see that you are pulling your own weight and not dumping all of the "grunt work" on him or her.

Following the six strategies above can really save time and make your important planning period feel less hectic. How might that new and improved planning period look? Figure 4.2 illustrates the improved time. Additional tips to maximize your planning period have also been provided.

Figure 4.2   Fifty Minutes of Planning Time Well Spent

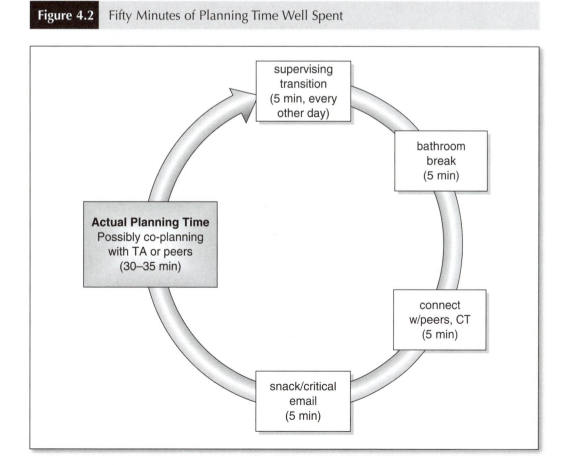

MORE TIPS TO STAY ON TOP OF PLANNING

✓ *Find an organizational mode that works for you.* Observe other teachers who seem to have it together, then develop your own style. Note: Chaos is a state, not a style.

✓ *Find good templates and stick with them.* Templates save time and help ensure consistency and completion in your documents. Thousands of templates (e.g., for lesson plans) can be found online and downloaded for free.

✓ *Prepare your lessons a week ahead of time for feedback.* Your CT might be able to give you a little insight about what will/won't work—and you'll have enough time to make changes if necessary.

✓ *Prepare your classroom in the afternoon before you leave.* Never trust that there will be time in the morning, because it is likely that something will come up—an emergency faculty meeting, a flat tire—and you'll end up prepping your room while simultaneously fielding questions from students who arrived early for school.

✓ *Think about long-term plans.* Keep a folder to collect materials for upcoming units and activities. When the time comes to write the plans, you'll already have an idea of what you're doing.

CLASSROOM STRATEGY 3: DEAL WITH DEADLINES

As we said before, student teachers comment every semester about the amount of paperwork they are responsible for during the internship. Here are a few ideas for taming the paperwork beast:

1. *Carry a calendar to all meetings, and keep it by your side as you check your e-mail.* When you hear of or read about a new responsibility, add it to your calendar immediately. Don't assume that you will remember to jot it down later. Chances are, later your mind will be on something completely unrelated, and you won't remember it again until later has become too late.

2. *Make sure you are clear on what is expected, when it is due, and how and to whom it should be submitted.* Often, school administrators (and even teachers) forget that student teachers are still learning about how schools truly function (even though you have the advantage of having read our advice on school culture). Consequently, instructions aren't always provided clearly. It's quite likely that you've transitioned so well into your teacher role that others in the school assume you know what they're talking about, but if there's something you don't know, ask. However, don't expect everything to be explained to you. It's not uncommon for others in the school to expect you to find some things out on your own. Just think how much more powerful and lasting the learning will be because you discovered it for yourself.

3. *Use your technology to set reminders.* Take advantage of what you can do with your cell phone, e-mail alerts, and electronic calendars. Even the most basic cell phone can remind us of our family members' birthdays if we program them in. So, it would be just as easy to set a cell phone reminder such as "March 30, Benchmark data due—Mr. Sanders—5 p.m." Cell phones and other gadgets with even more sophisticated capabilities are widely available and more affordable than they used to be. And some computers even have their own electronic version of sticky notes—which many people have found to be life changing. There's no reason you should miss a deadline.

4. *Use your filing system to keep your critical paperwork organized.* Did you forget already? If so, go back and reread the section above on organization.

_____ **BALL #2: UNIVERSITY DEMANDS**

This is the part of the juggling act that student teachers dislike the most. In fact, for many, it's the first ball to get dropped. The problem is that once the internship begins and student teachers are in their classroom environment, they feel they have "arrived" and are finally doing what they were put on this earth to do. "Now," they think, "If I could only get rid of those pesky university requirements, everything would be great." Not true. Your university or licensure program is still responsible for you and your learning during this training period. They have to make sure they have told you everything, prepared you for everything, and given you the very best instruction they could possibly provide; in most cases that lasts right until the very end with program completion and/or graduation. And you do receive a grade for this period in your teaching program, so you will want to make sure you keep up with your requirements. Our recommended strategies for your university responsibilities fall under three different categories: researching the internship, communicating with university faculty, and collaborating to get jobs done.

University Strategy 1: Research the Internship

What exactly is required of you by your university or licensure program? Are there on-campus sessions to attend? Is there a portfolio or other culminating project? Do you have official forms to complete? Below are tips for staying at the top of your game during the internship.

1. *Talk to recent graduates of your program.* Based on our past experiences within student teaching programs and our communication with faculty at other universities, we know that assignments and requirements usually don't change drastically from semester to semester. Thus, it's a good idea to communicate with someone who has recently completed the program regarding what you can expect. This person can give you hints about how to get the work done in the most efficient way and certain pitfalls to avoid.

2. *Go to class.* Talking to a recent program completer can be helpful, but it can also provide a wealth of misinformation, so beware. In order to get the full picture, you should also attend all scheduled meetings and seminars so you can be crystal clear on what your requirements are for the semester. Most instructors have a website or Blackboard page where information is housed and announcements are posted. Take advantage of this resource.

3. *Be an early bird.* In the beginning of the semester when your load is light, you should spend time reading over your requirements and beginning to chip away at all that you're expected to do. Student teachers who don't do their research or get the ball rolling early often find themselves overwhelmed—when it would have been so much easier to get started while the load was lighter. Completing as much work as possible in advance allows you to experience a more balanced internship—with fewer periods of panic and fewer all-nighters.

> Things You May Consider Tackling in Advance
>
> ✓ Studying for and/or taking Praxis II (if it's required for your program area)
> ✓ Writing papers, especially those not directly related to your classroom instruction
> ✓ Collecting and organizing items to be used in your final portfolio or other culminating projects
> ✓ Filing paperwork for graduation
> ✓ Organizing paperwork needed to apply for licensure

Simply getting one or two of these items out of the way can yield a more comfortable and manageable pace for completing the other tasks involved with student teaching.

UNIVERSITY STRATEGY 2: COMMUNICATE WITH UNIVERSITY FACULTY

You are still connected to the university or licensure program, so please don't abandon your supervisor for 15 weeks (or however long your internship lasts), then return for graduation. Here are a couple of tips to avoid seeing your face on the back of a milk carton:

1. *No disappearing acts.* You should be in regular communication with someone from the university, whether it be your supervisor, a student teaching seminar leader, or your academic advisor. Someone needs to know where you are and how you're doing, so be sure to share any information such as sickness or family emergencies that cause you to be absent or otherwise difficult to reach. In some instances, the university supervisor may be in the school quite frequently, and may pop in just to say hi between observations. However, with larger programs and limited faculty resources, supervisors are often stretched thin and unable to visit you outside of the required observations. Don't panic. Just make sure that your supervisor has provided you with a reliable and preferred method of contact—whether it's phone, e-mail, or text—and use it wisely, tactfully, and professionally.

2. *Check in periodically.* If you have concerns, of course, contact your supervisor right away. But it's also okay to simply check in to share brief information about how you're doing and what you're teaching, and to offer suggestions of good times to see you in action. If nothing else, the supervisor will know you are alive and well and still teaching in his absence. A good rule of thumb here, since the parts of the internship are so connected, is to copy your seminar leader (or whomever you report to in addition to your supervisor) on all e-mails so that this person can also be aware of your status. If you are experiencing challenges or need help, be sure to communicate your concerns early on, before they mushroom into problems that are larger than life or too difficult to fix within the remaining weeks of your internship.

UNIVERSITY STRATEGY 3: COLLABORATE TO GET JOBS DONE

You are not alone in the internship, and we don't expect that you will try to complete every task independently. Instead, we strongly recommend you seek out advice, resources, and assistance from others around you. This of course includes university faculty, but we also suggest that you band together with your peers in the program to get jobs done.

For example, if you're studying for Praxis II, work with a few of your peers to set up a study group. Quiz each other, share ideas, even talk about how you are dealing with the stresses related to the test. For assignments, talk with your peers about the criteria to make sure you are clear on the instructor's expectations. Once a first draft has been written, trade papers with your study group so your work can be edited with a fresh pair of eyes. You can even collaborate on larger projects. We have seen students set up gatherings that were part work related, part social—such as a portfolio party (complete with laptops, a scanner, pizza, and *American Idol* on the television) so no one felt alone in the process. We love this idea in particular because it allowed the students to do double-duty: working on a very important and potentially overwhelming task while in a relaxing environment with colleagues.

BALL #3: HOME DEMANDS

Another phrase in moms' arsenals is, "You can't take care of anybody else if you don't first take care of yourself." While moms probably still took care of everybody's needs before their own, they really were onto something with this advice. This is true of most of the moms we know (and plenty of dads responsible for caring for their children), although they have different ways of showing it. When you finish reading this chapter, call your parents—and/or others who looked out for your needs—and thank them. As a teacher, if you haven't met your own needs (i.e., "taking care of home"), you may be doing a disservice to your students.

Managing your responsibilities at home involves:

✓ Making healthy choices,

✓ Staying connected with family and friends,

✓ Doing things that make you happy, and

✓ Saying no to jobs that you can't handle at the moment.

HOME STRATEGY 1: MAKE HEALTHY CHOICES

First among your home demands is *personal health*. Be sure you're getting enough sleep (about 7½ hours per night), eating properly (not too much junk), taking any medications your doctor has prescribed, and exercising (about 30 minutes per day). We know you probably don't have a lot of time and that gym membership you bought may go completely unused during your internship, so consider walking before school, during your lunch break, or immediately after school. Even if you can only fit in two 15-minute periods or three 10-minute periods of exercise, it all adds up to a healthier you. Some teachers even participate in walking clubs at their schools. Consider joining them. The conversation that emerges can help you destress and remind you that there is life outside of your classroom.

HOME STRATEGY 2: STAY CONNECTED

The next home demand you'll have to address is *your need to be connected with family and friends*. Trust us—the internship isn't easy, and you can't do it alone. To survive, enlist the help of your personal support team. Whether it's through actual visits, phone calls, e-mails, Skype, or status updates on Facebook, you need to talk to people who are old enough to vote or rent a car. And you need your support team now more than ever, just in different ways. First, you'll have to make sure they understand the demands of student teaching. They need to know that you won't be as available for social calls as you were in the past, and that even though you (probably) aren't getting paid, this is a real job with real student outcomes at stake—not the fantasy gig with nights, weekends, and summers free that many uninformed people imagine when they think of teaching. So, tell them a little bit about what you're doing—but don't overdo it or they may stop listening or interject with a brand new conversation topic. Don't worry—you don't need your support team to listen to you go on and on about teaching. That's what teacher friends are for. What you can do, however, is get their help with other tasks, such as walking your dog on Wednesdays because you'll be home late after grade-level meetings, or picking your child up from dance class because you'll be at Open House. Chances are, they'll be happy to help.

HOME STRATEGY 3: GET A LIFE

The third home demand you must focus on is *your need to have a life*. We will say it over and over: Student teaching is a huge undertaking. It requires a lot of your time and energy. After you've spent the day teaching, the afternoon planning, and the early evening taking care of some basic personal needs (e.g., exercise, dinner), then what? More planning? Well, yes, if you are behind. But if you follow our advice and plan ahead, you will have a few minutes to focus on you and the things you used to have lots of time

for in a previous life. So pull out your scrapbooking, grab your Guitar Hero, or watch some totally guilt-free TV. You've earned it. Just spend this time doing something you enjoy. Remember: All work and no play may make you a very grouchy teacher.

HOME STRATEGY 4: JUST SAY NO

What about those projects you promised to work on? Remodeling the bathroom? Starting a neighborhood babysitting co-op? This might not be the time for those jobs. You should seriously reconsider most big projects for now, but you do have a couple of options.

You can postpone some projects by prioritizing your list and defining the critical items, then . . .

- ✔ If the task absolutely must be done, figure out a way to break it into manageable chunks, or enlist the help of your support team to complete it.
- ✔ If the task can wait, write down a realistic time to revisit it, and try your best to stick to it.
- ✔ If the task can be completely passed on to someone else—hooray. Cross it off your list.

It is quite possible that after you've prioritized your list and come to terms with what you can and can't take on right now, someone may come along and try to add another item to your list. What should you do? Most people's gut feeling is to say no, but they say yes anyway, so as not to disappoint others. Sometimes it's okay to accept the new job—if you can honestly give it the time and attention it needs. But what if you really do need to opt out? When you just can't take on one more task, you'll need a respectful way to say "No" or "Not right now." In Appendix A, you will find a list of 20 ideas for doing just that, plus a rationale for each response that makes the exchange guilt free.

_____ WHEN THE DEMANDS ARE MORE THAN YOU CAN HANDLE

Sometimes, the internship just doesn't work out. This typically happens when financial challenges, personal or family health issues, or perhaps even the loss of a family member or dear friend is too much to handle during the internship. If this happens to you, you will have to take a moment and honestly consider how you are doing and what you can feasibly take on for the next several weeks. Whether or not you choose to remain in the internship is a personal and respected decision, but you must be honest with yourself, and remember that there are real children in this equation who deserve 100% from their teacher, whoever it may be. Sometimes it is best for all involved for a student teacher to step away and return to the internship when he or she is emotionally capable of handling the demands of teaching.

Occasionally, a student teacher who is struggling with the demands of teaching may be put on an action plan by his or her university supervisor or even asked to take some time off and revisit the internship after reviewing aspects of teaching in which he or she needs to grow. This does not happen often, but we want to be sure that you are aware that it is a possibility in extreme cases.

_____ SPECIAL FEATURE SECTION FOR NONTRADITIONAL STUDENTS

"You Think You Know, But You Have No Idea"

We asked student teachers to share their thoughts on the myriad responsibilities that come with student teaching. Here's what they had to say. Notice that the majority of their comments had little to do with actual teaching, but instead with the ability to juggle all of the many tasks that are part of the student teaching experience as a whole.

Got Stress?

"Stress does not even to begin to describe how I feel. Life . . . what's that? Didn't even know that existed. My stressors are, no. 1, student teaching; no. 2, money and work; and no. 3, family. I feel as if there isn't much I could balance, because I don't have the time to. My life revolves around this student teaching experience. I feel as if I could've prepared better, but I had no idea it was going to be like this."

"My areas of stress are finding the time to pull my materials together to get my taxes done, spend time with my husband and family, and to get enough rest. When I get enough rest, I relate better to the children in the class and really enjoy them. When I'm dragging, I just want to get through the day and I really feel like I'm cheating the students."

Keeping Up With Family and Friends

"I have a 2-year-old daughter and it is so hard sometimes when I don't get to do as much with her as I want to because I am sitting at a computer (this is what drives me crazy). However, I am dealing with it and I am loving my experience."

"There has been a huge change in the amount of time that we are used to spending together. So what I've come up with is focusing on my daughter from the time I get home until she goes to bed. After I put her to bed, it's back to hitting the books. The only problem with that is that I have to retrain my brain to think during that time of night. I'm already pretty exhausted when I get home."

"It hit me a few weeks ago that I'm not really even a college student anymore. Even my weekends are taken up with writing lesson plans and pacing back and forth thinking about how I can get my struggling students to achieve these objectives."

"I try to keep Friday night as a fun night and do not do any student teaching stuff. Of course my house always looks a wreck nowadays. My kitchen table is covered with piles of teaching manuals, textbooks, lesson plans, etc."

MAINTAINING PERSONAL HEALTH

"I think that my two best friends are my daily vitamin and my extra dose of vitamin C. I swear if I miss a day, I can feel the germs creeping in."

"This experience has made me change the way that I eat (sorry, Steak n' Shake). I need more fruits and veggies just to make it through my day."

"Last week I slept. I went to bed every night by—if not before—9:30, and it felt good. . . . I found the kids a lot easier to deal with, and I was able to let almost everything roll off of my back."

DEALING WITH DISORGANIZATION

"I am very organized but I have one area lately that I need to focus on. During teaching, I've been laying down stuff and then forgetting where I put it. Or I do put things away and then can't remember where I put it. Help."

"My kitchen table is no longer used for eating but for storage. I also find myself laying papers down in my classroom and forgetting where I put them. One time a student accidently took them and luckily returned them the next day. My organizational skills have gone into overdrive with all I have to keep up with."

Words of Encouragement

"Stress is a word that has become entirely too frequent in my vocabulary. However, I have been able to deal with it because I know that this experience will not last forever."

છ૭   ૦૨

"One real important thing that helped me through the late nights and weekends on the computer was Starbucks. Starbucks is a great place to go relax and work. A hot peppermint latte calms you and gets those lesson plans flowing."

છ૭   ૦૨

"My advice to all is to stay focused on the bigger goal—remember that this, too, shall pass and that we all have a lot to be grateful for and proud of. All of us know what it took to get to where we are now and we have come too far to let this exhaustive student teaching process get us down. Keep your heads up, continue to take care of you—you are the priority here because you cannot be an effective teacher, mother, counselor, caregiver, etc., etc., etc., unless you are taking care of you."

FINAL THOUGHTS

This chapter has been full of strategies for managing the numerous demands student teachers often encounter during the internship. We want to reiterate the importance of organization and time management and their crucial role in keeping up with the day-to-day items and tasks involved in the internship. Moreover, we want to remind you that you are not expected to progress through the internship without the help of others. In addition to calling on your village to help with certain activities, it is equally important to remain in close contact with your supervisor so that there are no "surprises." Clear organization of outside factors can help you focus more closely on those factors directly related to teaching and learning. The next chapter addresses our final area of management—dealing with student behavior—which, when handled effectively, can lead to increased time-on-task during instruction

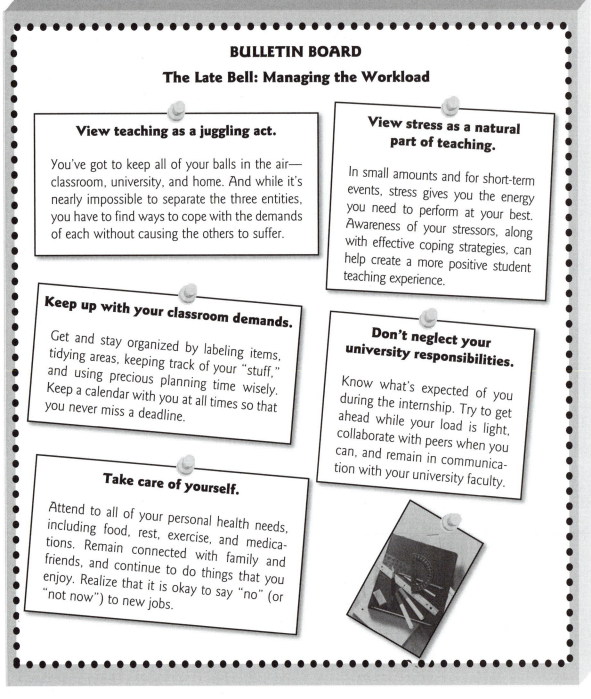

BULLETIN BOARD

The Late Bell: Managing the Workload

View teaching as a juggling act.

You've got to keep all of your balls in the air—classroom, university, and home. And while it's nearly impossible to separate the three entities, you have to find ways to cope with the demands of each without causing the others to suffer.

View stress as a natural part of teaching.

In small amounts and for short-term events, stress gives you the energy you need to perform at your best. Awareness of your stressors, along with effective coping strategies, can help create a more positive student teaching experience.

Keep up with your classroom demands.

Get and stay organized by labeling items, tidying areas, keeping track of your "stuff," and using precious planning time wisely. Keep a calendar with you at all times so that you never miss a deadline.

Don't neglect your university responsibilities.

Know what's expected of you during the internship. Try to get ahead while your load is light, collaborate with peers when you can, and remain in communication with your university faculty.

Take care of yourself.

Attend to all of your personal health needs, including food, rest, exercise, and medications. Remain connected with family and friends, and continue to do things that you enjoy. Realize that it is okay to say "no" (or "not now") to new jobs.

EXTRA CREDIT

READ ABOUT IT

Stress

Creel, R. (2009). *Twenty ways to say no.* OnlineOrganizing.com. Retrieved from http://www.online organizing.com/ExpertAdviceToolboxTips.asp?tipsheet=16

Davies, L. (n.d.). *Coping with stress: Tips for educators.* Retrieved from http://www.kellybear .com/TeacherArticles/TeacherTip16.html

How to manage your stress. (2008). The University of North Carolina at Chapel Hill Campus Health Services. Retrieved from http://campushealth.unc.edu/index.php?option=com_content&task=view&id=670&Itemid=167

Parks, B. (1997). ABCs for a low-stress school year. *Instructor Magazine.* Retrieved from http://content.scholastic.com/ browse/article.jsp?id=4020

Ranskin, D. G. (1989). *The doctor told me that my stress caused my . . . (headaches, insomnia, burning stomach, or whatever your symptoms are).* Kansas State University. (Revised for online version by D. Lambert in 2000.) Retrieved from http://www.k-state.edu/counseling/topics/stress/drstress.html

Wilkins, B. (2008, August 1). *101 ways to cope with teaching stress.* SmartTeaching.org. Retrieved from http://www .smartteaching.org/blog/2008/08/101-ways-to-cope-with-teaching-stress

Organization

Katz, M. (2002). *Managing paperwork: Top priorities for organization.* LearnNC. Retrieved from http://www .learnnc.org/lp/pages/741

Smith, K. J. (2005, August 19). *Templates to help you with paperwork.* LearnNC. Retrieved from http://www .learnnc.org/lp/editions/firstyear/254

Springer, S. (2005). *The organized teacher: A hands-on guide to setting up and running a terrific classroom.* New York: McGraw-Hill.

Thompson, J. G. (2009). *The first-year teacher's checklist: A quick reference for classroom success.* San Francisco: Jossey-Bass.

THINK ABOUT IT

1. Think about the internship so far. Overall, what have you found to be the most challenging aspects of teaching? For each aspect of teaching you listed, name two steps you can take to make the item less of a challenge for you.

2. What kinds of outside demands (university, home) might compete with your ability to do well in the classroom? Think of a plan for dealing with those demands. Use the chart below to jot down your ideas.

University Demands		Home Demands	
Demand/need	Who can help me, and how?	Demand/need	Who can help me, and how?

University Demands		Home Demands	

3. List at least five leisure activities that you would like to engage in during your free time. These cannot be related to teaching.

TRY IT

1. Revisit Figures 4.1 and 4.2 on planning time. For one week, track how you spend your planning time. After the first 3 days, reevaluate how you spend your time. Are you wasting a lot of time, or is your time well managed? Make changes as needed, and make an effort to stick with those changes. At the end of the week, check how you spend your time again. Are you making progress? Are your minutes used wisely? Are you getting a lot done? Write about your growth in your reflection journal or log.

2. Develop your organizational system. Get started with a three-ring binder, several dividers, and a few three-hole pocket folders. Add whichever materials you need to create a system that works for you—one that will allow you to keep up with all of the parent notes, faculty memos, paperwork, deadlines, and general stuff that teachers must hold on to. (Resist the temptation to file your lesson plans here; they actually work best in a separate notebook.) At the end of each school day, when you are clearing your desk, be sure to file away any of these miscellaneous pieces in their appropriate sections. If you find that you are still struggling to locate items, either your system isn't working or you haven't given it a good try. Reevaluate and try again.

3. Revisit the chart you created above for tackling home and university demands. Get the ball rolling by contacting those who can help you with the task. Be sure to provide them with the necessary information and materials to get the job done the way you want it done—or be prepared to have it done their way. Either way, it will be done. In your reflection journal or log, write about how it feels to ask and allow others to handle some of your responsibilities. Is this something you're comfortable doing? Why or why not? Determine the level of support that feels right for you, and move forward.

4. Each day after the students leave, try to focus on tackling an important job related to the internship, other than writing lesson plans and pulling resources together. For example, you might tweak your resumé, review for your specialty exams, or create an interactive bulletin board for your students. Also, each day when you leave the school, make a point of engaging in at least one activity that is about you and not your students—even if it's only for 15 minutes. For example, you might work in your garden, shoot hoops with a friend, or catch a quick nap—whatever makes you feel temporarily indulgent. Keep a running tally of these activities in your journal or reflection log so that you can remind yourself of all you have accomplished and all you've done to maintain balance and keep your sanity.

The Principal's Office

5

Classroom Management During Student Teaching

Dear Student Teacher,

Welcome to one of the most challenging parts of student teaching—classroom management. There is simply no way to sugarcoat this—classroom management can be hard, really hard. Although you've taken on a great deal of responsibility in the classroom (lesson planning, teaching, grading papers, creating bulletin boards, completing running records, and so on) and you really are doing much of the work of a "real" teacher, the truth is you are not the "real" teacher. The students know this, your CT knows this, and you know this. Moreover, nothing is more fun for students (no matter the grade or age) than to test a new teacher.

So, what's a student teacher to do? How do you manage a classroom that's not totally yours to manage? How do you discipline students when you really want them to like you? How do you enforce your CT's rules, especially those with which you disagree? In this chapter we'll provide you with strategies to help you and your students stay out of the principal's office. We'll help you to optimize the student teaching experience even though management is to some extent beyond your control.

Although classroom management will be challenging (as it is for many of the most experienced teachers), you can implement strategies that will eventually allow you to focus less on managing and more on teaching.

Sincerely,

Your Management Mentors

CLASSROOM MANAGEMENT

Classroom management is a colossal concern for new teachers. Other than content knowledge and effective pedagogical skills, we believe nothing is more integral to academic achievement than successful classroom management. We know your teacher education program provided instruction and training regarding classroom management. Still, now that you are actually in the student teaching internship, we thought a review of classroom management basics might be invaluable to your overall success.

WHAT EXACTLY IS CLASSROOM MANAGEMENT?

There are many definitions for classroom management, and often it's confused with discipline. However, it's important to understand that discipline and classroom management are not synonymous. According to Dictionary.com, **discipline**, or the act of training or punishment to obtain a certain behavior or outcome, is merely one of the many components that make up classroom management. Wong (2009) defines classroom management as "all of the things that a teacher does to organize students, space, time, and materials so that instruction in content and student learning can take place" (p. 81). Now ask yourself—don't you need more than discipline to be able to teach and for your students to learn? Of course you do. So, it's nonsensical to think of classroom management and discipline as the same. In truth, **classroom management** is a complex, yet organized, matrix of variables that teachers arrange to manage behavior and classroom processes, such as instruction and social interactions. Although only you can determine the exact variables necessary for your effective classroom management plan, let's review briefly what most educational researchers agree every good plan should have: procedures, rules, rewards, and consequences. (See Table 5.1.)

Table 5.1	Classroom Management Basics
Rule (rool), noun. A principle or regulation governing conduct, action, procedure, or arrangement.	Every effective classroom management plan must have rules. In other words, you need a way to regulate actions and behavior in your classroom. Students should know what is expected of them; thus, classroom rules should be clear, concise, and consistently implemented and enforced.

Reward (rĭwôrd'), noun. The return for performance of a desired behavior; positive reinforcement.	Rewards are often used as incentives for positive student behavior and/or excellent academic performance. Rewards should be developmentally appropriate and distributed fairly. Some examples of rewards are homework passes, extended recess time, free time, and assignment choices.
Consequence (kon-si-kwens, -kwuhns), noun. Something that logically or naturally follows from an action or condition.	Consequences in classroom management plans are most often enacted as a result of inappropriate behavior or breaking the rules. Consequences should be clearly communicated to students, appropriate for the infraction, and consistently enforced.
Procedure (prə-sē'jər), noun. A series of steps taken to accomplish an end.	This is the "how to" portion of the classroom management plan. You should clearly explain how to turn in papers, ask a question, label papers, sharpen pencils, get and return supplies, work in groups, complete seatwork, behave during interruptions, etc. Your class procedures could be extensive. The key is to make certain you explicitly teach and practice them with the students. Also, be sure to review class procedures when necessary.

POPULAR MANAGEMENT PLANS

A QUICK REVIEW OF POPULAR TRIED-AND-TRUE PLANS

You'll need more than just the basics to have a successful classroom, and there are a number of classroom management plans and philosophies which are very effective in helping teachers to manage their classrooms. In fact, during your pre-service training, you were probably introduced to several key players in the classroom management field. Just in case your memory is a bit fuzzy on the strategies, Table 5.2 provides a quick review of a few plans.

Table 5.2   Popular Classroom Management Plans Transformed for Student Teaching

Wonderful Wong		
Title & Author	**Strategies**	**Transform for Student Teaching**
The First Days of School by Harry and Rosemary Wong	• The first day will make or break your entire school year. • Have a plan with procedures and routines in place. Explain, rehearse, and reinforce procedures and routines at the beginning and throughout the school year. • Consistency is crucial. • Greet students at the door, have a seating chart, and get them to work quickly. • Post the schedule and assignments in a visible location. • Manage the classroom rather than disciplining the classroom. • Structure is needed in well-managed classrooms. • Create a supportive community of learners.	• Make a good first impression on your CT and students. • Learn the class management plan and the flow of the class. Ask your CT questions about class routines. • Always have a warm-up activity. • List due dates and assignments on the board. • Create an organized environment. • Encourage all students to value each others' opinions.

(Continued)

(Continued)

Magnificent Marzano		
Title & Author	**Strategies**	**Transform for Student Teaching**
Classroom Management That Works: Research-based Strategies for Every Teacher by Robert Marzano	• Educational research is used to create Action Steps. • Establish effective rules and procedures. • Implement appropriate disciplinary interventions. • Foster productive student–teacher relationships. • Develop a positive mental set. • Help students contribute to a positive learning environment. • Activate school-wide measures for effective classroom management.	• Read educational journals to stay current with the latest education research. • Reflect upon class rules and procedures. Revise those that are least effective. • Create a positive environment through your actions and attitude. • Read the school's faculty handbook, and align class rules with school-wide policies.

Can't Miss Canter		
Title & Author	**Strategies**	**Transform for Student Teaching**
Assertive Discipline by Lee Canter and Marlene Canter	• Catch students doing good. • Use no more than five clear rules written in positive form (e.g., Do your own work instead of Don't cheat). • Consequences should be on a spectrum directly related to the punishment. • Develop an appropriate rewards system. • Never embarrass students in front of their peers.	• Praise student accomplishments (e.g., behavior, academic achievement, peer interactions, etc.). Discuss sensitive issues with students privately. • Review your CT's consequence system. Identify which consequence goes with which inappropriate action. • Discuss your CT's reward system. Help to expand or update the system.

Amazing Albert		
Title & Author	**Strategies**	**Transform for Student Teaching**
Cooperative Discipline by Linda Albert	• Identify why the student is misbehaving: attention, power, revenge, or avoidance of failure. • Handle misbehavior immediately. • Use encouragement strategies that build self-esteem and motivation to cooperate. • Build strong partnerships with students and parents.	• Students misbehave for a reason. Discuss behavior issues with your CT to learn more about the student's history. • Address misbehavior the first time (even if you are nervous). • Use cooperative learning and team. building activities to promote students' self-efficacy. • Write a letter or email to parents introducing yourself and your role in the classroom. Invite them to participate in your lessons (e.g., discussion of travels, reading tutor, etc.).

Count on Kounin		
Title & Author	**Strategies**	**Transform for Student Teaching**
Discipline and Group Management in Classrooms by J. S. Kounin	• The teacher has "withitness" and knows what the students are doing and what is going on in the classroom. • Overlapping or attending to different events without being totally diverted by disruptions is a critical skill. • Lessons should be brisk and cues should be given to keep students focused. • Group alerting should be practiced to keep all students "alerted" to the task at hand. • Provide students seatwork activities that have variety and offer challenge.	• Don't stand at the board or sit for long periods. Circulate. • Visualize lessons to prevent unexpected events from distracting you. • Create signals to make students aware of transitions. • Differentiate assignments and allow student choice.

Judicious Jones		
Title & Author	**Strategies**	**Transform for Student Teaching**
Positive Classroom Discipline by Fred Jones *Tools for Teaching* by Fred Jones	• Use body language and physical proximity to prevent and correct misbehavior. • Help students to support their own self-control. • Focus on instruction to lessen management issues.	• Stand near students who are misbehaving or move the student near you. • Create student contracts to encourage self-monitoring of behavior and achievement. • Review the developmental stages of your students. Design lessons appropriate and relevant for them.

Controversial Kohn		
Title & Author	**Strategies**	**Transform for Student Teaching**
Punished by Rewards by Alfie Kohn	• Manipulating students with incentives only works in the short run. • Rewards only produce temporary obedience. • Build a classroom community to lessen management issues. • Curiosity and cooperation are encouraged—not competition. • Engage in discussions about actions rather than focusing on positive reinforcement.	• Don't rely solely on incentives or rewards. Help students make connections between the content and their personal goals. • Encourage students to work together and to resolve their own conflicts. • Create class goals and celebrate class progress. • Speak privately with students and discuss how their actions impact the class community.

Talented Tate		
Title & Author	**Strategies**	**Transform for Student Teaching**
Shouting Won't Grow Dendrites by Marcia Tate	• Create a classroom environment conducive to learning. • Develop a proactive plan. • Deliver brain-friendly lessons. • Deal with chronic misbehavior.	• Create a bulletin board, student display, or student work zone. • Anticipate challenges and create strategies to deal with them. • Review your lesson plans and use strategies to increase student engagement and minimize misbehavior.

All of these theories have a great deal to offer. Just remember: You will not fully be able to figure out what works for you until you have your own classroom and can create or utilize a plan that works best for you. The goal is always to optimize academic achievement and positive social interactions. This means you must have a sense of order in your classroom. Order doesn't mean you blow a whistle or put names on the board every time a student fails to follow a procedure or breaks a rule. According to Doyle (1986), "Order in a classroom simply means that within acceptable limits the students are following the program of action necessary for a particular classroom event to be realized in the situation" (p. 396).

WHO'S IN CONTROL HERE, ANYWAY?

Now that we've reviewed the basics of classroom management, let's discuss a fantasy you might have regarding student teaching. During your teacher education program, you may have studied Wong and Wong's "give me five" technique to quiet down a classroom or Marzano and colleagues' "action steps" (Marzano, Pickering, & Pollack, 2003; Wong & Wong, 2009). Perhaps you envision yourself (in your best teacher outfit) at the head of the class of students sitting in perfect rows, with raised hands, in your quiet but busy classroom. Or, rather than fantasizing about a perfectly managed classroom, perhaps you're on the opposite end of the spectrum and imagine names written in red on the board, students in time-out, or directing students to the hallway for a private conference about expectations? Whether you're fantasizing about the

perfect class or agonizing about possible behavior problems, there is a common theme. You're attempting to alter students' behavior. You're either trying to get them to do something or to stop doing something so that instruction can take place. You want control.

However, in order to have control, you must have power. As a student teacher, you must come to grips with the fact that your power is limited. Everyone at the school knows you're not the "real" teacher. Consequently, you don't have the same power as your cooperating teacher or other teachers in the building. Still, even knowing you have limited power, you are required to demonstrate your understanding of basic classroom management concepts. So, with very little power, you will be held accountable for how students behave and how the classroom functions. You will be asked to implement a set of rules and steps to get the students to do what you want, how you want it, where you want it, and when you want it. You can imagine how inherently difficult this can be. How easy is it to get your significant other, child, parent, or sibling (or cousin, fraternity brother, congressman, eccentric neighbor, etc.) to do what you want, how you want it, where you want it, and when you want it? It's not very easy, is it? Now, how easy is it to get 25 school-age children to do what you want them to do, how you want them to do it, where you want them to do it, and when you want them to do it—every single day of the school year? Is this even possible? Is this even a reasonable expectation? How, you might ask, can you be responsible for student behavior and what happens in your classroom at all times when you have no true power or control?

Here is a hard truth—control during student teaching is an illusion. However, even though you may not be able to control your students' behavior and what happens in your classroom at all times, you will nonetheless be accountable for it. That's right. You read that sentence correctly. Even though you cannot control it all, you will still be held responsible for it all. You are ultimately responsible for everything that happens in the classroom because it affects academic outcomes. The goal of education in the United States is to prepare children to be productive citizens in our society. As a practice, schools push mastering curriculum concepts and social relationships as a means to that goal. Thus, classroom management truly plays an integral part in the infrastructure of the entire United States. If you can't manage your classroom, then students might not be able to master fractions or become friends with other students. These failures might prevent them from becoming productive citizens in our now global economy. Without productive citizens to contribute to this global economy, our entire world order could collapse. Consequently, it could be argued that the success of the entire world depends on your ability to manage your classroom.

In truth, the success of the world doesn't depend on effective classroom management, but the success of your classroom does. According to Moskowitz and Hayman (1976), once a teacher loses control of his or her classroom, it becomes increasingly more difficult for that teacher to regain control. Also, research from Berliner (1988) and Brophy and Good (1986) shows that teachers' taking time to correct misbehavior caused by poor classroom management skills results in lower rates of academic engagement in the classroom. It is extremely important that you understand the role classroom management plays in the learning process and, consequently, your internship. A great deal is at stake: your reputation, your CT's reputation, instructional time, academic achievement, a potential job, your stress levels, and your sanity. So, with all of this at stake, yet still factoring in the fact that you cannot consistently control student behavior, how can you succeed at classroom management?

Apple (1995) explains that teachers have a great deal of power when it comes to influencing student behavior. So, even though you don't have the power of a "real" teacher, you do have the power to influence behavior and implement basic classroom management skills. The key is to remember that your job is to manage your classroom, not control it. Managing infers you can prevent and handle issues as they arise because you have a plan in place. It doesn't mean problems won't ever arise—quite the contrary. It just means that when (not if) they arise, you are ready.

HOW DO I PRACTICE CLASSROOM MANAGEMENT DURING STUDENT TEACHING?

Right now, you are a guest in your CT's classroom. He or she has already established a set of classroom rules that most likely you will be expected to implement. Still, the student teaching internship gives you a chance to discover what works for you so when you get your own classroom, you'll have the confidence to implement your own system. However, as your management mentors, let us repeat that now is not the time to do a lot of experimenting with classroom management strategies. Stay focused on your ultimate goal—demonstrating that you possess the knowledge, skills, and disposition necessary to join the teaching profession. Ultimately during student teaching, your only goal regarding classroom management is to show you can handle the very basics of managing your classroom. Now is absolutely not the time to test every strategy you've ever read about or witnessed during classroom observations. This doesn't mean you shouldn't try some of the strategies you've learned. The point is that this is not the time to try everything. You'll get the chance to integrate any management strategy you wish when you have your own classroom (and even then you'll probably find it wise to focus on just a few strategies at a time). We know you're full of enthusiasm and energy, and we know you've been anxiously waiting to test out all the ideas you've collected during your teacher education program. We promise you that you will get the chance—just not now. For this very brief and finite period of time, keep in mind the strategies reviewed earlier, but stay focused and ultimately follow the steps discussed next.

KNOW THYSELF

It seems simple enough to say to begin with yourself; still, it can be difficult during student teaching to reflect because you are so incredibly busy. However, beginning within requires you to take a long honest look in the mirror (literally and figuratively) and assess your confidence level. You must believe in yourself and your abilities to successfully manage a classroom. This is not an option. If you don't believe in you, your students won't believe in you either. It is completely normal to be nervous about classroom management. All student teachers are worried about managing the classroom. However, not all student teachers show it. Instead of projecting insecurity and worry, they appear self-assured and confident (even though they are not).

It's certainly natural to have some anxiety about being an authority figure in the classroom. Still, there is a difference between feeling nervous and lacking confidence. So, if you are feeling a little weak in the knees about managing the classroom, we'd like to suggest a strategy called "practice and pretend." This strategy involves practicing confidence. How do you practice confidence? In classroom management terms, you follow a procedure and a rule. The procedure involves pretending to have a conversation with your students while practicing your tone of voice (projecting your voice and speaking clearly), perfecting your posture (standing up straight, shoulders back), and maintaining eye contact (talking to yourself in the mirror and looking yourself in the eye). The rule is that you must practice this routine every morning when you wake up and every night before you go to bed. Practice and pretend introducing yourself to the class, reviewing classroom expectations, giving the directions for an assignment, or redirecting a student. The topic of the practice and pretend exercise can vary; just pretend to have a conversation and practice your tone, posture, and eye contact. Regardless of where you are on the confidence spectrum, remember you would not have made it to student teaching if you were not qualified. Confidence in your abilities is a key step in executing effective classroom management. Believe in yourself and your students will believe in you too.

Know Your Cooperating Teacher

If you haven't already read the chapters about the importance of a positive relationship with your CT, we'd like to encourage you to stop now to read them. Remember, in general, cooperating teachers are chosen because they are highly qualified to guide you through the entire teaching process, which includes all aspects of classroom management. Immediately familiarize yourself thoroughly with your cooperating teacher's classroom management plan. Recognize that your CT may not have an actual classroom management plan written down in a document like commercial management plans or like one you might have created for an assignment in your teacher education program. Consequently, you'll need to ask some very specific questions to make certain you understand your CT's system. Refer to questions in the Crucial Management Questions Guide (Figure 5.1) to help you discuss this with your CT.

| Figure 5.1 | Crucial Management Questions Guide |

Directions: During the student teaching internship, you'll need to know as much as you possibly can about your cooperating teacher's classroom management plan. Schedule some time with your cooperating teacher to find out the answers to the following questions:

✓ Can you tell me a little bit about why you've set up the room this way? Are you flexible with this arrangement, or do you want it to remain the same?

✓ What are your rules? How did you come up with them? Do the students follow them most of the time? Which rule is the most difficult for them to follow and/or for you to enforce? Are there any rules you're thinking about changing or adding? Are you open to me creating a new system? Can you give me some parameters?

✓ What happens when a student breaks a rule?

✓ Are you using any kind of rewards system? Can you explain it to me? How do you track it? What happens to students that do not get rewards frequently?

✓ What has been the parent reaction to your system? What do you do if a parent disagrees with the way an issue is handled?

✓ What organizing techniques are you using to keep the classroom flowing smoothly? How do the students know what to do and when to do it?

✓ How do you handle students who refuse to comply with your requests but they haven't broken a rule?

✓ What do you do if there is an emergency such as a fight breaking out or a student getting sick in the classroom?

✓ How did you find out what motivates your students? What strategies did you use to get to know them?

Truly, one of the most successful strategies you have at your disposal for success with classroom management is simply to have a serious in-depth discussion with your CT about his or her management system. You need to know more than just what to do if a student is defiant. Also, you need to discuss in an open way any rules you think you'll have a hard time enforcing. Sometimes just having a deeper understanding of why your CT has the rule in place can give you the fortitude to enforce it.

For most CTs, classroom management has become second nature. They're not always conscious of their system—what they do and why and when they do it to keep the classroom running smoothly. Consequently, you'll need to put on your detective hat and do some investigating. Keep asking questions so that you can learn as much as you can.

What If My Cooperating Teacher Is Bad at Classroom Management?

As your management mentors, it's time for us to give you another bit of hard truth. Not all CTs are experts at classroom management. Because the spectrum of expertise can vary and this is an issue many teachers find challenging, it is possible (but not probable) that you are working with a CT who is not equipped to assist you in fully mastering the basics in classroom management. Still, even if your CT is struggling to implement an effective management system, you can learn from him or her. Take the time to reflect upon what is not working. Perhaps there is no clear management plan in place, perhaps the rules are not clear or not consistently enforced, or perhaps your CT is more concerned about being the students' friend than teacher. Use this information to think about how you might handle these issues when you have your own classroom. Finally, carefully ask your CT whom else you should observe in the building to learn about effective classroom management. If you think this might offend your cooperating teacher, be sure to explain that you need to observe several teachers in key areas such as classroom management in order to fulfill your university's requirement. Once you know the experts in your school, spend some time in their classrooms. Ask them questions about their systems and share your findings with your CT. The information you gain will be beneficial to both you and your CT. Your CT might even be willing to try or let you try some of those ideas.

KNOW YOUR STUDENTS

Great performers know their audience. As a teacher, you already know the students are your audience, and it's imperative you learn as much as you can about them. First and foremost, learn their names. It does not matter if you teach 5 students or 500 or if they have easy names or very difficult names. You show your students that you value who they are when you learn their names and pronounce them correctly. Create a seating chart with the students' names on them, use mnemonic devices, or make associations that will help you to remember. For example, you have a student with red hair. The red hair makes you think of Lucille Ball, which makes you think of your Uncle Robert who watched the *I Love Lucy* show when you visited him in Georgia as a child during the summer. You remember that the capitol of Georgia is Athens, which sparks you to remember that your student's name is Athena. It might read like a long process, but this all happens in your amazing brain in mere seconds. Whatever strategy you choose, just learn their names correctly and quickly.

Second, make an extra effort to get to know what your students value. The only way to find out what your students are passionate about is to talk to them. Rather than writing lesson objectives on the board as your students are arriving in the morning, take the time to chat with them. Ask them basic questions: How was your weekend? Do you have any pets? What have you been doing since I saw you last? How are the rest of your classes going? Is there any good food in the cafeteria today? As your management mentors, we'd be remiss if we didn't remind you to be strictly professional in your approach to get to know your students. Be careful *where* (not alone in the bathroom) and *how* (not like a peer) you approach a student, as the location and manner of approach can impact how the student perceives your attempts to get to know him or her. It should be crystal clear that your intention is to build a teacher–student relationship and absolutely nothing more.

We are not suggesting that you waste instructional time by chatting with your students the entire period. However, taking some time to get to know your students is imperative. Do your best to make a connection with every student, even those students with whom you find it difficult to connect. Building positive relationships with your students will help to minimize management issues, thereby maximizing instructional time.

KNOW YOUR SPACE

In the world of architectural design, form follows function. We don't have a total grasp of the complexity of that concept (because we're management mentors, not designers), but we're pretty sure it means your space should work for you. In other words, you need to make certain the classroom is organized to facilitate teaching and learning. Your CT has already organized the classroom, so pay careful attention to how it is arranged. Make note of where information is posted, where students store their items, teacher and student work areas, resources and supplies, and lighting options. Depending upon your CT's flexibility, you may or may not be able to change much of your environment; however, having a greater awareness of it will help you to manage your classroom more effectively.

KNOW YOUR LESSON

You'll read all about instruction in Chapter 6. Still, it is worth stating now how important it is for you to have engaging lessons for your students. Tate (2007) explains that effective managers plan lessons that minimize classroom disruptions; they don't have any special magical talents. In our years of supervising student teachers in the field, we've sat in classes filled with perfectly obedient students until the lesson began. However, once the student teacher began to teach a poorly planned lesson, the students became bored and decided to entertain themselves. Once the students disengage, more likely than not, you will have management issues.

You must do your best to create lessons that will engage your audience. We don't mean you have to turn flips to explain gravity or light your hair on fire to explain the principles of heat. What we do mean is that you need to make certain you are employing brain-friendly strategies that will engage your students. Also, pay close attention to your students while you are teaching. If you see them begin to disconnect (you'll know this because their eyes are glazing over, they're passing notes, or they're sleeping), change your teaching strategy. Don't keep teaching a bad lesson just because it took you all night to create it and it's written in ink in your lesson plan book. It's a plan, not a binding legal contract. As the teacher, you get to make adjustments to your lesson as necessary.

KNOW THE SYSTEM

What we're calling "the system" includes the systems of both your CT and the school. Effective classroom management requires a plan, preferably a clear and concise plan that works for you and your students. Whether you are using your CT's plan, a popular plan, or creating and implementing your own, you must be clear about its components. Really know it in order to show it and enforce it. However, if you see that you need to make changes to your plan, by all means, make those changes. Just beware: Don't make changes all day, every day. You'll confuse yourself and your students. You are the expert in your classroom, and you know yourself and your students. Take advantage of professional development opportunities, talk to seasoned teachers, and consult other student teachers. Do whatever you need to do; just be confident enough to consistently implement your plan and to make small changes when your system is not working.

AVOID THE MOST COMMON MISTAKES STUDENT TEACHERS MAKE

Now that you have some ideas about what to do with classroom management, we want to give you some advice on what not to do during student teaching.

Teaching Is Not a Popularity Contest

As your management mentors, we want to warn you of the number one classroom management misstep that student teachers make—they want to be friends with their students. Many student teachers have a powerful desire for their students to like them. It can be hard not to fantasize about being the engaging, challenging teacher who is also beloved by all the students. We in no way think it's bad for your students to like you; however, teaching is not a popularity contest. If your students like you, that's great. If they don't, continue to do your best to make personal connections with them while staying focused on your goal to deliver meaningful lessons and to create an environment conducive to learning. Think back to your motivations for becoming a teacher. Some common reasons people join the teaching profession are a love of their content and a love for working with children. Your motivation to become a teacher was not to become friends with 25 kindergartners. If you are in need of increasing your social network, there are many avenues you can explore for expanding your friendship base. However, becoming BFFs (best friends forever) with all of your students is not one of them.

So, even though the plot line in many popular movies about teachers involves phenomenal breakthroughs once the teacher cultivates authentic friendships with the students, remember that is not reality. You can be friendly without focusing on being their friend. You are the teacher. Friendship just is not your primary objective. Nowhere in the job description of teacher will you see "befriend the students." In addition, I dare you to find one teacher evaluation instrument that lists befriending students as a requisite. So, be friendly. Rapport matters, but being a friend does not. Get to know your students. Ask about their lives and care about them—just don't depend on them to be your social network. If you focus on friendship, you'll do them and yourself a disservice; plus, your ability to effectively manage the classroom will be severely compromised.

YELLING IS TELLING

As a student teacher, we know you are often unsure of yourself. However, you would never tell the students, "Class, I'm not sure of myself today, and I'm feeling really nervous inside. I don't know if I have what it takes to be a teacher. I'm really terrified you'll figure out I'm not sure what I'm doing. Sometimes it just feels like I'm winging it." Most of you would never say this aloud to your students because it would simply confirm your inexperience. However, when you resort to raising your voice (also known as yelling) in the classroom in an attempt to gain control—that is exactly what you're doing. Your yelling is telling. It is a clear (and very loud) signal to the students that you don't know what you're doing.

If you find yourself yelling to get your students' attention, stop and take a deep breath. Recognize the need to review and enforce the management system. Do not talk over the students; just wait (with your best "I mean business" face) for them to listen to you. Do not talk until the room is silent. The students will eventually stop talking (this might take 2 minutes or 10). Now, calmly and quietly review your rules, consequences, and classroom policies. Ask the students to repeat them back to you, resumé your lesson, and consistently enforce your system.

USE, DON'T ABUSE, YOUR CT

We have strongly suggested that you work cooperatively with your CT when tackling classroom management. However, make certain you do not rely on your CT to handle all of your discipline issues. This may be really hard for you and extremely hard for your CT. It could be hard for you because you're probably a little nervous and afraid about implementing your consequences. If your CT is willing to handle behavior disruptions, it might be easier for you to let him or her take over than to face your fears of disciplining students. On the other hand, it might also be extremely challenging for your CT to let go of the reins he or she is so used to holding. Sometimes, it's just hard for your CT to hand over all aspects of classroom management, especially those involving discipline, to an inexperienced student teacher. Your CT understands that instructional time is extremely valuable, so it could be difficult for him or her to completely turn over the reins to you while you figure out the realities and complexities of management. Also, because your CT will ultimately be held responsible for the management of the classroom, he or she will often jump in to rescue you rather than risk invaluable instructional time being lost.

Nonetheless, whether you are using your CT's system or not, you simply must not rely solely on your CT to enforce the consequences for misbehavior or enforce classroom procedures. If you constantly look to your CT when misbehavior or procedural issues occur, you will lose all credibility with your students. Effective teachers position themselves as confident leaders in the classroom. It is important that you demonstrate your ability to confidently and consistently guide procedures in your classroom and implement consequences if problems arise.

SPECIAL FEATURE SECTION _____

If You Are a . . .

TEACHER'S ASSISTANT → Make the shift from assisting to leading. Don't rely on your CT to handle management issues for you. Be sure that you and your CT explain your new role as "teacher" to the students.

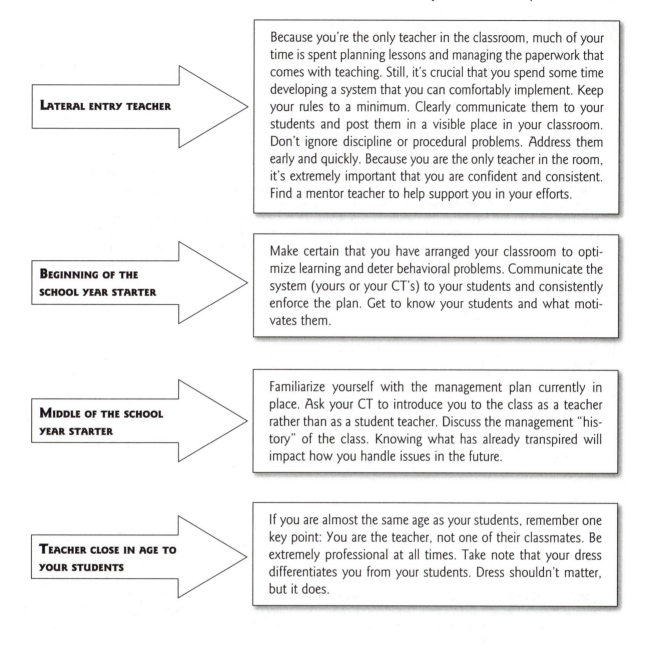

LATERAL ENTRY TEACHER

Because you're the only teacher in the classroom, much of your time is spent planning lessons and managing the paperwork that comes with teaching. Still, it's crucial that you spend some time developing a system that you can comfortably implement. Keep your rules to a minimum. Clearly communicate them to your students and post them in a visible place in your classroom. Don't ignore discipline or procedural problems. Address them early and quickly. Because you are the only teacher in the room, it's extremely important that you are confident and consistent. Find a mentor teacher to help support you in your efforts.

BEGINNING OF THE SCHOOL YEAR STARTER

Make certain that you have arranged your classroom to optimize learning and deter behavioral problems. Communicate the system (yours or your CT's) to your students and consistently enforce the plan. Get to know your students and what motivates them.

MIDDLE OF THE SCHOOL YEAR STARTER

Familiarize yourself with the management plan currently in place. Ask your CT to introduce you to the class as a teacher rather than as a student teacher. Discuss the management "history" of the class. Knowing what has already transpired will impact how you handle issues in the future.

TEACHER CLOSE IN AGE TO YOUR STUDENTS

If you are almost the same age as your students, remember one key point: You are the teacher, not one of their classmates. Be extremely professional at all times. Take note that your dress differentiates you from your students. Dress shouldn't matter, but it does.

FINAL THOUGHTS

As your management mentors, we've done our best to advise you on the components and challenges of classroom management. Work closely with your CT, be confident, and know your plan. Our hope is that you now have a better understanding of what to do and what not to do. Still, we've supervised long enough to know there are a few common classroom disruptions most student teachers will encounter. So, we'll provide you with Figure 5.2, which will offer some solutions to a few common classroom disruptions many student teachers encounter.

Figure 5.2 Solutions for Common Classroom Disruptions

Disruption

Solution

Excessive talking, talking during inappropriate times, and/or a student dominating discussions

Remind students of the appropriate times for talking; then, redirect them back to the assignment. See if you can determine why the students are talking. Are the students hungry because it's right before lunch? Are they tired because it's right after recess? Are they distracted because of an upcoming event? Sometimes you need to adjust your lesson based on the reason for the talking. When a student dominates class discussions, meet privately. Express your pleasure at his or her level of enthusiasm and involvement in discussions. Explain that you'd like other students to have the opportunity to participate as well. Ask the student to help you create strategies to involve more students in class discussions.

Disruption

Solution

Two students disrupting the class and interfering with your lesson

Move over to the disruptive students and quietly remind the students of the appropriate behavior. Ask for their cooperation. If the disruptive behavior continues, ask one of the students to be your assistant or helper during the lesson. Removing one of the students and engaging him or her actively in the lesson will minimize disruptions. After class, speak to both students about the disruptive behavior and review expectations for the next class.

Disruption

Solution

A student making fun of you or talking back to you

Stay calm. Do not take the comments personally. Do not get angry or show emotion. The student is testing your authority. Remind the student that the comments are inappropriate and redirect attention back to the class activity. If the comments or behavior continues, speak with the student privately and implement classroom consequences.

Disruption

Solution

A student sleeping in class

Walk near the student's desk and speak loudly. If the student continues to sleep, once the other students are working, kneel down by the student's desk. Ask the student if he or she is feeling well or if something else is wrong. The student may be sleeping for a legitimate reason. If the student is merely disengaged, review lesson concepts quickly and focus the student back to the task. Remind the student how the task relates to upcoming or past lessons.

BULLETIN BOARD

The Principal's Office: Classroom Management During Student Teaching

Know your system.

Whether you're following your CT's system, a popular management plan, or using your very own creation, be very clear about its components. The key to classroom management is a reasonable plan you will consistently enforce. However, don't be afraid to make adjustments if necessary and allowed by your CT.

Familiarize yourself with popular classroom management plans.

There are many effective management plans that have already been developed. Spend some time researching and/or reviewing current popular plans so you have a basic understanding of management theory.

Control is an illusion.

Expect for issues to arise, and have a plan in place to handle them. It's an impossible task to expect students to behave the way you want at all times, so be as proactive as possible.

Avoid common management speed bumps.

Don't yell at your students or let your CT implement all of the discipline. It's okay to be friendly, but don't rely on your students to be your friends.

Teach engaging lessons.

One of your best deterrents for misbehavior is your ability to engage your students. Engage them before they begin to entertain themselves. Don't be afraid to adjust your lesson when necessary.

Get to know your students.

Learn their names and pronounce them correctly. Make a personal connection with every student. Knowing who they are, what motivates them, and what they value will help to minimize discipline issues and help you to adapt your management plan to suit their needs.

Know the classroom environment.

Make certain you understand the function of all areas in your room. Students should also understand the flow of the classroom and any systems used for the smooth operation of the class.

Work with your cooperating teacher.

Your CT is a valuable resource, so use him or her. Your goal is to demonstrate competence. Wait to implement ambitious management strategies until you have your own classroom. If your CT has weak management skills, be sure to observe the experts in your building.

Be confident.

Confidence is an absolute necessity. Believe in yourself. If you're feeling insecure or inadequate, take immediate actions to boost your confidence.

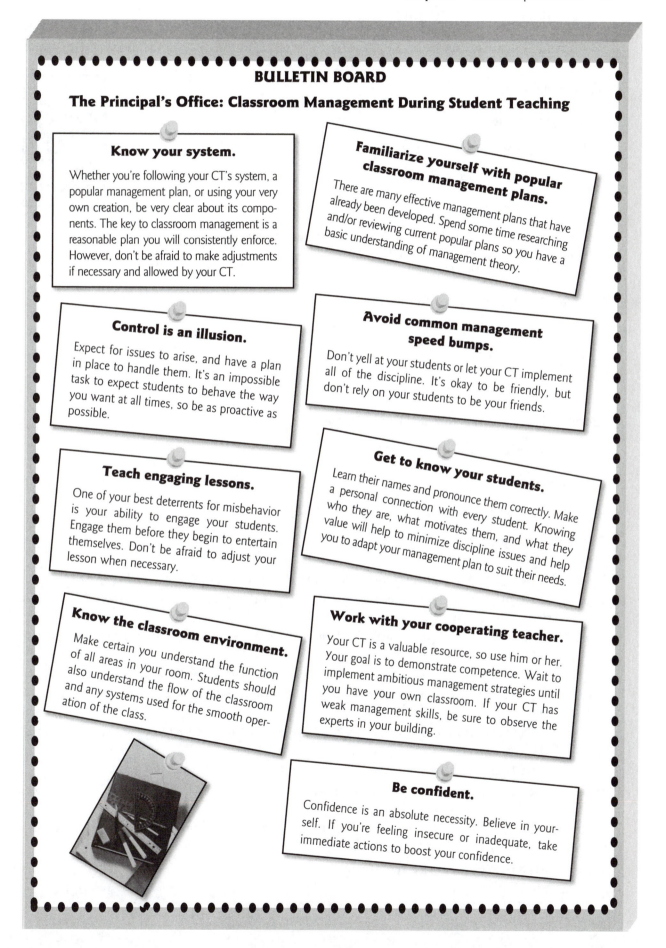

EXTRA CREDIT

READ ABOUT IT

Behavior Management

Dr. Mac's Behavior Management Site

http://www.behavioradvisor.com/11583.html

Classroom Management

http://www.education-world.com/a_curr/archives/classmanagement.shtml
http://www.nea.org/tools/ClassroomManagement.html
http://www.teachervision.fen.com

Classroom Management Video Tips for Teachers

http://www.edutopia.org/classroom-management-video

Confidence

http://www.mindtools.com/selfconf.html

Education Information for New and Future Teachers

http://www.adprima.com/managing.htm

Student Teachers

http://www.inspiringteachers.com/beginning_teachers.html

Classroom Management

Brophy, J. E. (1983). Classroom organization and management. *The Elementary School Journal, 83*(4), 265–285.

Burden, P. R. (2000). *Powerful classroom management strategies: Motivating students to learn.* Thousand Oaks, CA: Corwin Press.

Burke, K. (1992). *What to do with the kid who: Developing cooperation, self-discipline, and responsibility in the classroom.* Thousand Oaks, CA: Corwin Press.

Canter, L., & Canter, M. (1993). *Succeeding with difficult students.* Santa Monica, CA: Canter & Associates.

Crawford, G. B. (2004). *Managing the adolescent classroom: Lessons from outstanding teachers.* Thousand Oaks, CA: Corwin Press.

Davis, B. M. (2006). *How to teach students who don't look like you: Culturally relevant teaching strategies.* Thousand Oaks, CA: Corwin Press.

Divinyi, J. (2003). *Discipline that works: 5 simple steps.* Peachtree City, GA: The Wellness Connection.

Docking, J. (1982). The impact of control and management styles on young children in the early years of schooling. *Early Childhood Development and Care, 8,* 239–252.

Emmer, E. T., Evertson, C. M., & Anderson, L. M. (1980). Effective classroom management at the beginning of the school year. *The Elementary School Journal, 80*(5), 219–231.

Glasser, W. (1999). *Choice theory.* New York: HarperCollins.

McEwan, E. K., & Danner, M. (2000). *Managing unmanageable students.* Thousand Oaks, CA: Corwin Press.

Smith, R. (2004). *Conscious classroom management: Unlocking the secrets of great teaching.* San Rafael, CA: Conscious Teaching.

Tileston, D. W. (2004). *What every teacher should know about classroom management and discipline.* Thousand Oaks, CA: Corwin Press.

Workman, E. A., & Williams, R. L. (1980). Effects of extrinsic rewards on intrinsic motivation in the classroom. *Journal of School Psychology, 18*(2), 141–147.

THINK ABOUT IT

Directions: Read the following real "stories from the field" while imagining you are the student teacher. What could you have done to prevent the issue from arising? What is the best course of action now? Are there any behaviors that will make the situation worse?

1. Your CT announces to the class she is leaving the room for a few moments. She reminds the students of the classroom rules and informs them all that you are in charge. She explains that any student who breaks a rule will bear the consequence of not being able to participate in the class pizza party on Friday. Still, as soon as she leaves the room, all of the students start talking to each other and stop working. You remind them of the rules, but they ignore you and continue to talk. You walk to the front of the class and wait for the class to quiet; yet, they continue to talk. So, you clear your throat and remind them again that their teacher will return momentarily and they all need to be working. A few students begin to work, but most of them continue to talk. Your CT returns to the room, and all students immediately quiet and begin working. She asks you how the class behaved while she was out, and all of the students turn to look at you.

2. Two students are talking loudly across the room to each other. You've already reminded them of the class rule of no talking during seatwork, and you have asked them nicely to work quietly. They apologize for talking and begin to work quietly. However, they start passing notes to each other instead.

3. It's your first day teaching full-time, and you're very excited. You start your lesson and everything is going very well. The students are working cooperatively in groups, and you are circulating to offer feedback and remediation when necessary. One student asks to go to the bathroom. You remind him that bathroom breaks are not allowed during class time and he will have to wait for the period to end. You continue circulating, but when you return to his group, he asks more frantically, "Please, I really have to go. I just can't wait until the break." Since you've been in the internship, this student has been very helpful to you and has never been a discipline problem. With this in mind, you respond, "Okay, I'll let you go this one time during class, but you need to hurry. Come right back." The student agrees. Five minutes pass, and the student has not returned. You step into the hall, but there is no sign of the student. Fifteen minutes pass, and the student still has not returned. Suddenly, another teacher on your hall appears at your classroom door with the student in tow, and asks, "Does this student belong to you?" The entire class laughs as you thank the teacher and usher the student to his desk.

4. You are reading a story to the class during circle time. All but two students are paying attention and participating in the lesson. Rather than interrupt the flow of the entire lesson, you decide to continue reading. However, although you planned to address their talking after class, their talking is becoming difficult to ignore. You pause during the reading and say, "I need your eyes on me and your lips closed. This is a great story, and I don't want you to miss a thing. If you can't keep quiet, you know what will happen." One student replies, "Alright, I'll be quiet." The other student, however, replies, "Why'd you choose such a boring story? Our teacher always chooses good stories. You're not a real teacher anyway. I don't have to listen to you or do what you say."

5. Before class begins, you spy one of your students talking on a cell phone in the hall. She sees you watching her as she talks on the phone. You motion to her to put the phone away and come to class. Still talking on the phone, she turns her back to you and continues talking. As the bell rings, she starts to walk to your class. As you hold the door open for her, you say, "Thank you for joining us today. You know it's against school policy for you to talk on your phone during school hours. I'm going to pretend I didn't see you, okay? Just go ahead and take your seat." The student takes her seat, and you begin reviewing the previous day's lesson. While you are talking, a phone begins ringing. Everyone looks around, and the student who was talking on her phone in the hallway takes out her phone and answers it. She says quietly, "Hello? Yeah, I'm in class right now, so I'll call you back after class." She hangs up the phone and puts it back into her bag.

TRY IT

Cultivating Confidence Activities

Directions: Review the following list carefully. Choose three activities to complete within the next 2 weeks.

1. Make a list of every success you've had with classroom management during the student teaching internship. Now, post the list on your desk, in your lesson plan book, or some other place where you will see it often. Continue to add your successes to the list and watch it grow.

2. Review your CT's classroom management plan and other management plans of teachers in your school. Also, review the summaries of popular classroom management plans listed in Table 5.2. Now, using all of this information and reflecting upon your experiences in the classroom, create your own classroom management plan.

3. Make a list of your strengths. List all of your positive attributes. Ask your significant other, family members, and/or close friends to help you add to your list. Keep your list in a visible space and read it daily.

4. Make an "I Did It" or vision board (Byrne, 2006). Cut out pictures from magazines and make a collage celebrating all of your accomplishments and/or goals. Place your board where you'll see it often.

5. Create a playlist of songs that make you feel strong and powerful. Listen to the songs on your way to work, during your planning period, and at any other free time.

6. Watch teacher movies such as *The Ron Clark Story, Freedom Writers, Stand and Deliver, The Great Debaters,* and *To Sir With Love.* Take the time to identify qualities in yourself that are similar to the teacher heroes in the movies.

7. Spruce up your look. Go through your wardrobe and identify five professional outfits that make you look and feel great. Work out, get a new haircut, or do something else that will make you feel good. Take the necessary steps to look your best on the outside so that your confidence will radiate from the inside.

8. Get in touch with your fans. Pretend you're a rock star, and figure out your fan base. Is it the Cub Scout group you led, or is it your 6-year-old son? Find all of the people that think you rock and spend time with them often.

SOURCE: Byrne, R. (2006). *The secret.* Hillsboro, OR: Artria Books/Beyond Words.

PART III

Planning

The Planning Period

Strategies for Effective Teaching

Dear Student Teacher,

At this point, you've had a chance to figure out how you fit into your school's big picture, how to manage your multitude of new responsibilities, how to work effectively with your cooperating teacher, and how to keep the students from being totally out of control. That just about covers it, right? Wrong. You still have to teach.

Undoubtedly, the methods classes you took in your teacher education program provided you with a wealth of ideas for teaching in your subject area or grade level. Having experienced this from both sides of the teacher–learner coin, we are well aware that this information often doesn't make the transition to long-term memory because (a) it hasn't become "real" yet and (b) your brain has been overloaded with information from so many courses that you haven't had a chance to fully process it yet.

In this chapter, we provide a review of strategies that are currently considered best practice in the field of education. While our assumption is that these strategies are not new to you, our hope is that revisiting them during the internship will not only help you remember them but also ignite your desire to try them out with real students and a very real responsibility for student learning. With our combined years of experience teaching and observing learners from preK through adult, we feel confident that you'll finish this chapter with a repertoire of tried-and-true ideas (and perhaps some new and innovative ones) for keeping your students engaged, challenged, and constantly learning.

Signed,

Your Strategy Support Team

CHAPTER OBJECTIVES

After reading this chapter, you will be able to:

- Explain why lecture is a good instructional strategy in small doses,
- Define brain-friendly learning and share several strategies that fit this philosophy,
- Discuss the relevance of infusing technology into instruction for 21st-century learners, and
- Develop engaging ideas and activities that fit your personal style and (we hope) try some of them out in your internship classroom.

Few of us can focus for extended periods of time. That is, except for activities we have chosen and find enjoyable. Sadly, school does not top (or even appear on) most people's lists of "Favorite Ways to Spend a Little Free Time," so consider the context for the following section to be a traditional learning environment.

LIMIT YOUR LECTURES

A common saying in the field of education is that "the average attention span, in minutes, is a person's age divided by one." So, according to this revolutionary mathematical concept, 5-year-olds in a kindergarten class can focus their attention for . . . 5 minutes. The typical teenager in a civics class has drifted off to la-la land in less than 15 minutes. And, what about adults? Do you remember that last meeting, lecture, or conference you had to sit through? Your mind probably started to wander long before the first 20 minutes passed. Of course, we all come up with strategies to keep focused, such as voluntarily taking notes or secretly checking text messages, but it's so easy to succumb to the millions of thoughts racing through our heads at any given point in time—no matter what our age.

With so many media available, instant access to information, and constantly changing images on TV and computer screens, children and adolescents essentially expect to be entertained—and if they aren't, they quickly lose interest (Elias, 2005). Moreover, young people also more adept at multitasking, prompting some to suggest that children's and adolescents' brains are changing—allowing them to multitask more efficiently than those in previous generations (Elias, 2005).

Don't get us wrong—we're not suggesting that screen time is the root of all short-attention-span evil. However, when you think about it, the average television show has commercials approximately every 8 minutes, which allow us to regroup, get a glass of water, or run to the bathroom. Even if you have a digital video recorder (DVR) or personal video recorder (PVR), you still have the option to bypass the advertisements or to channel-surf to see if anything better is on. You can even rewind and fast-forward if you want to see or hear the program again, or if you want to skip a segment. When surfing the Internet, you have the ability to immediately switch pages with the click of a mouse. We can't think of a single person who has ever uttered the words, "Gosh, I was so bored surfing the Internet today. There was nothing new or interesting." More often, we hear, "I have no idea how I lost 3 hours surfing the Internet today."

Students in a classroom environment aren't so fortunate as to be able to change channels or click a mouse to regain interest and attention. In fact, they're pretty much held hostage for the learning period and punished if they try to escape in any way. So, our advice is: Give your students a commercial break. In other words, about every 7 to 10 minutes (perhaps less for younger learners), stop talking and let them do something—even if it's simply a 30-second task (Bowman, 2008). This "doing" could be partner-to-partner sharing of what was learned so far, tossing a small beach ball around so several students can provide an example of a concept, or answering a reflective question in small groups. When your students learn to expect this "commercial break" (and the understanding that it will be content related rather than random chit-chat), they will be more likely to pay attention during your presentation.

With this knowledge in mind, we can start on the path to effective teaching by no longer implementing "death by lecture" (Bowman, 2008) and beginning to think realistically about how much information our students can digest before they begin to gloss over or fade completely. Consider this additional common quote from the field: "The one doing the most talking is doing the most learning." We believe that this is true—so who wins in a lecture format? The teacher wins. The students, however, are tying their shoelaces in a knot, decorating their notebooks with graffiti, planning an escape to the bathroom, and secretly listening to their iPods under their hoodies. They are not learning the difference between *homonym* and *homophone* or the cell structure of a plant. When too much time is spent with the teacher at the forefront, that time is, unfortunately, wasted. (Cue the commercial. Quick!)

So, if prolonged lecture is taboo, what are your options? We have compiled a review of strategies to move your teaching from dull to dynamic and to move your students from fast asleep to fascinated. In the following sections, we'll cover two of the hottest topics in schools today—brain-based learning and technology infusion.

BRAIN-FRIENDLY TEACHING AND LEARNING

On July 17, 1990, President George H.W. Bush proclaimed the years from 1990 to 2000 as "The Decade of the Brain." In the years that followed, millions of dollars were spent on activities and programs that enhanced "public awareness of the benefits to be derived from brain research" (Presidential Proclamation 6158). Over time, practical application of research on the structure and function of the brain has become quite common in educational settings as teachers and administrators use this information to positively impact their learning communities (Jensen, 1995, 2000, 2001; Sousa, 2001; Sylvester, 1995).

Brain-friendly (or brain-compatible) teaching and learning helps increase student engagement and retention through instructional methods, which are grounded in research and understanding of how the brain functions. As a quick review, here are the main components of this approach, along with some of the underlying principles.

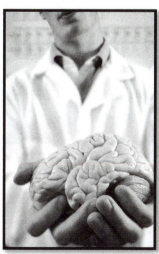

Nuts and Bolts of Brain Research

- *The primary function of the brain is to learn.* That's precisely what it does—what it was made to do. As a parallel processor, the brain is capable of completing multiple tasks at once—so many that we don't even realize when our brain is doing its job. So, not only can everyone learn, but everyone does learn. The problem arises when the brain's natural needs are stifled. What does the brain need then?
- *The brain craves novelty.* To satisfy the brain, we must learn and do things in new and different ways. When activities become monotonous or routine, our brain tunes them out. In a sense, it says, "Been there,

done that. Engage auto-pilot." However, when a new element or mode is introduced, it serves as a wake-up call for the brain: "Hey. This is new. Pay attention."

- *The brain must make connections.* It is constantly searching for patterns and ways to map new information onto what is already known. This is how the brain makes meaning. When you have an idea of how information is organized and its relationship with your prior knowledge (e.g., similarities, differences, and hierarchies), it is easier to both store and retrieve the information when it's needed.
- *The brain must actively process new information to assure retention.* In other words, we must do something relevant with the information to make it stick. When teachers provide opportunities for choice, collaboration, and reflection, information is able to move from short- to long-term memory. But how do we make it stick? Table 6.1 provides some examples.

Table 6.1 Make It Stick

	What Happens	**Why It Matters**	**How It Looks**
Choice	The teacher provides activities that allow students choice in how they will process and store knowledge	Choice leads to motivation (Guthrie, 2001) Learners are more invested in their work when it is meaningful	Students choose what to learn (within parameters) Students choose activities Students choose how to work (alone, with peers) Students' activities include "must dos" and "may dos" The teacher gradually introduces more choices for students
Collaboration	The teacher orchestrates a variety of opportunities for students to work together to solve a problem or complete a task	The brain is social Collaboration increases students' interest in the content (Hootstein, 1995; Zahorik, 1996) Collaboration leads to sustained active participation in learning (Nolen & Nicholls, 1994)	Students work together as partners, triads, or small groups Student groups are self-selected or preestablished Groups are heterogeneous or homogenous The teacher uses peer helpers (experts) to capitalize on student strengths The teacher periodically makes changes in groups depending on the activity's purpose
Reflection	The teacher intentionally and frequently includes opportunities for students to reflect on both the process and the product of their learning	Reflection is a powerful tool for self-assessment Students' awareness of their performance on a task can lead them to continued success or to make changes that might bring about success in the future	Students write in journals Students practice visualization Students and teachers engage in class discussions Students create reproductions of objects and simulations of events Students use interactive notebooks The teacher uses graphic organizers Students do guided note taking

What does "making it stick" mean for educators?

- It can make teaching and learning fun. (It may increase student engagement.)
- It can reduce behavior problems. (Engaged students are less likely to be off-task.)
- It can increase achievement for all. (Isn't this the ultimate goal, anyway?)

A FEW IDEAS TO GET YOU STARTED

Some of you may already be in a school setting in which the instruction is quite brain-friendly. This environment creates a sense of safety and well being, which influences cognition (thought processing), which in turn affects interest, motivation, and recall. That's great. However, some of you may find brain-friendly teaching to be a foreign concept because you have no real-world models for it. The next section provides specific ideas you can use to develop a positive classroom climate where students feel comfortable and are willing to take risks.

SETTING THE STAGE: CREATING A BRAIN-FRIENDLY ATMOSPHERE

Use music in your classroom. It alters brain chemistry—and can be used to energize students or help them relax, depending on the BPM (beats per minute).

Use sound. Vary your tone, volume, and rate of speaking to fit your activity or purpose. You can use books on tape, sound effects, and even think-alouds to model a process.

Use color. You can use it on transparencies, on the whiteboard, and around the room. Print important documents on colored paper. Teach students to use different colors of highlighters or sticky notes to indicate important information on a page.

Use humor. It reduces stress and increases alertness and memory. Funny stories, jokes, and cartoons—very brief ones—can do the trick.

Use movement. It increases the flow of oxygen to the brain. Have students stretch, move into groups, or provide physical responses to your questions (e.g., with thumbs up or thumbs down, "Every Pupil Response" cards, standing to share their answers).

Hydrate. The brain functions more efficiently when it's properly hydrated. Allow students to bring bottled water or provide water breaks to decrease lethargy and inattention.

When possible, give students a choice. This lowers stress and triggers the release of good brain chemicals. And, as stated before, it leads to increased interest and motivation for learning.

THE BIG INTERACTIVE PERFORMANCE: TEACHING IN A BRAIN-FRIENDLY WAY

Remember—brain-friendly teaching involves choice, collaboration, and reflection. As a result, students are more interested in their learning, more accountable for their learning, and more likely to recall and retain their learning. Need a few ideas?

Start class with a ritual. The ritual can be as simple as a greeting or an overview. Dr. Shepherd on *Grey's Anatomy* begins each surgery with the line, "It's a beautiful day to save lives." Some teachers begin with "Good morning. Today is a Magnificent Monday (or Terrific Tuesday, etc.). I'm so glad you're here." Be creative. Think of ways to make the greeting interactive, and have your students join in.

Begin with meaningful information. Save the "housekeeping" items (e.g., taking attendance, collecting homework) for later, once the class has gotten started on a purposeful and relevant task.

Set a purpose for learning. Knowing the big picture can help students follow along appropriately because they have an idea of where they're going. Furthermore, purposes should be revisited throughout and at the end of a lesson or activity, in order to rethink and revise expectations.

Start with the known so that new learning can be linked to students' existing knowledge. Additionally, it is helpful to begin with familiar contexts and gradually move on to new and/or unfamiliar contexts. Try using analogies to link known and new information.

Use graphic organizers. **Graphic organizers** (such as Venn diagrams, bubble maps, and flow charts) are powerful visual tools for helping students recognize what's important and understand how all the bits and pieces fit together. Consider using advance organizers for content-heavy courses, because these frameworks allow students to see ahead of time (and focus on) the important information as it is being provided. This is far easier than how most students take notes: writing down everything the instructor says or writing nothing at all. When used appropriately, the organizer can be used later as a study guide.

Pose a problem for students to attack in small groups. This strategy is effective because the brain grows by trying to solve problems. With brain-friendly learning, the goal is the attempt rather than finding a correct answer, so seek out problems that have more than one right answer, or more than one way of getting there.

Use affirmations to keep students thinking positively. Employ a few stock phrases (e.g., "Great thinking," "Way to go," and "You rock") to let your students know their participation is appreciated and that their responses are valid. Make them responsible for the positive climate by having them give a neighbor a high five or a fist bump, give themselves a pat on the back, or say a group cheer.

Add some spice to your presentation. Remember, the brain craves novelty. In addition to the ideas mentioned in the section above, you can also use games, props, role play, simulations, group work, challenges, and so on. However, be sure to change your activities often (even in small ways) so that they don't become old and boring.

Incorporate nonlinguistic representation. Information is stored in the brain both linguistically and visually. The linguistic (spoken) forms usually come naturally for teachers. However, according to brain research, the nonlinguistic forms are the ones that have been shown to increase brain activity. To keep the brain alert (and to make learning stick), use images, models, and movement—by you and your students—to represent the information and relationships you're teaching.

Provide lots of opportunities for practice. After modeling has taken place, it's the students' turn to give it a try. We suggest many tries, because practice leads to increased speed and accuracy with a given concept. Students can try activities out in small groups or complete work independently.

Use collaborative and cooperative learning. **Cooperative learning** incorporates small-group work that requires input from each member to complete a task or solve a problem. When set up effectively, it can help students feel comfortable and supported. Each student must be accountable for some part of the team's work, and students must depend on each other to complete the task successfully.

Review often. Weave repetition and practice with lots and lots of review to see if your students are "getting it." Review can be done in pairs, on paper, or even chorally. Rather than you providing the recap, make your students accountable for sharing key information. If they make mistakes or leave out critical points, that's a good time to chime in with clarification.

Provide regular feedback. Let students know how they're doing and if they're on the right track. Use checklists, rubrics, and even verbal comments to give students an idea of how their understanding and application of the content measures up to your expectations.

Encourage self-evaluation. Find out what students think about their own learning and processing. Have them discuss their strengths, areas for improvement, and insights gained.

THIS SOUNDS A LOT LIKE LEARNING STYLES

At this point, you might be thinking that quite a bit of brain-friendly teaching is similar to strategies focusing on learning styles (Dunn & Dunn, 1978). **Learning styles** refer to learners' strengths and preferences for taking in information. Like brain-friendly teaching, an awareness of students' individual learning styles can help teachers modify the learning environment to increase the likelihood that learning will transfer to long-term memory. In a nutshell, the Dunn and Dunn model (1978) outlines five categories (environmental, emotional, sociological, physical, and psychological) that help teachers think about 18 or so modifications (e.g., sound, lighting, seating arrangement, groupings, level of structure, ability to get snacks/drinks) that can impact how well students are able to receive and remember information. Some reports even suggest that using the learning styles approach can lead to higher scores on achievement tests for average students, struggling students, and students with special needs (Dunn & DeBello, 1999).

If you think that it sounds difficult to try to meet each of those 18+ individual needs for every child, every lesson, every day, you are not alone. You probably won't want to spend your first days of school mapping out learning styles for your entire class. Rather, we think it's more useful to

- Know that different learning styles exist,
- Be aware of and provide the types of modifications that appear to be critical for some of your students, and
- Think about learning styles from a broader perspective (e.g., visual, auditory, and kinesthetic preferences) so that you can meet your students' needs without becoming overwhelmed.

There are numerous assessments and inventories available online that can help you quickly determine your own and your students' learning styles. One link is provided in the "Read About It" section at the end of this chapter. Additionally, there is an opportunity for you to think about the relationship between your style, your preferred mode of instruction, and modifications you might need to put in place to make sure you are reaching all of your students.

We hope you have a better picture of what brain-friendly, learner-centered instruction looks like in the classroom. Now is a good time to talk about technology, which is actually a very brain-friendly tool. The next section of this chapter deals with ways to use technology to keep your students engaged and to maximize time spent on teaching and learning.

TECHNOLOGY-BASED INSTRUCTION

Being "in the know" requires a lot of work. And as our global community grows, we have access to increasingly more information—information that changes from day to day, hour to hour. (We still find it hard to believe that we are more than 10 years into the 21st century. It seems like just yesterday we were stockpiling bottled water, canned goods, and cash in preparation for Y2K.) We are reminded of how quickly times are changing as we observe the students who enter our classrooms each day. These students, born between the mid-1990s and the late 2000s, are often referred to as Generation Z, **"digital natives"** (Prensky, 2001) and "new millennium learners" (OECD, 2008) because they have spent a majority of their lives surrounded by and using technology. They have a voracious appetite for technology and expect instant gratification. They appear to be constantly connected to devices—laptops, iPods, iPads,

and MP3 players, hand-held gaming systems, and smartphones, just to name a few. Additionally, these students are constantly connected to each other through e-mail, instant messaging, status updates, texting, and social networking. And between the time this book is written and the time it reaches the bookstore shelf, even more exciting technological advances will undoubtedly be made and in the hands of your students.

With all of the glitz and glamour of technology, how can teachers compete? We say, jump on the bandwagon. Technology is not the enemy. In fact, it can bridge the gap between you (the dinosaur) and your students (the ones who have always had instant access to everything). There are many ways that you can use technology in your instruction—as well as for student practice and sharing of knowledge—that can keep you in tune with the interests and learning needs of your students. And, as a nonlinguistic representational tool (remember—images, models, and movement), technology can be a wonderful way to boost your students' brain activity.

The first thing you need to do is find out what is available at your school. Most schools have the basics (computers, DVD and CD players) in either the classroom or a lab. Perhaps there are also digital cameras, document cameras, and laptop carts that you can reserve or check out. Many schools have whiteboards available as well. Make an appointment with the school's technology specialist to see what your options are. And if some new type of technology is mentioned, make an appointment to learn how to use it. In many schools, the equipment is in a room collecting dust because no one knows it's available or has the time to figure out how it works. Be a pioneer. You might even be able to teach your CT a thing or two.

The Tried and True—and Possibly Overused

When it comes to activities, there are the traditional technology forms, such as educational software and websites. These are great, especially if you find programs and activities that allow you to tailor the content to meet individual students' needs and to keep track of their progress.

Then, there's the other all-time favorite—PowerPoint. Remember when we told you that the brain craves novelty? Well, after a while, listeners often begin to tune out these presentations, particularly if the slides are bland, too busy, or being read verbatim. To spruce up your PowerPoint presentation, try adding color and sound—but don't overdo it. Also, try some other ideas, such as embedding related video, linking to a related webpage, making the presentation interactive, and/or breaking it up with small-group activities.

Dig In to the Digital Age

If you're pretty good at scheduling individualized computer time, you can efficiently search for and bookmark appropriate links for your students, and your PowerPoint presentations aren't referred to by your students as "coma inducing," you could also try the following:

Virtual Field Trips

Can't afford to take the class to China to learn about the Great Wall? Need to go back in time, but your time machine is on the fritz? A virtual field trip may be right up your alley and in your budget. A **virtual field trip (VFT)** is a guided exploration of pre-screened and thematically based webpages (including any combination of text, images, video, and audio content) that, when woven together appropriately, can create an effective online experience. Some VFTs are arranged in a logical thread with prompts and questions to guide the learner through the process; others merely provide links and leave the rest up to the teacher. Either type can be effective. However, we do believe that the best VFTs are created and reviewed by educators who understand child and adolescent development.

Internet Scavenger Hunts

This is a new take on an old concept. The interactive **Internet scavenger hunt** allows individuals or small groups to learn about and review concepts. Essentially, they include a set of questions followed by links to teacher-approved Internet sites where the answers can be found. The hunt can be as simple or as complex as you wish. Many hunts are readily available on the web. In addition to being engaged in a fun activity, the students are able to learn content and practice technological skills simultaneously.

WebQuests

Similar to an Internet scavenger hunt, a **WebQuest** allows students to participate in a scaffolded learning experience using teacher-approved web resources to investigate a topic. However, unlike most scavenger hunts, a WebQuest includes (a) an authentic, meaningful task, such as a problem or a challenge, and (b) a structured group environment in which each member takes on a specific role and is responsible for searching for, discovering, and sharing specific information with the group. There are many WebQuests available on the Internet, as well as sites for helping teachers develop their own.

Multimedia Projects

Technology is great for use during instruction. How about using it for students to share their knowledge with others? We all remember the dreaded book report, the poster, and the brochure. And don't forget the dioramas—you know, the scene in the cardboard box. Is there anything else out there? Sure, there is. A **multimedia project** is a method for sharing knowledge, which may include any combination of text, graphics, animation, video, and sound. In the earlier grade levels, these projects may require more adult assistance and may even be completed as a whole class or small-group collaboration. However, many older students (intermediate grades and beyond) are technologically advanced and need only to be provided with the parameters of the project. Your job as teacher would be to set up the guidelines, create the rubric, and watch as your students' creativity blooms.

PODCASTS, WIKIS, AND BLOGS—OH, MY

Our final section on technology in the classroom deals with strategies that may be a little less common and may require a little more technological prowess. Here, we address three of the more recent and innovative ways you can elevate your educational technology use— through podcasts, wikis, and blogs.

Podcasts

Have you ever wondered how to catch students up to speed after they were absent or have otherwise missed out on important information? How do you make your lectures available to a group of students? What if some of your students require audio or visual support as they are participating in your class? A **podcast** may solve this problem. It is a digital recording that can be made available electronically for future viewing or listening. You can record your critical lessons and activities (audio or video) and make the podcasts available for your students to download online. In addition to using podcasts to catch up, students can also create podcasts (e.g., radio-style shows) to share their learning each week with parents and others in the community.

Wikis

A **wiki** is an online database (or a collection of webpages) that allows users to freely add and edit content. Yes, it can be edited by anyone, at any time, from anywhere with an Internet connection. Consequently, the pages you pull up may not be accurate or complete, so you should regularly use other sources to check your facts.

Some claim that wiki stands for "what I know is . . ." while others state that wiki is the Hawaiian word for "quick." Either definition applies because a wiki allows users to add their own content to a community page, and it's pretty instant. Many of you are familiar with Wikipedia, the free online encyclopedia that uses wiki software. This site can be a great resource for teachers because it provides instant, up-to-date answers to thousands of questions that you or your students may have. So—how can you use a wiki in your class? Simply put, it could be a class webpage where everyone is allowed to add content—such as photos, video, lecture notes, handouts, articles, discussion, links to related websites, and so on. The wiki becomes a repository of information that your students can access and add to as needed.

Blogs

Some of you may remember the good old days of journaling in a spiral notebook or a composition book with a black-and-white marbleized paper cover? Well, technology has allowed us to move forward past this archaic (though, for many of us—nostalgic) practice. Today, many teachers are setting up a **blog** (or online journal or discussion board) for students to write about what they are reading and learning. The advantage of a blog is its interactivity: Students are able to respond to each others' posts, as opposed to simply receiving feedback from the teacher. Dialogue causes the learner to feel more engaged in the process and more connected with others in the class—including the teacher. Blogs aren't only for literacy, however. Teachers can also set up theme-related blogs where students can post their connections to and reflections on their learning. Just remember that you will have to set up guidelines about how to respond to each other and what types of comments and exchanges you will allow. Some older students may be familiar with open blogs on the Internet, in which respondents "slam" each other or post other negative remarks. Remind your students that they are part of a classroom community and that only positive comments and constructive feedback are permissible.

SPECIAL FEATURE SECTION

There May Be no "I" in TEAM, but It's Time for "U" to Step Up to the Plate

If you're a teacher's assistant or lateral entry teacher, you're in a bit of a unique situation when it comes to being innovative, engaging, and effective. And just as in other chapters, we're here to guide you through the murky water. Table 6.2 illustrates how your expectations and reservations may differ from the traditional student teacher's, then provides suggestions on how to move past these feelings in order to find your voice and provide the best instruction for your students.

Table 6.2 Differing Expectations for the Teacher's Assistant and Lateral Entry Teacher

	How your situation differs from the traditional one	Strategies for making the most of your experience
Teacher's Assistant (TA)	You have a previously established role in the school, which typically has not been a leadership role.	*Think like a teacher.* Drop the role of TA (as much as your administration will allow) and become a (student) teacher. This means that you are learning, but you are increasingly capable of taking on more instructional responsibilities.
	You may be used to being told what to do, as opposed to making suggestions for what to do.	*Act like a teacher.* As you begin to view yourself as a teacher, start to take more initiative with instruction. You have years of methods classes (and your professors) to back you up.
	You may not have been involved in classroom instruction at all.	*Be a teacher.* Now is your time to show what you know. You are a professional, and you can do more than make copies and check homework. Share some ideas that you have wanted to try. Speak up at grade level meetings. Do not disappear into the background.
	You may be uncomfortable with the role reversal (i.e., delegating responsibilities to your CT while you engage in instruction).	*Be part of a team.* By all means, don't let your discomfort lead you to doing everything on your own. Instead, talk sincerely with your CT about how this makes you feel. Your CT may feel weird about it too. Be aware of your tone when making requests of your CT. Also, remember that the environment is more positive when the two of you work as a team. This is even more important for you than for traditional student teachers.
	Your CT has a distinct style, and up until now, you basically followed it.	*Be mindful of your tone when making suggestions.* This is tricky. Making suggestions can cause your CT to think that you believe something is wrong with how he or she handles instruction—and to wonder why on earth it is wrong all of a sudden. To prevent this reaction, be careful how you express your ideas. Rather than saying, "Your style stinks" (because often it really doesn't), perhaps try saying that you'd like to try some other strategies to help discover your personal teaching style. "I'd like to try some new strategies to fulfill the requirements of my university. I hope you don't mind."

(Continued)

(Continued)

	How your situation differs from the traditional one	Strategies for making the most of your experience
Lateral Entry Teacher	You are the teacher, and this can be overwhelming.	Give yourself some time to be in survival mode, but not too long. You will probably begin with some tried-and-true instructional strategies, but we encourage you to gradually introduce some of those new and innovative ones you've been meaning to try. And you've got it made—because there's no one to tell you that you can't.
	You haven't gotten a chance to see what others are doing.	Capitalize on your in-school planning period to visit other teachers to observe their instruction. If this isn't possible, simply ask them what they're doing.
	You've seen what others are doing, and it's nothing to write home about.	Don't fall into the rut with them. You have a wonderful opportunity to break the mold.
	You've seen what others are doing, and it's amazing.	You will be expected to follow suit. Give yourself some time to get in the flow, but make time to learn the strategies and technologies that are important to your school.
	You may be worried that the other teachers will call you a "radical" or reject you from the group if your instructional ideas are different.	Let's be honest. You really do want to fit in. Fitting in is part of the job. You wouldn't have picked this job if you didn't want to be part of the team. This doesn't mean that you leave your own personal style at the door, but it does mean that you have to be careful not to "flaunt your new-fangled teaching styles" as if everyone else was out of touch. You have to find a balance where you can be yourself within the group. Start by tapping into the different areas of expertise in the group. It may sound a bit like brown-nosing, but it can be effective if it is sincere. As always, be mindful of your tone.

FINAL THOUGHTS

We hope we have held true to our word—that by the end of this chapter, you would have a wealth of ideas for creating an engaging, brain-friendly, and technology-infused classroom environment. Now that you have these great ideas, it is time to think about how to pull them all together in a clear and effective format called—you guessed it—the lesson plan.

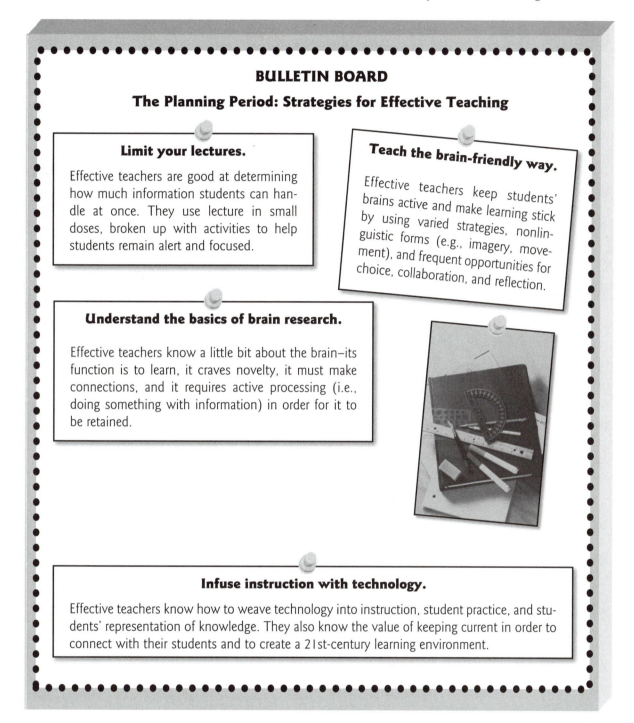

BULLETIN BOARD

The Planning Period: Strategies for Effective Teaching

Limit your lectures.

Effective teachers are good at determining how much information students can handle at once. They use lecture in small doses, broken up with activities to help students remain alert and focused.

Teach the brain-friendly way.

Effective teachers keep students' brains active and make learning stick by using varied strategies, nonlinguistic forms (e.g., imagery, movement), and frequent opportunities for choice, collaboration, and reflection.

Understand the basics of brain research.

Effective teachers know a little bit about the brain—its function is to learn, it craves novelty, it must make connections, and it requires active processing (i.e., doing something with information) in order for it to be retained.

Infuse instruction with technology.

Effective teachers know how to weave technology into instruction, student practice, and students' representation of knowledge. They also know the value of keeping current in order to connect with their students and to create a 21st-century learning environment.

EXTRA CREDIT

READ ABOUT IT

Brain-Friendly Teaching Strategies

Dr. Spencer Kagan's *Structures for Cooperative Learning:*
  http://www.kaganonline.com

Kathie Nunley's *The Layered Curriculum:*
  http://www.help4teachers.com

Dr. Marcia Tate's *Worksheets Don't Grow Dendrites:*
  http://www.developingmindsinc.com

More Teaching Strategies

Marzano, R. J., Pickering, D. J., & Pollack, J. E. (2001). *Nine essential teaching strategies.* Alexandria, VA: Association for Supervision and Curriculum Development.

Learning Styles

Learning Styles: The Dunn and Dunn Model—Learn about the different domains and what their implications for classroom environment and instruction.
  http://fc.lovett.org/~kkalnin/studybuddies/Learning%20Styles%20GISA.pdf

What's Your Learning Style?—Take the quiz and determine what your results mean.
  http://people.usd.edu/~bwjames/tut/learning-style

Technology

American Tapestry—The Millennial Generation
  http://www.knightdigitalmediacenter.org/resources/powerpoint/200812Tapestry-Shutte.ppt

Blogspot—Create your own blogs, free.
  https://www.blogger.com

Wikis in Education—Create your own wikis, free.
  http://wikisineducation.wetpaint.com

WebQuest.Org—Learn about and search WebQuests.
  http://webquest.org/index.php

More on Web Tools

Richards, W. (2009). *Blogs, wikis, podcasts, and other powerful web tools for classrooms* (2nd ed.). Thousand Oaks, CA: Corwin Press.

Warlick, D. (2007). *Classroom blogging: A teacher's guide to blogs, wikis, & other tools that are shaping a new information landscape.* Raleigh, NC: The Landmark Project.

THINK ABOUT IT

1. What are some ways you see teachers in your school engaging in brain-friendly teaching and learning?
   - Novelty in learning
   - Making connections
   - Active processing
     o Choice
     o Collaboration
     o Reflection

2. What might be some barriers to using brain-friendly teaching and learning? How can teachers overcome those barriers?

3. Prior to student teaching, how did *you* use technology in the classroom?

4. What might be some barriers to using technology in the classroom? How can teachers overcome those barriers?

5. Develop a list of at least three new ways you will try to use technology in your classroom during student teaching, using the resources you have available.

TRY IT

1. *Review the brain-friendly strategies for classroom atmosphere and instruction.* Select three to try out within the next week. How did your students respond? Did you notice any differences? Write about your observations in your reflection journal. Consider whether you will stick with these strategies or add new ones. Be sure to reflect after attempting each new strategy.

2. *Take a learning style inventory.* (We recommend the "What's Your Learning Style?" test listed in the "Read About It" section above.) What kind of learner are you? How might this impact your teaching style? What strengths does your style bring to the classroom? What might you need to do to meet the needs of your students who have different learning styles?

3. *Become familiar with the technology in your building.* Who is the technology specialist at your school? Make an appointment with this person. Discover the technology available at your school:
   - in the classrooms
   - in the media center
   - in the computer lab

4. *Make an appointment with your school's technology specialist to be trained in at least one piece of equipment that is unfamiliar to you.* At the end of the training, be able to list at least three ways you could potentially use the equipment in your upcoming lessons. To take it a step further, plan to teach someone else (e.g., your CT, a fellow student teacher) how to use the equipment, and demonstrate how you will use it to deliver your lesson.

5. *Search the Internet for a WebQuest, Internet scavenger hunt, or VFT that is related to an upcoming lesson or unit.* Follow through the steps of the activity to determine if it is appropriate for your students. If so, share it with your CT, and if you get approval, incorporate it into a lesson. Be sure to reflect on your use of technology in your reflection journal.

6. *Help your CT develop a wiki, blog, or podcast related to a unit of study.* Set up the parameters of use, and model your expectations for students. It might be a good idea to begin with a small group rather than the entire class, but allow everyone in the class to view your product. As students become familiar with the concept and process, they can teach more students in the class how to participate. In your reflection journal, write about what worked well and what you might do differently next time.

The Lesson Plan

Preparation and Performance

Dear Student Teacher,

We hope you finished Chapter 6 feeling satisfied with a variety of ideas for stimulating your students' brains with instruction that is interesting, innovative, and challenging. Now, it's time to take those ideas and organize them in a coherent and complete format—a lesson plan—that shows that you can carefully design a full activity from start to finish. This activity, by the way, should include a variety of effective instructional strategies to meet the needs of a diverse group of learners. That doesn't sound so bad, does it? Writing lesson plans involves thinking through an entire process, and great strategies such as wikis and WebQuests are only a piece of the process.

You may have heard horror stories about the dreaded lesson plans required for student teaching: They are long (we've seen faculty members with 17-step plans), you must write them for everything you teach (which is true), and you spend all of your waking moments composing them at the computer while your friends are in the next room playing Wii Resort (that is totally up to you—and depends on how much you follow the advice in this chapter).

Once you become armed with the information we provide, we feel very confident that you will be able to wow your CT and your students with some fantastic lessons that showcase all you've learned. Good luck, and go get 'em.

Sincerely,

Your Power Planning Pros

CHAPTER OBJECTIVES

By the end of this chapter, you will be able to:

- Describe the relationship between assessment and instruction;
- Discuss ways in which assessment-driven instruction can help teachers get the most out of their instructional time;
- Explain the importance of differentiation and individualization for optimal student learning;
- List and define the essential components of lesson plans;
- Compare and contrast different formats for writing lesson plans, and discuss the extent to which different formats address the essential components; and
- Develop written lesson plans based on state standards.

THE LESSON PLAN: BEST BASIC PRACTICES

Effective instruction involves very thoughtful planning. During student teaching (and even once you've landed your dream teaching job), you should have a written plan for everything you teach. In the beginning, your plans will need to include substantial detail, but over time, you will become more at ease with teaching, and your instruction will flow more naturally with less of a reliance on step-by-step, word-by-word plans. Even though the plans required by your CT may look different from the structure you were taught at your university, you should know that all good lessons have some very basic elements that focus on content and grade-level expectations prescribed by your state and/or the needs of your particular students. In the sections that follow, we provide a brief overview of critical elements for developing sound instructional plans. Additionally, we provide an overview of differentiation and how it can also lead to effective instruction.

KNOW THE EXPECTATIONS: STATE STANDARDS AND SCHOOL PACING GUIDES

In order to be an effective teacher, you have to know what is required for the different subjects you teach, from the state all the way down to your school level. To begin, review the state standards for students in each grade and subject you teach. In the United States, education is a local issue; therefore, each state has its own set of standards, or uniform guidelines for the major curriculum areas in Grades K–12. These standards outline the specific skills students need to master in order to progress to the next grade or course. Often, the standards are available online through your state's Department of Education website.

To be most effective, familiarize yourself with at least one grade level above and below the grade with which you are working. In addition to helping you to better understand the learning sequence, it also helps you build up your repertoire of skills and strategies for working with students who need more or less challenge in a particular area.

Next, ask your cooperating teacher if there is a **pacing guide**, which outlines the topics to be taught at different points in the school year for a particular grade or course. Sometimes, pacing guides are set up by grade-level teams within a school, using state standards as a guide. Other times, pacing guides may be set up system-wide and available online for teachers to access and use. However, if no official pacing guide is available, you should ask

your cooperating teacher to give you an overview of the topics that will be covered during your time in the internship, and ask approximately how much time is devoted to each topic. (Sample pacing guides have been included in Appendix B.)

USE ASSESSMENT TO GUIDE YOUR INSTRUCTION

Once you have a clear idea of what you are supposed to teach and when you are to teach it, you can begin thinking about how to teach it. To determine more precisely the level and scope of instruction necessary, you will need to implement one or more carefully chosen assessment measures. **Assessment** involves the formal and informal collection of information used to make judgments about what students know, have learned, and should learn next. In Figure 7.1, note how assessment and instruction are related in a recursive process.

Figure 7.1	The Assessment–Instruction Cycle

- *Assess:* Use formal pretests, discussion, KWL charts, and other quick methods for determining your students' current level of understanding. (Recall that a KWL chart is a student-driven visual representation of what they already **know** [K], what they **want** to learn [W], and eventually what they have **learned** [L] about a given topic.)
- *Instruct:* Locate or develop lessons and activities to teach and reinforce the concepts and skills your students are lacking or need more help with.
- *Assess:* Use discussion, post-tests, projects, and other activities to determine if your students "got it" or not.
- *Instruct:* If the students "got it," move ahead to the next concept. If they didn't "get it," reteach the challenging concepts in new and different ways.
- *Continue with the assessment–instruction cycle until you are able to move on to the next major concept or unit of study.* Keep in mind that all of your students are entitled to learn, even if they have already mastered the concepts you had planned to teach. If you are unable to move on because some students are not yet ready, consider using a combination of remediation for some and extension and enrichment for others until the class is ready to move forward.

Think of this cycle as a time-management tactic: If you know what your students know, you can focus your sacred planning time and valuable teaching time on areas that actually require additional instruction. Furthermore, you can tailor your lesson specifically for those students who need it, and provide other instruction for those who don't.

Another key point to consider regarding assessment is that you are actually expected to demonstrate a positive impact on student learning during the internship. When you analyze your pre- and post-assessment data from the subjects you have taught, you should be able to clearly show how well your students learned the content you presented. Table 7.1 provides several key questions to ask yourself as you are examining your impact on student learning.

By examining what your students have learned in light of what you presented and how you presented it, you can determine whether or not you are really meeting the needs of all of the young people who fill the seats in your classroom each day. And, as the assessment–instruction cycle tells us, your instructional plan has to be different for the different levels of understanding you discover.

Table 7.1 Examining Impact on Student Learning

Measuring Students' Prior Knowledge	• What did the students know before I began this unit? • How was this measured?
Assessing Students at or Near Mastery Level	• Did some students already have a full and clear understanding of the content? • Did I make sure that these students continued to learn? How?
Assessing Students Requiring Additional Instruction	• Were misconceptions noted? If so, were these pockets of errors or widespread confusion? • What was most problematic for the students? • Did I choose lessons and activities to address these students' needs? What were they?
Assessing Students' Gains	• What gains did my students show by the end of the unit? • Did all students have an opportunity to be challenged and increase their learning?

Examining Lessons I Learned	• What have I learned about:
	  ○ my efficacy as a teacher?
	  ○ my students' learning styles?
	  ○ how my students and I work together in our learning environment?

DARE TO DIFFERENTIATE

Have you ever been in a classroom where the teacher spent a considerable amount of time teaching the entire class using the same type of instruction? What was the behavior of the students? Our guess is there were three distinct categories:

1. One group of students was paying attention. They were able to learn from both the type of instruction and level of challenge provided.

2. Another group of students had initially paid attention, but perhaps became confused with the content or bored with the presentation, and they began to engage in off-task behavior.

3. A final group of students stopped paying attention long before the instruction even began. Perhaps they already understood the content, or the lesson didn't present a challenge for them—so, like their confused and bored peers, they also tuned out and began to engage in off-task behavior.

Likewise, when the entire class is offered the same exact type of practice activities, projects, and products for assessment, only a fraction of the class is motivated or able to complete the tasks set before them. This is a serious problem, but one that can certainly be overcome through the use of **differentiated instruction**. When teachers differentiate, they adapt instruction so that all their students can reach their potential. This instructional strategy is very useful, for example, for learners with a wide variety of learning styles, students with learning disabilities or exceptionalities, academically gifted students, and English-language learners.

According to Elksmin (2001) and Whitaker (2001), teacher education programs often fail to demonstrate the use of differentiation strategies in their own teaching. Consequently, we're willing to bet that many of you have never seen an actual model for differentiation in your own schooling or your teacher preparation. We admit it—allowing differentiation in your classroom is an invitation for "organized chaos" (Sands & Barker, 2004); however, effective teachers recognize that they cannot have a "one size fits all" philosophy of instruction because their students have different interests, learning styles, and learning needs.

In classrooms with **differentiated instruction,** the teachers modify the materials, content, projects, products, and assessments to meet those varying and student-specific needs. They use **flexible grouping procedures,** which means that the groups are monitored and adjusted as needed, based on student interests, learning styles, and readiness. Sometimes groups and assignments are selected by the teacher to make sure students get what they need; at other times, students are allowed to choose assignments that appeal to their own particular strengths and interests.

STRATEGIES FOR DIFFERENTIATION

- ✓ Breaking coursework into more manageable chunks
- ✓ Accelerating coursework for those who need it
- ✓ Focusing on curriculum basics
- ✓ Extending the curriculum for students who need more challenge
- ✓ Guiding small groups through tasks
- ✓ Encouraging independence
- ✓ Promoting higher-level thinking for *all* students

Remember: Your students will not all fit a predetermined mold, so refrain from "teaching to the middle." Provide activities that engage all of your students, and encourage them to work to their potential. Admittedly, it takes work to figure out what your students need, then to tailor your instruction to the groups that emerge, but the more you do it, the easier it becomes. Trust us on this one.

LESSON PLAN BASICS

A **lesson plan** is a framework for presenting instruction in a clear and cohesive manner. However, if you ask five different people what should be included in a lesson plan, you are likely to get five different answers. Actually, the answers may seem different on the surface, but they are probably very similar at the core—with different names or a different order for each of the components, and some extra stuff added to fit personal styles. We believe that there are some "must-haves," or nonnegotiables, when it comes to lesson plans:

- *Objective/Purpose.* There must always be a purpose for the lesson or activity—even if you want students to discover it during the lesson rather than having it stated up front.

- *Teacher Input.* You must have a role, whether you are providing instruction, modeling, or facilitating. Your level of guidance and direction will vary depending on the type and purpose of the lesson. During input, you can try some of the instructional strategies mentioned in the previous chapter.
- *Opportunities for Practice.* This is where the students get to do things—to move around, to discuss, to write, to explore, to experiment, to share, and to play (yes, we said play) in ways that help teach and reinforce the target skills and content. This practice can be guided, where you literally walk students through a task, or independent, where students demonstrate skill mastery on their own.
- *Checks for Understanding.* You have to include these checks periodically throughout your lesson to make sure students are on track, they understand the content, and they understand what they are expected to do. If students seem to have missed the boat, you must go back and reteach the content in new and different ways; then, check again to see if the group is back on track.
- *Closure.* This is a must, and even though it's a simple concept, it is often misunderstood or completely left out. Every lesson needs a wrap-up to remind students what the point was. We recommend having students take the lead on closure by taking turns sharing the lesson's main points or concepts.
- *Assessment.* You must have a way to determine whether or not the class "got it" overall. This could be based on students' verbal or written responses, observations of their performance on a task, or even (at times) a test or quiz. Consider using rubrics or checklists (which are typically made available to students ahead of time) to clearly indicate areas of mastery and areas of need.

TIME-SAVING TACTICS

NEED A WHEEL? IT'S ALREADY BEEN INVENTED

Like most of you, we are fairly busy people with plenty to do and not enough time to do it. Consequently, we are firm believers in finding someone else's wheel rather than reinventing it. By this, we mean finding someone else who has already created a template or model of the item you need. Of course, you will need to tweak the preexisting material to make it useful for you and your particular style, and in certain cases (i.e., to avoid plagiarism) you'll definitely need to give credit to the original authors, but that's so much easier and less time-consuming than starting from scratch. We recommend that you use templates to save time and minimize accidental omissions (such as forgetting to include the "check for understanding" and "closure" procedures in your lesson plans—which seems to happen a lot). Sample templates are provided for you in Appendix C.

MAKE YOUR PLANS "SUB-PROOF"

In addition to using templates to streamline your lesson plans, we also recommend that you make your lesson-plans "sub-proof." No, this doesn't mean that you guard your sacred lessons from substitute teachers with Fort Knox–level security. On the contrary, it means that with short notice and very little effort, a substitute teacher (or parent volunteer) could pick up your plan book and teach your lessons almost exactly as you would. When you make your plans sub-proof, you don't have to develop a set of extra "sub plans"—which usually involve a lot of worksheets and pointless activities meant to keep the sub's head from exploding or to make sure the sub will agree to come back in the future. When your plans include engaging lessons that the sub can actually follow, the sub may even see the job as that of a teacher rather than as a babysitter for your class while you are away. There's an added bonus: When you do return to the class, you won't have to double up on or skip lessons, or extend your unit to make up for lost time.

____ TIPS FOR TEAMWORK—OR HOW NOT TO STEP ON YOUR CT'S TOES

By now, your bag of tricks is bulging at the seams, you've got multiple strategies on a variety of levels, you know what's nonnegotiable in a lesson plan, and you're ready to hit the classroom. You walk through the door, bright-eyed and ready to take on the world (or at least a group of fourth graders), and you're hit with one of the following realities:

1. It's everything your professors said it would be. *Woo-hoo. Bring it on.*

2. It's nothing like your professors said it would be. It's all lecture, worksheets, skill, and drill. *Beam me up, Scotty.*

3. It's kind of like what your professors said, but these teachers are in overdrive. You're going to have to spend some evenings and weekends catching up on the new programs and technology that your all-knowing professors somehow failed to mention—yet you need to have these strategies incorporated in your lesson plans by the end of the week. *Can you say "energy drink"?*

If you walk into the first situation, we're happy for you. That's the best-case scenario. And if you walk into the third situation, that's not bad, either. It just proves that different schools have different materials and programs and structures, far too many for us to teach, and that we were at least on track with the foundation we provided for you. But if you walk into the second situation, we feel your pain.

Every year, at least a handful of students inform us that "the teachers aren't doing this stuff" (and by "stuff" they mean brain-friendly teaching, infusing technology, differentiating instruction, etc.). Even though we've tried to expose our students to cutting-edge strategies for teaching and learning, sometimes a disconnect exists between what is learned at the university level and what is experienced in the actual classroom. Now, we hope that this is more the exception than the rule, but it does happen, and we would like to offer a few suggestions for how to move beyond the feeling that somehow you have been hoodwinked.

TAKE INITIATIVE—BUT GET PERMISSION

Sometimes teachers (and entire schools) get in a rut. They've been doing things the same way for years. It is quite possible that their methods have been successful, too. You know, "If it ain't broke, don't fix it." But, really, there's nothing wrong with adding a little variety to teaching—so long as the results remain positive. Perhaps you are just the right person at the right time to come in with some fresh ideas. We have even heard from cooperating teachers who list this as one of their reasons for agreeing to host student teachers. If you see an opportunity to try some of the strategies and activities that you've heard and read about, find a way to tactfully suggest this to your CT. Try infusing some of the teacher's current practices with some of your new ones. For example,

> "Ms. Smith, I am thinking about adding about 10 minutes of role play to Thursday's social studies lesson. After the class reads the first three pages of the chapter, I want to let them work in groups of three to act out what they've learned. Then, they can answer questions 1 and 2 individually in their journals, as usual. Does that sound okay to you?"

or

> "Ms. Price, I am so excited. I found an amazing website on the Amazon rain forest that includes a virtual field trip with pictures, sounds, and unbelievable video. I've also borrowed the LCD projector from the computer lab so that I can display the screen for everyone to see. Would it be alright if I showed this website to the class next week? I have the link in case you want to look at it ahead of time."

(Notice that in these scenarios, the CT is given the final say as to whether or not you should move forward with your idea. Also, the idea is introduced with enough time to create Plan B, if your CT's answer is no.)

We hope the answer will be yes. If you plan the activity just right, and give students reasonable expectations for behavior in the modified learning environment, it might actually go really well. You might be asked to share your success with others on your grade level. On the other hand, you might get no response. But no response is a far cry better than "Don't ever do that again"—so don't worry.

Make Reasonable Modifications

Always keep in mind that you are a guest in your CT's classroom for a limited period of time. With that in mind, you should never attempt a complete overhaul of your CT's current program. When your time ends, your CT has to continue instructing the students, and no one wants to have to reteach an entire class. Reasonable modifications might include slight changes to the teaching and learning environment, such as adding a "think-pair-share" component that partners students to share responses or some other slightly different approach to the way the work has traditionally been done:

> "Ms. Brown, I bought several small dry-erase boards and markers on clearance at the drug store. For tomorrow's math lesson, I want to try letting the children use the individual boards to work out the problems that will be written on the board. That way, more than one student gets to do board work. And they'll probably enjoy using the boards, too. Do you mind if I try that?"

Work *With* Your CT

A positive student teaching environment—for you, for your CT, for your students, and their parents—comes about when you and your CT work as a team. During your initial period, as you are phasing into full responsibility, find ways to work alongside your CT to get the job done. While the two of you are team teaching, this is a great time to bounce ideas off of each other about new or different strategies. Your CT will appreciate that you acknowledge her expertise—and your acknowledgment should be genuine, of course—but you are also developing a relationship of mutual trust and respect. As a result, your CT may be more likely to let you try some of the strategies you've highlighted, bookmarked, and tagged for the past 2 years. Furthermore, if you and your CT are team teaching, you can try new strategies with a small group first to see how well they work or to determine how you might need to modify them for next time.

ASK FOR FEEDBACK

In every situation, but especially when you are trying a new strategy, always ask for feedback on how it went. It might help if you start by reflecting on it first, then asking your CT what she thought:

"Ms. Smith, I'm so glad you agreed to let me try out role play in today's lesson. The kids really got into it. I did realize about halfway through the activity, though, that I probably need to set up the groups ahead of time, rather than let the class pick their groups. But I do think they paid more attention overall and got more out of the chapter because their performances were pretty accurate, and their written answers were clearer than they were last week. What did you think of the lesson?"

If you reflect on the lesson first, it lets your CT know you have processed the lesson, and you are not merely looking to her to tell you everything. In other words, you can think for yourself, but you also value her input. (Note: This little golden nugget will take you very far in student teaching.)

SPECIAL FEATURE SECTION

Determining Your Level of Detail for Lesson Planning

If you are a teacher's assistant or a lateral entry teacher, you already have an established role (and numerous additional responsibilities) within your school before the internship even begins. This role affects a good portion of your experience—even down to the type of lesson plans you're expected to prepare. Figure 7.2 provides a handy flow chart to help you determine how to proceed in this often tricky area.

FINAL THOUGHTS

We hope that this review of lesson planning basics has served as a helpful tool as you begin to develop your instructional program. You have a clear idea of what to teach, the bare minimum components of a lesson plan, the importance of differentiation for the most effective teaching and learning, how to function as part of a team. Now that you have the essentials of planning under your belt, you can think about performance. The next chapter focuses on the process of student teaching, how you will grow and change as you reflect on the process, and the role that formal observations play in this transformation.

Figure 7.2   Determining Your Level of Detail for Lesson Planning (Daniels, Patterson, & Dunston, 2010)

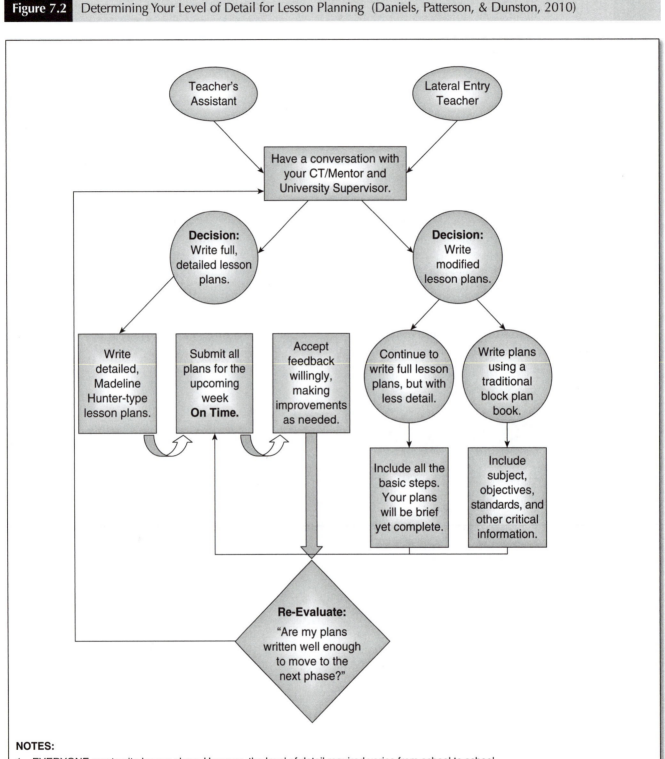

NOTES:
1. EVERYONE must write lesson plans. However, the level of detail required varies from school to school.
2. Your role does NOT matter! The process of determining your level of detail always begins with a conversation.
3. Before moving on to the next level of detail you must always return to the conversation step.
4. Be aware that your CT/Mentor and University Supervisor reserve the right to require MORE detail if your lesson plans are not satisfactory!
5. For more information on what to include in your "Madeline Hunter-type lesson plans," revisit the section called *Lesson Plan Basics* at the beginning of this chapter.

BULLETIN BOARD

The Lesson Plan: Preparation and Performance

Utilize the assessment–instruction cycle.

Before teaching, effective teachers use assessment to fine-tune their instruction. After teaching, they use assessment to determine what has been mastered by whom and what needs to retaught to whom. They then repeat as necessary—saving time and energy by focusing on what the data say the students need to learn next.

Include lesson plan basics.

Effective teachers include the "must-haves" in their lesson plans: (1) objective/purpose, (2) input, (3) practice, (4) check for understanding, (5) closure, and (6) assessment. They use templates to save time, and they make their plans sub-proof so that learning continues if they have to be absent.

Be a team player.

Remember that you are a guest in your CT's classroom, and you can't institute a complete overhaul of any of the procedures that are already in place. Get permission, start small, and show some respect, please.

Differentiate to meet the needs of diverse students.

When planning, effective teachers keep their students' learning styles, preferences, and abilities in mind. They provide opportunities for learners to work in their strong areas, but also encourage them to branch out and work in those areas that don't come as naturally for them.

EXTRA CREDIT

READ ABOUT IT

Ready-Made Lesson Plans

The Educator's Reference Desk

http://www.eduref.org/Virtual/Lessons/

Scholastic—Timely Lessons and Units for All Your Teaching Needs

http://www2.scholastic.com/browse/lessonplans.jsp

Teachers.Net Lesson Plans

http://teachers.net/lessons

Planning Guides and Templates

10 Steps to Developing a Quality Lesson Plan

http://www.lessonplanspage.com/WriteLessonPlan.htm

How to Develop a Lesson Plan

http://www.eduref.org/Virtual/Lessons/Guide.shtml

Scholastic: How to Develop a Unit of Study

http://www2.scholastic.com/browse/article.jsp?id=3749710

Differentiation

Differentiated Instruction—Theory, planning, links, etc.

http://www.Internet4classrooms.com/di.htm

How to Differentiate Instruction

http://www.teach-nology.com/tutorials/teaching/differentiate/planning/

THINK ABOUT IT

1. **View the pacing guides provided in the Appendix B.**
   - In what ways do these pacing guides build on prior knowledge and extend concepts? Why is this so important for learners?
   - Why is it helpful for educators to develop and use pacing guides? What might be some barriers to effective instruction in the absence of such guides?
   - Find out if your school or district has developed pacing guides for the content you teach. If so, find out how to get a copy. If not, ask your CT to help you create a "big picture" for the content you'll be teaching during the internship.

2. **Take some time to explore the concept of lesson planning.**
   a. What are the principal's expectations for lesson plans?
      - How often are they submitted?
      - How detailed must they be?
   b. How does your CT prepare for instruction?
      - Does she write full plans or use a block-style planning book?
      - Has she been teaching so long that she can teach without the written plan, notes, or teacher's manual on hand? What evidence do you have to support this assumption?

c. Examine the lesson plans used by teachers on your hall.
- What level of detail is used?
- Is differentiation addressed? If so, in what ways?

d. How will **you** prepare for actually teaching **your** lessons?
- Will you read and re-read your plans until they become familiar?
- Will you practice in front of a mirror?
- Will you use an agenda on your board or note cards to help you recall key points from your lesson?

3. **Observe your CT's approach to determine what to teach.**
- Does your CT use assessment to guide instruction? How do you know?
- What forms of assessment does he use

  o *before* instruction?
  o *after* instruction?

- Are instructional strategies chosen to meet students' specific learning needs? If so, provide some examples.
- If you are **not** observing a CT who uses assessment to guide instruction, what opportunities do you see that easily lend them to informal assessment? How comfortable are you with suggesting these tactics during your teaching time?

Try It

1. *Examine lesson plans for inclusion of "the basics."* Visit one of the ready-made lesson plan sites listed in the "Read About It" section above. Select at least three lesson plans written by different authors. As you read through the lessons, see if you can identify the basic components that should be included in every lesson plan. Does the author label the lesson components using the same language you were taught in your teacher education program? In what other ways is the lesson similar to or different from your own plans? What structural designs have the authors used that you might consider incorporating into your own plans?

2. *Begin to plan for your students.* Have a conference with your CT to determine what you will be teaching. You may want to refer back to the pacing guide as an additional resource. Ask if there are any preferred strategies (e.g., assessment, instruction, practice) that are nonnegotiable for the upcoming lessons and which ones you can choose freely. Make a list of potential assessment measures you can use before and after instruction, as well as brain-friendly strategies to make the content engaging for your students.

3. *Write your own lesson plan(s) tailored for your students.* When you have the go-ahead, write a lesson plan (or a series of plans) that includes at a minimum: the basics, a mode of delivery that is reasonably engaging, and ideas for differentiation of instruction based on what you discover from your pre-assessment measures. Submit your lesson to your CT several days before it is to be taught, and ask your CT for feedback. Make suggested modifications in a timely manner.

4. *Teach your lesson, then reflect on it in a reflection journal.* Consider how well your students mastered the objectives you outlined in your plan. Did they "get it"? How do you know? Was there a part of the lesson that went particularly well? Or a part that didn't go well at all? Why do you think this happened?

5. *After teaching a unit, consider your impact on student learning.* How well did your students meet the objectives set forth in your unit? Did they master the broader content? How do you know? Revisit Table 7.1 to address the key questions.

6. *Add your plans and reflections to your lesson plan notebook.* This notebook was introduced in Chapter 4. Be sure to separate your plans using labels such as "Current," "Past," and "Upcoming"—or other labels that make sense and keep you organized. Additionally, use your lesson reflections to begin to determine what you will teach next and how you will teach it.

PART IV

Performance

The Evaluation

Developing Confidence in Your Teaching Ability

Dear Student Teacher,

As Student Teaching Gurus, it is our job to help you have a successful and enjoyable experience by giving you the inside secrets. Well, hold onto your hats because this chapter will really be an eye opener. As a student teacher you will go through many phases within your internship. Although there are formal phases (which will later be defined and explained), we like to compare the student teaching experience to a carnival ride. You know, the one roller coaster ride that only a few brave men and women want to get on. It goes too high, too fast, has too many loops, and looks like a lot of fun. Your university supervisor and cooperating teacher are willing to help you manage the ride. It is through their guidance (and your willingness to accept it)  *that you will build confidence in your ability to not only successfully complete student teaching but also to transition into a full-fledged solo teacher.*

Additionally, we will offer even more strategies to help you get organized, create balance, and reflect on your strengths and challenges. Expect to make mistakes, but more importantly expect to grow. Remember, at the end of the day, the Loop-de-Loop is just part of the roller coaster. Student teaching should be fun and rewarding. Make sure you're not so wrapped up in trying to be perfect that you aren't taking the time to truly enjoy and appreciate the experience.

Good luck,

Your Student Teaching Gurus

ROLES AND RESPONSIBILITIES

Ask teachers about their memories of the most challenging yet rewarding experience of their teacher education program and we're sure (hands down) most will share stories about their student teaching experience. Historically, student teaching has been, and continues to be, the capstone experience. So much so that all 50 states require a student teaching practicum, testifying to the significance of the experience. This experience has a significant impact on you as you juggle the responsibilities of being a student and teacher (and all that it entails), while establishing and developing relationships with cooperating teachers, principals, additional school staff, and a university supervisor. Thus, student teaching is a complicated emotional and interpersonal experience that is critically important to the making of a great teacher.

> *"Student teaching is one of those things that will make you and break you. I have learned so much about myself—more specifically, I feel I am now a better judge of how far to push myself. I realized during student teaching that I do have limits and I should be aware of them, not afraid of them."*
>
> —Henry, Elementary Education major

As mentioned earlier, you are guided through this full-time teaching experience by a knowledgeable and resourceful university supervisor and cooperating teacher. Their roles are extremely important during the internship, as they will be responsible for the almighty observation. Some of you have already broken out into a cold sweat just thinking about being

observed. Well, we wish we had the magic pill to relieve your anxiety, but we are only your student teaching gurus, not pharmacists. However, we can offer you this bit of advice: Take a deep breath, try to relax, and stay positive. We know this may be hard to do, but you'll have less anxiety if you are well organized (revisit Chapter 4).

Your CT and US are there to help you learn how to be a great teacher. They can't provide you with constructive feedback unless they actually watch you in a variety of teaching settings. It's really okay if your US drops in to observe you while you are lining the kids up to go to lunch (this will inform him or her as to how you handle transitions). This is just as important as when your CT observes you teaching a geometry lesson. Both of these observations will give each of them insight into your knowledge, skills, and dispositions. Just face it—evaluation will be an ongoing part of this experience. People will talk about what and how you are doing, so you may want to get used to living in the fish bowl for a while. Regular conferences between you and your CT or US (or with all three of you together) are an integral part of the student teaching experience. The university supervisor should be kept informed of any problems or challenges that are identified and your cooperating teacher should discuss your performance with the university supervisor on a regular basis.

Defino (1983) notes numerous reasons for evaluating student teachers during their experiences in K–12 settings. Among them, certification programs need to prove to state or national program approval agencies that student teachers are doing what the institution said they would during the field experience (remember the NCATE conversation from Chapter 2). While this reason is important, more significant is that evaluation is used to inform you about skills that need to be strengthened. If all goes well, you will receive both formal and informal feedback from both parties that will provide positive reinforcement and constructive criticism along with communication of clear goals and expectations. Later in this chapter we'll discuss how to use their feedback to your benefit. Teacher education programs will vary, but Figure 8.1 provides you with a handy checklist to help understand the roles and responsibilities of your support team.

Your successful completion of student teaching is determined by your meeting not only the expectations of your CT but also the performance expectations established by your teacher education program. Trust us—you should not hesitate to seek out the guidance of your US or CT. Think about it: If you do well, they get to claim some of the credit.

Figure 8.1 Roles and Responsibilities

Cooperating Teacher	University Supervisor
Regular supervision includes the following:	Regular supervision includes the following:
✓ Communicating clear expectations regarding planning, classroom management, curriculum, student assessments, and performance;	✓ Visits (often a minimum of 3) to the classroom to observe and discuss performance in accordance with state and teacher education program guidelines;
✓ Weekly observations (at a minimum) of performance in the classroom along with communication/reflection of those observations;	✓ Continuing availability to both the student teacher and the CT for consultation regarding any issues that may arise during the course of the internship;
✓ Weekly discussions (as a minimum) to address expectations regarding planning, classroom management, curriculum, student assessments, and performance; and	✓ Completion of formative assessments of the student teacher's performance, in accordance with state and teacher education program guidelines; and
✓ Completion of a formative assessment provided by the teacher education program and participation in collaborative feedback conference(s) with the student teacher, CT, and US.	✓ A summative assessment of performance at the end of the student teaching internship in accordance with state and teacher education program guidelines.

PHASES AND STAGES _____

We know many educators who think that the best way to support student teachers and provide them with experience is to just "throw them in." But in most cases, this can be a recipe for disaster, which is why teacher education programs usually proceed with a gradual immersion marked by **phases** or distinguishing events that are part of the internship. These plans will vary widely, depending upon the state department of education and/or accrediting institution, although the typical student teaching experience begins with a phase plan that transitions you into and out of full-time teaching. The overall plan should include a negotiation and clarification of the expectations, needs, and desires of both you and your CT—this facilitates the process of gradually increasing your responsibility until you're able to fly solo.

PHASES OF RESPONSIBILITY

Phase In

Due to the many variables involved in student teaching placements, phase-in plans may vary, but they typically begin with your observing your CT, handling classroom routines, and assuming non-instructional duties, and then gradually increase to your teaching one or more subjects. A specific plan should be established during the initial meeting or during the first week of the placement.

Typical duties may include but are not limited to

- Managing transitions (e.g., taking students to specials, lunch, bathroom breaks, etc.),
- Cooperative planning involving you and your CT (or other teachers),
- Team teaching with your CT,
- Preparing and administering assessments,
- Teaching part of a class, and
- Teaching one or two subjects or one or two class periods.

As you progress through this phase, responsibilities will increase in preparation for full-time teaching.

Full Responsibility

Whether it is 1 week, 4 weeks, or more, this is when you take control of the classroom and you are the full-time teacher. When this takes place, and when you are ready to handle it, this responsibility is negotiated by you and your CT (and sometimes your university supervisor will be a part of the process). You name it, and most likely, you are in charge of it. Your CT may still reserve some crucial tasks to be handled solely by him or her, such as parent conferences and report cards, but this doesn't mean you shouldn't still be close by to learn best practices.

Phase Out

During this time, you begin to gradually release the responsibility and "give back" the teaching reins to your CT. You may still teach some subjects, but this will decrease as the semester comes to an end. Some programs may want you to include visits to other classrooms and/or schools during this time to gain additional exposure to other grade levels, teaching styles, and school cultures.

STAGES OF DEVELOPMENT

While teacher education programs may vary as to courses, schedules, and student teaching phase plans, within these three broad components of your experience, research shows us that the student teaching experience is universally similar (Moir, 1990). Moreover, it is marked by five developmental stages that every new teacher is guaranteed to pass through. We'll get to these technical terms in a moment, but first, we'd like to help you visualize these stages using our previous roller coaster analogy.

The Student Teaching Roller Coaster

If you've never been on a roller coaster, hang tight (you'll understand the analogy really soon). In this case, we like to refer to the five stages as

- *Raring to Go*—You want the ride to begin, but first you have to observe the people who successfully got on and off the ride before you (preferably, studying the ones who managed to keep their lunch down).
- *Climbing*—You finally get on and you're slowly inching your way up to the top, enjoying the view, and taking it all in as you go along.
- *The Loop-de-Loop*—It's here. You are at the top (and sometimes the bottom), twisting and turning. Sometimes you want to scream, laugh, shout, and cry. You want to get off, but there is still a long way to go.
- *Coasting*—You see the end in sight. It's all slowing down and you're not so sure that you are ready for it to be over.
- *Relief*—Time to exit and reflect on the best parts of the ride. It doesn't hurt to remember the parts that didn't go so well either—as long as you learn from your mistakes (e.g., by not sitting in the front car next time).

SOURCE: Adapted from Moir, E. (1990). Teaching Phases. This article was originally written for publication in the newsletter for the California New Teacher Project, published by the California Department of Education (CDE).

PHASES OF TEACHING

Moir (1990) offered the following developmental stages to characterize the first year teaching experience: *anticipation, survival, disillusionment, rejuvenation,* and *reflection*. The research refers to these stages as first-year teaching experiences, but we have adapted the ideas to reflect the student teaching experience. It should not be surprising that these stages also follow a similar "bumpy" (albeit exciting) ride. Figure 8.2 gives you an idea of how the phase plan is related to the developmental stages. Keep in mind that this is a general example, as your specific student teaching experience may differ in number of weeks. We will discuss each of the stages and give you important tips and strategies to help build your confidence as you move through each stage. Confidence comes from being prepared. Recognizing and understanding these stages and knowing "how to deal" with them is essential to being prepared and having a positive experience.

Figure 8.2   The Student Teaching Experience

Weeks in the Student Teaching Internship														
1	2	3	4	5	6	7	8	9	10	11	12	13	14	15

Raring-to-Go:
You want the ride to begin, but first you have to observe the people who go on 10 times in a row.

Climbing:
You finally get on and you're slowly inching up to the top, taking it all in as you go along.

Phase In:
Observation
Non-Instructional Duties
Gradual Teaching
Responsibility

The Loop-de-Loop:
It's here! You are at the top (and the bottom), twisting and turning. You want to get off, but there is still a long way to go.

Full-Responsibility:
Full Control
The Content Becomes Real
The Children Become Real
The JOB Becomes Real

Coasting:
You see the end in sight. It's all slowing down, and you're not sure that you are ready for it to be over.

Anticipation Phase:
Excitement and anticipation of what your ST experience will be like.

Survival Phase:
Your textbooks didn't prepare you for everything! You are trying to keep up with a lot of new information, routines, and teach effective lessons.

Phase Out:
Decrease Teaching
Responsibility
Observe in Other Classrooms

Disillusionment Phase:
Planning, teaching, evaluating, more planning, teaching, and evaluating and not enough sleep or healthy eating. You may be thinking, What have I gotten myself into?

Rejuvenation Phase:
Renewed spirit and confidence

Relief:
Time to exit and reflect on the best parts of the ride. It doesn't hurt to remember the parts that didn't go so well either (i.e., next time don't sit in the front car).

Reflection:
Think about the various changes that you'd like to make during and after your ST experience.

ANTICIPATION PHASE

The anticipation phase begins during the semester before you actually begin your student teaching. The closer you get to student teaching, the more excited and anxious you become about the student teaching placement. You may spend a lot of time thinking about who your CT might be, the wonderful class of kids that you will have, the supportive families you will work with, and your equally supportive school staff. Student teachers enter their new role with a tremendous commitment to making a difference and a somewhat idealistic view of how to accomplish their goals. This feeling of excitement carries new teachers through the first few weeks of school.

"My student teaching experience was pretty great once I got comfortable with being in someone else's classroom. I was nervous when I first began because I didn't know what to expect from myself or the kids."

—Leslie, Secondary Science major

Potential Pitfalls (may include but are not limited to)

- A tendency to idealize the responsibilities of the teaching position
- Forgetting to have a formal meeting with your CT to negotiate his or her expectations of you in the classroom

How to Deal

Create a Plan. Be honest about your strengths and challenges.

Listen, Watch, and Learn. Basically, observe and ask a lot of questions to help you transition.

Be Flexible. Prepare for the realization that everything you think you know will probably change.

Reflect and Request. Think about how you can continue to grow and ask your CT, the teacher's assistant, and your university supervisor for feedback.

SOURCE: Adapted from Moir, E. (1990). Teaching Phases. This article was originally written for publication in the newsletter for the California New Teacher Project, published by the California Department of Education (CDE).

SURVIVAL PHASE

The first month or so of the student teaching experience is very overwhelming. You are observing, taking on new tasks, getting to know the kids and the school. As well, you are expected to learn a lot at a very quick pace. Most student teachers are instantly bombarded with a variety of unanticipated situations. Despite the A's and B's (and perhaps even an occasional C) that you received in your methods coursework and field experiences, you may still be caught off guard by the realities of teaching. You will find that you become very focused on the day-to-day routine of teaching and preparation (it is not uncommon for new teachers to spend up to 70 hours a week on schoolwork), and you may lose sight of other responsibilities, such as eating healthy meals. In spite of this, you will probably be surprised how your body will continue to function on sheer excitement, adrenaline, and commitment.

(Continued)

(Continued)

"My advice for future student teachers is to be open to new things. Yes, student teaching is the time to shine, but it is also time for experimenting and challenging yourself."

—Dean, Middle Grades major

Potential Pitfalls (may include but are not limited to)

- Difficulty finding appropriate times to talk with your CT (you both are always teaching)
- Constant struggling to stop and reflect on your experiences
- Creating a balance between schoolwork, teaching, and your personal life

How to Deal

Be Flexible. Remember that each school day will be different. Try to start every day with a fresh, renewed outlook.

Get Organized. Establish a plan to keep all of those little details in line (lessons, materials, extra responsibilities, etc.).

Think Again. Revisit subject content and pedagogy.

Ask for Help. Be honest about what you know and what you don't know.

SOURCE: Adapted from Moir, E. (1990). Teaching Phases. This article was originally written for publication in the newsletter for the California New Teacher Project, published by the California Department of Education (CDE).

DISILLUSIONMENT PHASE

After 6 to 8 weeks of nonstop work, you may enter the disillusionment phase. The intensity and length of the phase will vary, as it is typically defined by the ongoing reality of the particular job. The vicious cycle probably includes: lots of planning and teaching; sustaining your days with Red Bull, 5 Hour Energy, coffee, or some other caffeinated product; no leisure time; exposure to lots of sick kids; getting sick yourself; getting behind on work, having to make up days; getting stressed; lack of sleep; not eating; and so on. See where we're going with this?

This is a very difficult and challenging phase. You will surely be missing your regular schedule (when exactly was the last time you actually exercised or watched a whole episode of your favorite TV show?), and your family and friends are definitely missing you. In fact, getting through this phase may be the toughest challenge you face along your journey toward becoming a teacher.

"I was a teacher assistant at the school where I did my student teaching and at first I was afraid to ask questions because I thought that I should already know the answer. But my CT encouraged me to ask questions since I will only have one chance to be a student teacher. I'm glad that I did. It really helped a lot."

Bruce—licensure candidate

Potential Pitfalls (may include but are not limited to)

- Realizing the extensive time commitment and that things may not be going as smoothly as you would like
- Low morale, which may contribute to a period of disenchantment
- Questioning your commitment and competence
- Questioning your ability to manage the classroom

How to Deal

Keep Your Cool. There are going to be many opportunities to lose patience or get frustrated. But nothing will help you get through something more than holding your tongue and being patient. Remember the temporary nature of the internship and always be respectful to your cooperating teacher, to your students, to the staff, and to yourself.

Be Flexible. Clearly, we can't stress this enough. Don't get upset if things do not always go as you planned. Review your lesson plans for any missing instructional strategies and try to anticipate discipline problems before they arise so that you can have solutions already prepared.

Just Do It. Do something that you enjoy (but haven't thought about doing since you began your internship) at least twice a week. It might be working out, getting 8 hours of sleep, going to the movies, or just eating a meal that is not served through the window of your car. The unfinished plans will still be there when you return.

SOURCE: Adapted from Moir, E. (1990). Teaching Phases. This article was originally written for publication in the newsletter for the California New Teacher Project, published by the California Department of Education (CDE).

REJUVENATION PHASE

The rejuvenation phase is characterized by a slow rise in your attitude toward teaching. Sometimes all it takes is a long weekend, a teacher workday, or the realization that things do get easier with time. This breath of fresh air may give you a broader perspective that comes with renewed confidence. By now, you have completed your full-time teaching responsibility, have a better understanding of how the system works, have gained new coping strategies, have accepted the realities of the job, and most important, have a sense of accomplishment. Give yourself a pat on the back.

"One thing to take advantage of, are the people on your grade level team who offer to help you because every teacher is different and can help you in their own unique way."

—Monica, licensure candidate

(Continued)

(Continued)

Potential Pitfalls (may include but are not limited to)

- Having moments when you question your confidence (Did I teach the concepts correctly? Will they pass the test? Do my 1st graders know how to decode texts? Can they explain the life-cycle process?)
- Getting too comfortable (You are still in learning mode and this time is important, as it gives you an opportunity to still be a part of the classroom and to show your CT that you are still respectful of the learning environment.)

How to Deal

Put on a Happy Face. Try to exude confidence. Even if you aren't, act like you are. Confidence typically comes from a teacher's enthusiasm, excitement about the content, and genuine pleasure in teaching.

Go on Vacation. If possible, use this phase out time to visit other classrooms and/or schools. This will help to give you a better perspective. You may have always thought that you wanted to teach kindergarten, but spending time in a 5th-grade class might make you rethink your choices. Plus, at the end of the day, you are certified to teach a range of grade levels, not just one.

SOURCE: Adapted from Moir, E. (1990). Teaching Phases. This article was originally written for publication in the newsletter for the California New Teacher Project, published by the California Department of Education (CDE).

REFLECTION PHASE

Reflection should be taking place throughout the entire student teaching internship, so although it is called a phase, it really is interwoven in everything that you do. It begins the first day of your experience and in reality never ends. Reflection is the key to growth and sustaining a successful career. You should never be intimidated by the reflection process, as it will provide you with the most information for ways to improve your craft.

"Teaching is a real 'minds-on' profession. You have to be prepared to analyze and think about everything that you do. This is the only way to become a better teacher."

LaTanya—secondary candidate

Potential Pitfalls (may include but are not limited to)

- Only reflecting on the negative and not the positive
- Only reflecting at the end of your student teaching experience
- Throwing the baby out with the bathwater (You don't have to start from scratch every time you want to revise a lesson or idea or try a new strategy.)

How to Deal

Have a Vision. Reflect on all of the positive and negative experiences and think about how you will make changes for your own classroom. Write them down in a journal so that you won't forget your ideas when you get your new job. This will inevitably lead you right back to the anticipation phase where you will begin the whole cycle all over again, but this time you will be older and—more important—wiser.

SOURCE: Adapted from Moir, E. (1990). Teaching Phases. This article was originally written for publication in the newsletter for the California New Teacher Project, published by the California Department of Education (CDE).

_____ **EXPERIENTIAL LEARNING**

If you haven't realized it yet, all of these phases and stages converge in an effort to help you to think about how to improve and build upon the teaching skills you currently have. This also translates into helping you to build confidence in your abilities as a teacher. Those in the teaching profession understand that learning requires developmentally appropriate teaching and learning strategies along with a healthy dose of "trial and error." This idea can be equated to the theory of **experiential learning** (learning from direct experience) that was championed by Dewey (1933). He noted that it is possible for people to have different approaches to and/or ways of learning when they are presented with direct, well-designed, and facilitated hands-on experiences.

THE EXPERIENTIAL LEARNING CYCLE

As basic as it sounds, experiential learning helped to shape teacher education programs as we now know them. Over the years, many other theorists added to and updated Dewey's ideas in this area. Most notably, the educational philosophy of Lewin (1951) and the social psychology theory of Kolb (1984) have been merged to give us the _experiential learning cycle_ (ELC) model for understanding the process of learning. This model is distinct from other models of learning (such as behavioral models or social learning models), in that it views your experiences and how individuals reflect on them as integral to the learning process. According to this model,

- All experiences should be viewed as a continuous process;
- Each experience influences each future experience;
- Purposeful reflection, questioning, and planning bring about a transfer of learning; and
- The entire process may happen in minutes or over an extended period of time (days, weeks, or even months).

These ideas are displayed in Figure 8.3, which portrays the steps in the cycle. The technical, historical model suggests that you have a _concrete experience_, followed by a _reflective observation_, and then a formation of _abstract conceptualizations_ occurs before finally conducting _active experimentation_ to test out the newly developed principles, which leads to a transfer of learning. However, we also offer a nontechnical explanation in Figure 8.4.

A SIMPLER APPROACH

Even though this is the most commonly cited model and its popularity is widely accepted, there is considerable debate as to whether or not it adequately represents all learning situations. However, we think that the model has considerable value and merit in education. Although we understand that using this model sounds like a lot of work (and it is), so is teaching. And if you want to get better at it, you should think about how you can apply this model to your everyday experiences. To help you do this, we'd like you to abandon the technical terms in favor of our more streamlined approach to this learning process. Think of the model as the four easy steps in Figure 8.4.

_____ **STRATEGIC REFLECTION**

While it is important to understand all of the stages of the learning process, is much more to the "reflection stage." The art of self-reflection is probably the most overlooked learning process, we feel that it is most important to focus on the "reflection stage." Aspect of any teacher's day (or year for that matter). It receives less attention than collecting lunch money, parent conferences, administrative observations, and just plain sheer exhaustion. Let's be honest—we ask children to

Figure 8.3   The Experiential Learning Cycle

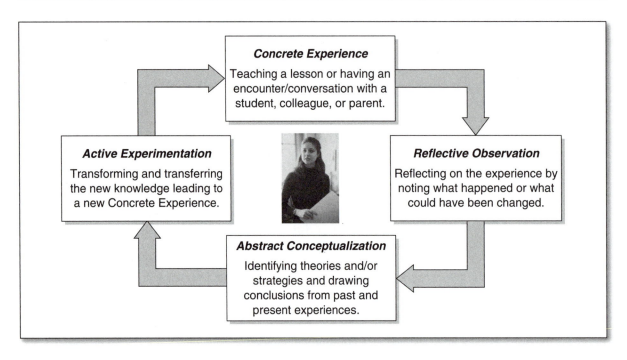

Figure 8.4   Four Easy Steps to Learning

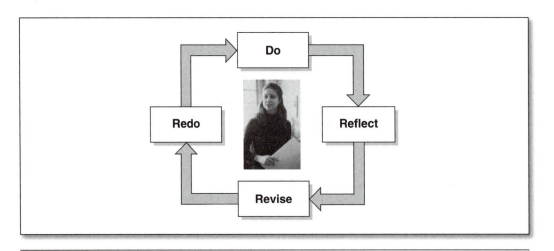

SOURCE: Adapted from Lewin, K. (1951). *Field theory in social science; Selected theoretical papers*. D. Cartwright (Ed.). New York: Harper & Row.

reflect on their behavior all day long: "Why did you solve the problem that way? Why did you skip Lisa in the lunch line? Why didn't you tell your dad to call me?" and so on. If we expect reflection from students, then perhaps we should at least take the time to understand better what it entails. *Reflection* has been defined in many different ways. It usually includes or is prompted by some level of uncertainty that needs to be resolved (Dewey, 1933). The process of reflection involves a continuum, which is defined as a gradual transition from one condition to another without any abrupt changes. You'll have days where you are actively reflecting all of the time, consistently questioning the choices that you've made. You might be jotting notes on a piece of paper about new activities, attending a professional meeting where you are collaboratively working in groups to solve instructional challenges, or a meeting with your CT after a lesson. However, some days you won't actively reflect at all, thereby saving your mental energy to just make it through the day.

WHY IS SELF-REFLECTION IMPORTANT?

Why reflect at all? Simply put, reflection can improve your practice. Your CT and US began the process when they provided you with constructive criticism and feedback about your knowledge, skills, and/or dispositions. But, you aren't doing anyone a favor if all you ever do is smile and nod your head as you are given priceless teaching advice. You must do something with the recommendations that are proposed. The initial step is easy—just do what is asked of you—but for long-term growth and development you will need to take additional steps and continue the process through the use of purposeful self-reflection. The use of reflection can

- Help you organize your thoughts and make sense of classroom events,
- Lead to goal setting and professional growth,
- Frame your teaching as an ongoing process of knowledge building, and
- Lead to conversations and collaboration with your mentors (Boreen et al., 2000).

LEVELS OF SELF-REFLECTION

Reflection is not so much about one day or a single event as about the process that occurs over time as you better understand your role and relationship to others (your students, their families, your colleagues, etc.). The ups and downs are to be expected; they typically go along with the job. The "aha" moment comes when you realize you must reflect in order to make changes.

Reflection, however, is more than "just thinking hard about what you do" (Bullough & Gitlin, 1995). The process should involve posing questions, searching for alternative answers, and seeking the deeper meaning of what you do. To be useful, reflection should include both individual and collaborative questioning about what you teach and how you teach it. Initially, reflection may focus on what you are doing. This is referred to as the *technical level,* where you may only be interested in refining teaching strategies. Typically the questions that occur to you are prompted by challenges you have about the quality of your teaching or the effects of your teaching on your students (e.g., "I thought those changes I made for Alicia in the math materials for today's lesson were exactly what she needed. . . . I wonder why they didn't work very well?"). You may also begin to ask yourself (and others) questions that focus on the relationship between your actions (and the actions of others) and specific situations that occur in your classroom, as well as in the context of a program, the school, and/or the community. This is the *contextual level,* which is marked by a realization of cause-and-effect relationships (e.g., "My response to Mary's behavior was great yesterday. I know what she did today is due to the same reason, but she didn't respond as well. I wonder what else was going on that could be getting in the way?").

Reflection also occurs when you find yourself contemplating issues about your teaching and its impact on larger systemic issues. This is the *critical level,* which is the broadest form of reflection and may focus on ideas such as social justice. Researchers have noted that these levels are developmental and not everyone will progress through all levels to reach critical reflection. For example, "How is access to healthcare related to how my students learn?"

But in order to progress and reach the critical level, there has to be a "method in the madness." Reflection should be strategic as well as systematic. Basically, this means you have to be organized and have a system in place that specifies how you will reflect. Will you keep a daily journal, keep a small tape recorder handy, use a flip camera to record yourself, or use some other recording method? These are all very simple ways to hold yourself accountable for the reflection process. Specifically, the goal is:

- To think about what you are doing,
- To challenge or validate your beliefs, and
- To develop and test cause-and-effect theories related to connecting what you do to outcomes for students (for more information on this process, see the Bridges to Success website: www.tr.wou.edu/bridges/contact.htm).

At the end of the day, (week, month, and year), if your goal is to become a better teacher, the process is simple. You may need to ask some hard questions, but the answers you get will help you to be more confident and productive; this ultimately benefits your students.

SPECIAL FEATURE SECTION

So now that you have a good idea of the scope and sequence of the student teaching experience, it is important to review what you've learned. In true teacher form, we felt it was important to leave you with something that you would find not only easy to read but also memorable. It is to this end that we provide you with Figure 8.5, The ABCs of Student Teaching. Figure 8.5 is an invaluable list, including everything from A to Z that you will want to keep in mind as you get started with and continue on in your student teaching placement. You will probably find that you will want to keep this list handy as a way to remind yourself of all the important points.

Figure 8.5   The ABCs of Student Teaching (adapted and updated from Lowman, 1984)

- **A**dmit your mistakes—and learn from them.
- **B**e flexible.
- **C**ommunicate with your cooperating teacher, university supervisor, and classroom parents.
- **D**ream a little dream (i.e., get a good night's sleep).
- **E**xplain, examine, expect, experience.
- **F**ind time to attend some after-school events.
- **G**et to know all the teachers in your school and make friends with the cafeteria staff, custodians, aides, and secretaries.
- **H**ave the courage to try something else if what you're doing isn't working.
- **I**nvest time in yourself—outside of the school day.
- **J**ust listen—both to what the kids are saying and to what they're not saying.
- **K**eep a journal.
- **L**earn your school's policies and procedures.
- **M**odel the behavior that you'd like your students to display.
- **N**obody's perfect.
- **O**verplan. You might just need it.
- **P**repare lessons that are exciting, innovative, creative, and engaging.
- **Q**uit worrying and just do your best.
- **R**eflect, reflect, and then reflect some more.
- **S**tay alert.
- **T**ake pictures (lots and lots of pictures).
- **U**nderstand that the learning process involves everyone—teachers, students, colleagues, and parents—and get everyone involved.
- **V**olunteer to share projects and ideas, and don't be afraid to ask others to share their ideas with you.
- **W**ork within your limits.
- e**X**pect the unexpected—and plan for it!
- **Y**ell if you need support.
- **Z**ero in on your strengths, not your weaknesses.

FINAL THOUGHTS

Having read this chapter, you should be feeling a bit more confident in yourself as a student teacher. You now know more about the roles and responsibilities of your cooperating teacher and university supervisor. Although their evaluations of and feedback on your performance may seem intimidating at first, they are an important part of the process. Each phase and stage of the internship is as exciting as a roller-coaster ride, and your CT and US are right there beside you with every slow climb and fast fall. But, in order to be adequately prepared, it is your responsibility to anticipate these ups and downs. This can be accomplished through active learning and strategic reflection. Remember: Do, reflect, revise, and redo—and then do it all over again. You are all set. You have the resources that you need to complete your internship with a smile. Now all you need is a job (well, most of you will need a job). Chapter 9 will get you one step closer to this goal.

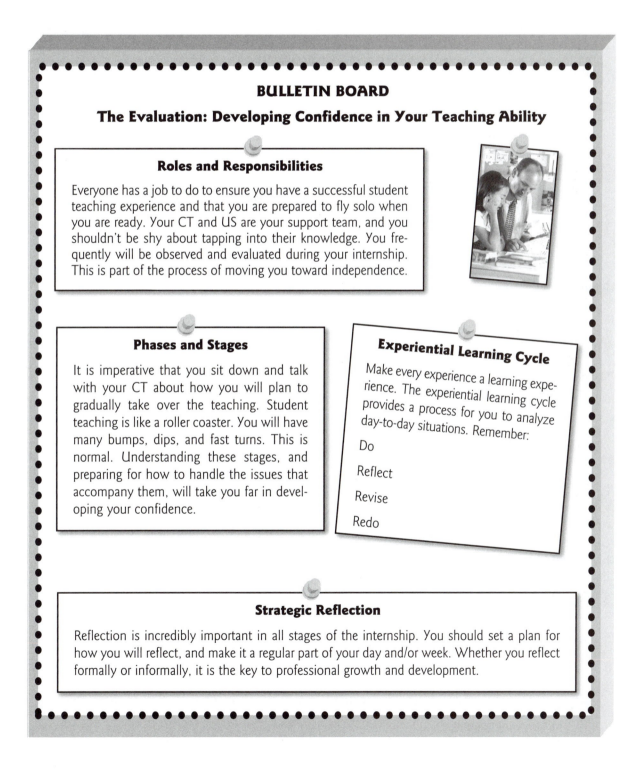

BULLETIN BOARD

The Evaluation: Developing Confidence in Your Teaching Ability

Roles and Responsibilities

Everyone has a job to do to ensure you have a successful student teaching experience and that you are prepared to fly solo when you are ready. Your CT and US are your support team, and you shouldn't be shy about tapping into their knowledge. You frequently will be observed and evaluated during your internship. This is part of the process of moving you toward independence.

Phases and Stages

It is imperative that you sit down and talk with your CT about how you will plan to gradually take over the teaching. Student teaching is like a roller coaster. You will have many bumps, dips, and fast turns. This is normal. Understanding these stages, and preparing for how to handle the issues that accompany them, will take you far in developing your confidence.

Experiential Learning Cycle

Make every experience a learning experience. The experiential learning cycle provides a process for you to analyze day-to-day situations. Remember:

Do

Reflect

Revise

Redo

Strategic Reflection

Reflection is incredibly important in all stages of the internship. You should set a plan for how you will reflect, and make it a regular part of your day and/or week. Whether you reflect formally or informally, it is the key to professional growth and development.

EXTRA CREDIT

Read About It

Student Teaching

http://www.education-world.com/a_curr/curr152.shtml
http://www.nmsa.org/AboutNMSA/PositionStatements/StudentTeaching/tabid/289/Default.aspx
http://www.middleweb.com/1stDResources.html
http://www.associatedcontent.com/article/28918/surviving_student_teaching_a_guide_pg2.html?cat=4

Observations and Evaluations

http://preservice-teacher-training.suite101.com/article.cfm/classroom_observations

Managing Multiple Responsibilities

http://www.associatedcontent.com/article/443012/student_teaching_how_to_keep_from_burning.html?cat=4

The Reflection Process

http://www.missteacha.com/?p=1083

Alternative Licensure

http://www.ncei.com/Alt-Teacher-Cert.htm

Research Article: Traditional vs. Nontraditional Undergraduates

National Center for Education Statistics. (2002). Special analysis: Non-traditional undergraduates. Washington, DC: Institute of Educational Sciences, U.S. Department of Education. (See Think About It below.)

Think About It

Special Analysis: Nontraditonal Undergraduates

Access and read "Special Analysis: Nontraditional Undergraduates," a research article that compares and contrasts confidence levels of traditional and nontraditional student teachers. If you are unsure of your status, reading this article will be especially important for you. Answer the following questions based on the findings in the article, and see how well you can interpret the results. Spoiler alert: The results are probably exactly what you'd expect.

1. Nontraditional students with children or child-rearing experience display fewer concerns for self than do others. True or False

   Explain your reasoning.

2. Twenty-five-year-old and older nontraditional students display fewer concerns across all stages. True or False

   Explain your reasoning.

3. Discipline issues surface more often for nontraditional career switchers. True or False

   Explain your reasoning.

4. There is no difference between groups in regard to higher levels of concern about student achievement and fewer concerns about interactions with adults (principal, other teachers, TAs, etc.). True or False

   Explain your reasoning.

5. Nontraditional student teacher groups are more self-confident than their traditional counterparts. True or False

   Explain your reasoning.

SOURCE: Adapted from Bray, J. (1995). *A comparison of teacher concerns for the non-traditional student teacher and the traditional student teacher.* ED390844

Understanding the Phases of Student Teaching

The student teaching internship is marked by distinct phases. We've provided you with an outline of these phases in the hopes that you will be prepared for the events that occur during your experience. Use the following activity to develop tangible strategies to help you identify and anticipate what may come next.

The *anticipation phase* is marked by the following:

1.

2.

3.

When I see these signs, I will do the following to avoid potential pitfalls:

1.

2.

3.

The *survival phase* is marked by the following:

1.

2.

3.

When I see these signs, I will do the following to avoid potential pitfalls:

1.

2.

3.

The *disillusionment phase* is marked by the following:

1.

2.

3.

When I see these signs, I will do the following to avoid potential pitfalls:

1.

2.

3.

The *rejuvenation phase* is marked by the following:

1.

2.

3.

When I see these signs, I will do the following to avoid potential pitfalls:

1.

2.

3.

The *reflection phase* is marked by the following:

1.

2.

3.

When I see these signs, I will do the following to avoid potential pitfalls:

1.

2.

3.

Experiential Learning Cycle

Use the case study to help answer the questions that follow.

The TA Who Wanted to Be a Teacher: A True Story

Pat always knew that he wanted to be a teacher. He loved learning as a child and always enjoyed school. In college, he wanted to major in education, but his parents talked him into majoring in business (they thought it was a more fitting occupation for a man). Even though he continued to take as many education courses as his schedule would allow, by his junior year he had declared a major in business management. Needless to say, those were two very long years. After graduation, he spent 10 years as a business consultant. While he enjoyed the job, he got the most satisfaction from organizing his company's community service events and volunteering at the local elementary school as part of the company's partnership efforts. Then, due to the failing economy, Pat lost his job. Although most of us would not welcome this situation, he saw it as a sign that he could finally enjoy a teaching career. He promptly started researching what he needed to do in order to become licensed as a teacher. While it didn't seem like it would be difficult, it did mean going back to school. After a bit of time, he was lucky enough to find a job as a teacher's assistant. It was hard in the beginning, working during the day and going to school in the evenings, but he felt like finally he was on the right track. Although there were some difficult days, he really enjoyed the classroom. He looked forward to going back each day. He spent a lot of time envisioning what it would be like when he had his own class: how he would do things differently (from the teacher who he worked with), what he would say to the parents, and the creative, engaging lessons he would plan. The teacher he worked with was great, and it was partially because of her and the rest of the staff that he asked the principal to let him stay and complete his student teaching experience. It also helped that he wouldn't lose his income, which he needed. He wasn't really sure how it was going to work, but he knew he would be able to stay at the school where he had already built relationships, and he wouldn't have to quit his job to fulfill the student teaching internship like many of his classmates. In any event, he looked forward to student teaching with more excitement than anxiety.

The first day of student teaching was a bit chaotic (and it didn't have anything to do with the kids). He was assigned to a class for student teaching, but the teacher was under the impression that he was there to be her new assistant. So he spent the better part of the morning talking to the university site supervisor in hopes of getting things resolved. Progress was made, and midway through the day he was moved to another class. Unfortunately, that was not the last time that problems occurred. On one occasion, the school building administration scheduled professional development training during class time, and they put Pat on the schedule to cover a kindergarten class. This took him away from his teaching duties. It wasn't when he had full responsibility, but he was teaching two subjects. He tried to be respectful and informed the administration that he should really stay with the CT's class, but they insisted that they needed him to serve his regular TA duties. Although Pat's CT supported him and echoed his concern about being pulled away from teaching duties, it didn't help to change the situation. He had to cover the class and figure out how to squeeze in teaching the two subjects that he missed. The situation was so stressful he decided that if he was ever put in that situation (or a similar situation) again, he would have to give up his position as a TA.

Answer the following questions:

1. How can you apply the experiential learning cycle model to Pat's unique situation?

2. This case study exemplifies many concurrent experiential learning cycles. Show the complete process by filling in the missing stages.

3. What are the strengths and weaknesses of this experiential learning cycle?

Pat's Assessment

"I really feel like in the end, the biggest issues seemed to stem from the administrators and teachers not realizing (or understanding) that I was now a 'teacher' (at least for 15 weeks). I also didn't always receive a welcoming response from other TAs. The response to my complaining was always the same, 'At least you still have a job.' In my school, teachers and TAs work together, but they definitely live in separate camps. Some of the TAs didn't feel respected, and that translates into resentment towards some teachers. I had to live in both camps. I got to hear the gripes of teachers about TAs and the gripes of TAs about teachers. I had to walk a fine line to appease both camps. This just added to my already full plate along with

(Continued)

(Continued)

lesson plans, classroom management, and trying to keep my CT happy. Although there were a couple of false starts and some stalls, I walked away from the ST experience feeling like I successfully completed my tightrope act. I learned a lot from my CT and the children, and I definitely feel like I am ready to be a teacher. But if anyone asked, I wouldn't be able to hold back my opinion on things that could have been done differently in order to make the process smoother. I could give you a long rant, or a laundry list of bewares, but it all really comes down to one thing—communication. My school doesn't usually have student teachers, and because of this, I don't think the administration fully understood the commitment they were making when they agreed to let me student teach. That lack of understanding sometimes put me in uncomfortable situations where I had to remind administration that there were certain responsibilities I had to fulfill as a student teacher. I think if my CT and I had sat down with the administration and worked out some of the important details about the role of a student teacher, some of the 'surprise responsibilities,' wouldn't have been such a surprise. It is worth the extra time in the beginning to lay everything out. Perhaps having your university supervisor in on the meeting could also help. All in all, I still really like the school, and the experience really helped me to understand how schools run from both perspectives (teachers and TAs) as well as some of the politics involved in schools. I'd even want to teach there. I look at it like this—every experience is different, and once you commit to being a great teacher, you take the good with the bad because in the end, you know that you are dedicated to the kids."

TRY IT

Strategic Reflection

Strategic reflection can prepare you to monitor your own thinking and make connections between your experiences, thoughts, and text readings. You've purchased a lot of books during the course of your program. It's now time to dust them off and crack the spines again. This activity helps you to document a variety of experiences to help you make concrete changes. Once you make the connections, you can document how you will change or alter your behavior to produce an alternative result (or you may decide to continue to do things the same way). In order to get maximum value out of this activity, be as specific as possible when completing the "I read . . ." column. Start by using this text, and when you have more time, branch out and use your other education texts.

Experience	I thought . . .	I read. . . .	I will . . .
I planned a great lesson, but midway through it some kids kept asking a lot of questions, which took my attention away from Sara. When she didn't get my attention, she ripped up her paper and refused to participate.	What is wrong with these kids? This lesson was awesome. I even had them working in cooperative groups and they didn't get into it. And what is up with Sara? She's going to have to do it for homework.	"Identify why the student is misbehaving: attention, power, revenge. or avoidance of failure Handle misbehavior immediately Use encouragement strategies that build self-esteem and motivation to cooperate Build strong partnerships with students and parents." (*The Ultimate Student Teaching Guide*, p. 88).	Think about planning better for all of the students next time. Maybe because the lesson wasn't differentiated, it made it too easy for some and too hard for others. Sara obviously maxed out on waiting for me to help her and got frustrated. I won't assign it for homework, since if she couldn't do it in class, she probably won't do it at home. I'll figure out a way to help her understand the lesson tomorrow.

The Last STEP

Student Teacher Exit Plan

Dear Student Teacher,

Congratulations. You've survived student teaching. We know the last few months have been very challenging. You've had to figure out ways to navigate school politics, plan and present lessons, assess students, cooperate with your CT, collaborate with parents, manage the classroom, and build your confidence. Way to go. Now that you've turned the classroom back over to the cooperating teacher, the students have thrown you a party, and you've completed all of your teacher education or licensure program assignments, you are finally free. Even if you're a lateral entry teacher, you're now free to concentrate completely on teaching rather than meeting certification requirements. No matter your category as a student teacher (e.g., traditional student, licensure-only, or lateral entry teacher), once you've completed the internship, you are free, free, free, right?

Actually, you're almost home free. The journey to become a teacher has really only just begun. Remember, the student teaching internship provides you with the opportunity to demonstrate that you've mastered the knowledge, skills, and dispositions necessary to acquire licensure. In order to actually get hired as a teacher (or keep your job if you are a lateral entry teacher), there are a few more hurdles you must jump. Some are higher than others, but you'll have to jump all of them in order to officially join the profession. So lace up your sneakers, and get ready to jump. The information in this last chapter will help you to step over these last few hurdles and actually be free—free to do it all over again, but this time you'll get paid for it ☺.

Sincerely,

Your Career Coaches

THE PROFESSIONAL PORTFOLIO

Before You Go, You Need a Portfolio

If there's one thing you've learned by now, it's that educators believe in documentation. This concept is no more evident than in the universally required teaching **portfolio,** a collection of artifacts that summarize major teaching accomplishments and strengths (Shore et al., 1986). Practically every student teacher in the United States must complete a portfolio of some kind by the end of the student teaching internship. This requirement is due in part to NCATE, which, if you recall from earlier chapters, is the professional accrediting organization for schools, colleges, and departments of education in the United States and requires teacher education programs to assess their programs (see www.ncate.org). Thus, programs use student teaching portfolios not only to document that they are preparing candidates with the knowledge, skills, and dispositions necessary to enter the teaching profession but also as assessment instruments to help them to revise and strengthen their programs. Consequently, practically every teacher education program requires candidates to compile a portfolio.

The portfolio serves as an assessment tool and documentation for teacher education programs, but more important, it serves as documentation for you. Your portfolio allows you to paint a clear picture of who you are as a teacher, your beliefs about teaching and learning, and how you facilitate learning in the classroom. It allows you to demonstrate your understanding of pedagogy, content, and classroom management. Additionally, the portfolio offers you the opportunity to show the full range of your professional self. This includes your involvement in the school community, professional development activities, professional goals, personal reflections, leadership and teamwork skills, technological expertise, and any other unique strengths and talents you bring to the profession.

Thus, your student teaching portfolio is extremely important, as it serves not only as a mechanism to document that you've met program standards but also as tangible evidence of your abilities as a teacher. This evidence will be needed once you begin the interview process, as most school districts require candidates to show a sample of their work during a job interview (Darling-Hammond, 2006; Delandshere & Arens, 2003; Zeichner & Wray, 2001). Consequently, the teacher portfolio is a multipurpose device essential to your success.

THE BASIC PORTFOLIO

In all probability, your teacher education program will provide you with a list of requirements for your teaching portfolio. However, at a minimum, all student teaching portfolios should include some basic elements:

✓ *Resumé.* This is the document where you list your education credentials, all relevant teaching experience (including student teaching, volunteering, and observing in the schools), other professional employment positions, and any other relevant skills, awards, and/or community service. A sample resumé is provided in Appendix C.

✓ *Educational Philosophy.* Explain your position regarding education and the kind of teacher you are. You can show your knowledge of educational theories, but your use of theory should be written so that it is clear and simple enough for anyone to understand. Remember, you are not writing for a class or a professor. Put a piece of yourself in your philosophy while grounding it in research and theory. Write it so that it's brief (preferably one page), clear, and memorable. Do this by using specific examples and anecdotes to support your thinking about education. Stay away from clichés such as "I think all children can learn," "I love children," and "I've always wanted to be a teacher." These sentiments are true for most people who go into the teaching profession. In a nutshell, explain your beliefs about education while infusing them with memorable anecdotes.

✓ *Classroom Management Plan.* Stakeholders reviewing your portfolio will want clear and convincing evidence of your ability to manage the classroom. Therefore, define your philosophy and plan for management in very simple terms. Explain your rules, consequences, incentives, and classroom procedures. If possible, show an example of your classroom layout through pictures or a simple diagram and provide a rationale for your setup.

✓ *Lesson/Unit Plans.* Be sure to include several examples of excellent lesson plans you have used (or will use) as a teacher. Include all assessments and supplemental materials (readings, handouts, tests, project guidelines, etc.) so that your lesson will come to life. Make certain you've included a variety of lesson plans that show how you incorporate technology, infuse diversity, differentiate instruction, and engage your students. If you've used the plans before, it is also helpful to include samples of student work with your feedback to students.

✓ *Student Teaching Observations.* During the internship, you will be observed by your university supervisor and often by your cooperating teacher and/or other teachers and school administrators at the school. Invite your supervisor or principal in to observe you when you are confident you have a superior lesson. Only include your absolute best observations.

✓ *Reflections.* Adding reflections will allow evaluators to see you as a reflective practitioner dedicated to improving your teaching. The reflections can be about your lessons, the internship, views on certain contemporary issues (diversity, technology, ESL learners, etc.), and/or your strengths and plans for improvement. Your reflections should do more than just describe and summarize; they should evaluate and analyze events and ultimately lead to insights in your teaching.

✓ *Accolades.* Show and explain your successes. Include letters of recommendation and/or appreciation. If you have received any educational awards or you presented at an educational conference, include those items as well. Include all relevant certifications. Most important, once you receive your teaching certificate, don't forget to include it.

PORTFOLIO ORGANIZATION

As there are so many elements involved in creating the portfolio, a strategy for organization is essential. Although it's most likely you'll receive some guidance from your teacher education program, we'd like to offer suggestions we've found most efficient for student teachers. Additional pointers on creating your portfolio can be found in Figure 9.1.

1. *Purchase your supplies,* You'll need quite a bit of stuff to organize your portfolio. Most portfolios are organized in a basic, two-inch, three-ring binder. You may also need some or all of the following: tabs to organize sections, paper for printing documents, ink for the printer, scissors or a paper cutter, a three-hole puncher, plastic sleeves to protect important items, labels, and photo paper for printing pictures.

2. *Find a space to work.* You'll need a place to work on the portfolio where you can lay out items, leave and take a break (you will definitely need one), and be sure that everything will remain untouched. Maybe it's the kitchen table, your bedroom floor, or your home office. You just need a spot where you can leave items and no one (not small kids, roommates, or pets) will disturb them. Choose this spot carefully and think about your needs while working. Do you like to watch television while you work? Is music a necessity? Do you need absolute silence? Taking all of your personal preferences into consideration while remembering you'll need the space to remain undisturbed, choose the best possible space for this project.

3. *Find your stuff.* Creating the portfolio can be a daunting task. Consequently, student teachers have a tendency to panic about locating the documents necessary to compile it. We want to  reassure you that you do have the necessary items to compile your portfolio; you just need to remember where they are. Most likely, you have access to your lesson plans, assessments, and all supplemental materials from student teaching. If you haven't been given copies of your observations, request copies from your supervisor and CT. If there is any item you can't locate or you just don't have that is critical for your portfolio, create or re-create it. Just do your best to locate existing materials so you don't start from scratch for every item. If you have not written your educational philosophy, it's perfectly fine to cut and paste ideas from preexisting documents you've already written and then add and revise to create the appropriate document for your portfolio. Be sure to photocopy all of the documents you'll use. Whatever you do, keep the originals (just in case something goes wrong).

    This approach also applies to pictures. You probably already have several pictures of yourself teaching and interacting with students. If, however, you failed to take photographs (because you were too busy concentrating on teaching), it's quite easy to go back and re-create them. Have a classmate meet you after the school day and pretend you're teaching at the board or creating a bulletin board. Or, you can ask your CT to take pictures of you while you're teaching. You can also take pictures of projects you assigned or initiated. If you created the school's recycling club or spearheaded a book drive, take pictures of that activity. Before you add any pictures to your portfolio, be certain that you follow your school and teacher education program's policy on photographing students. Make certain you have permission to use the photos for educational purposes.

4. *Organize your stuff.* You'll need a way to organize all of your documents. Our suggestion is to use a large accordion file and categorize your items. However, you may prefer piles on a table, a separate file cabinet, or some other method. What's important is that you organize your items so that you have a clear picture of what you have and where it will go. Use whatever method works best for you; just be sure to be very organized before you begin. This is a key step that will save you a great deal of time in the end.

5. *Find your time.* If you think you can compile your portfolio in one night or over the weekend, know that you absolutely can. However, we wouldn't be very good Career Coaches if we didn't make it clear that anyone reviewing your portfolio will absolutely be able to tell that you compiled it within 48 hours. In other words, the amount of time you choose to spend on your portfolio will be very apparent. Remember, everyone looking at your portfolio has probably seen quite a few (as Career Coaches, we've seen over 1,000). It is very easy to spot a portfolio put together at the last minute.

Also, the portfolio is a representation of who you are as a teacher. The portfolio is you in your absence. It represents all that you are as a teacher—your instructional style, your management style, and your overall approach to teaching. Don't you want to look good while you're not there? We know you do. That's why it's critical for you to schedule time to create your portfolio. As your Career Coaches, we'd like to warn you in advance that it's going to take much more time than you think, and often something will go wrong. Your computer will crash, your files will become corrupted, the printer will die, coffee will spill on your observations, your child will get the flu—you name it and we've seen it happen to student teachers. So, allow not only time to create the portfolio, but also allow time to deal with any problems that may surely arise.

6. *Find your reviewers.* You know to include only your best work in your portfolio; however, you are not always an objective judge of your own best work. So, before you submit your portfolio to any official audience (e.g., principal, university supervisor, or human resource representative), have objective reviewers look at your portfolio. The unit you taught on the duckbill platypus that culminated with your students making marshmallow sculptures might indeed be an engaging collection of lessons, activities, and assessments. Nonetheless, is it the best choice for your portfolio? Does it showcase your technology skills? Does it show how you incorporate reading across the curriculum? Does it show how you help your students to develop critical thinking skills? Does it show how you differentiate lessons? If you don't get some honest feedback on the documents you plan to include in your portfolio, you will do yourself a disservice. So, ask your CT to review your lesson plans, the principal to review your resumé, and a friend to read your educational philosophy. Don't overwhelm any one person by asking him or her to review all of your items. Enlist several people to review your portfolio, not just your friend, spouse, or classmate.

Figure 9.1   Particularly Pertinent Portfolio Pointers

✓ *Make it simple.* Don't go overboard. Your portfolio is not a memory book or a photo album. It is a professional representation of your teaching.

✓ *Make it relevant.* Don't include class assignments or irrelevant documents in your portfolio just because you have them. Your goal is not to include EVERYTHING. You don't have to add it just because you have it.

✓ *Make it manageable.* Organize your portfolio so that it is reader-friendly. Use a three-ring binder with tabs and plastic sleeves. Include a table of contents with page numbers so readers can access sections easily. Remember, quality is better than quantity.

✓ *Make it clear.* Every item you include in the portfolio should be well written and free of grammatical and mechanical errors. Include captions with pictures and documents; don't leave the reader to guess why you have included an item.

✓ *Make it engaging.* The portfolio stands for you, so it should leave a positive lasting impression. Make a cover that invites the reader to review it. Add pictures to help show your teaching.

Who Looks at the Portfolio?

You may have different types of audiences for your portfolio, and it will be extremely important for you to tailor it for the audience. For example, as part of your student teaching requirements, your university supervisor and your cooperating teacher might formally or informally assess your portfolio to verify you have mastered program competencies. Although your CT and supervisor have seen you teach and will have firsthand knowledge of your style and abilities, they'll still want concrete examples of your abilities to assess whether you can clearly articulate your ideas about teaching and education. You'll want to be sure to include the kinds of documents for which they are specifically looking.

Also, you'll want to be certain not to include any documents that show you or your CT in a bad light. For example, don't include any documents whatsoever that don't show you at your absolute best. Do not include any substandard lesson plans, below-standard observations, or items with spelling, grammar, and/or mechanics errors. Also, don't include personal reflections that express your frustration with your CT, the students, the profession in general, or how you'll do everything differently once you have your own classroom. Although this might be true (and most likely it's not entirely true), do you really want your CT to read negative assessments of his or her teaching before writing your reference letter and/or recommending you to those principals you hope will be calling soon?

Often, administrators and teachers will also review your portfolio during the interview process. This review can occur at any point in the interview process. Some systems review portfolios before the interview as a way to limit the pool of potential interview candidates. Others review portfolios during interviews and ask you questions based on your artifacts. Still other interviews might involve a review of the portfolio after the interview as a basis to confirm the decision to hold an additional interview or even to hire you. There is no way to determine how your portfolio will be used during the process, so it's better to simply prepare the best portfolio possible so you are ready for any and all potential scenarios.

The portfolio you submit should be edited and revised to show you meet the demands of the program or the position for which you are interviewing. For example, you might have completed your student teaching internship in a kindergarten classroom; however, you've received a call to interview for a fifth-grade teaching position. It will be important for you to tailor your portfolio for that particular grade level and school. Revise a few of your kindergarten lesson plans to fit the curriculum standards for a fifth-grade class. Moreover, if you know the school is focused on technology, include plans that demonstrate your expertise with integrating technology into the curriculum. Do you get the idea? You want to make certain your portfolio demonstrates that you can teach to the needs and mission of the school

for which you are interviewing. If the focus is technology, show them you're a computer whiz. If the focus is basic skills, show them how you make the basics engaging. Whatever the focus is for the school, make sure your portfolio shows you can do it (e.g., teach second-language learners, use cooperative learning, incorporate character education, focus on global learning, etc.). Your portfolio should show them you are exactly what they are looking for. Don't make them wonder if you're a perfect match; it should be obvious from their review of your portfolio.

Electronic Portfolios

When we joined the teaching profession (back in the Stone Age), it was expected that all of the documents for a student teacher's portfolio would be neatly typed, placed in page protectors, and compiled in a three-ring binder. Usually, this was the only copy, and the student teacher carried it along to every interview and job fair. Times have changed drastically. Luckily, you don't have to carry around a huge notebook as your portfolio. In fact, many schools are switching to electronic portfolios (Goodson, 2007). An electronic portfolio allows your audience to view the sections they deem most appropriate, but it also allows you a great deal of options when it comes to compiling representations of your teaching. Figure 9.2 provides a description of the benefits of an electronic portfolio and items to include in it.

Figure 9.2	Benefits of Electronic Portfolios
Video Clips	Adding video clips of your actual teaching to your portfolio will give you an edge over other candidates. You'll be able to not only talk about your teaching but also actually show your reviewers how you teach.
Pictures	Including pictures will transform your portfolio. Take pictures of student work, bulletin boards you've created, attendance at professional development workshops, service projects, and you teaching.
Testimonials	It may be appropriate to include interviews from your CT, university supervisor, and other teachers, as well as students and their parents, regarding your performance and successes as a teacher.
Hyperlinks	Hyperlinks within your electronic CD allow you to create links to detailed documents (e.g., lesson plans, unit plans, etc.) that a reviewer might want to access but that would cause a traditional paper portfolio to become too bulky. Hyperlinks also allow you to create links to websites and other resources on the Internet that you use as a teacher.
Portability	The best aspect of electronic portfolios is that they are lighter and easier to duplicate than traditional paper portfolios. You can make multiple copies within minutes and then leave them with potential employers. Also, consider buying an inexpensive software program that allows you to create CD covers, and use the CD to market yourself. Hand your portfolio cd out at job fairs, send them with cover letters to schools, and send them with a thank-you note after an interview.

Whether you choose to create an electronic or hard copy portfolio, do not believe the rumor buzzing about in educational discourse: Principals and hiring personnel don't take the time to look at your portfolio. Just like with most rumors, there is an element of truth in this statement. In all honesty, there are some school personnel who will choose not to look at your portfolio—hard copy or electronic. However, there are still so many who will expect to review your portfolio during the interview because it serves as concrete evidence of your knowledge and skills. Isn't it better to have one than not? Remember, you want to do all you can to differentiate yourself from all the other teachers who've just finished their programs as well. Don't show up empty-handed. This is just like a lesson plan; don't be caught without one.

Resumés Rule

Although the decision to create a traditional three-ring binder portfolio or electronic portfolio is up to you (or perhaps your teacher education program), you absolutely must have a hard copy of your resumé. Resumés still rule. Having a portfolio simply is not a substitute for having a stellar resumé. However, don't make the mistake most student teachers make when creating their resumés—the resumé reads like a student teacher's (or worse, a student's) resumé rather than an actual teacher's resumé. Keep in mind that you've completed your student teaching internship successfully. This means you have what it takes to enter the teaching profession. Your resumé should

reflect this huge accomplishment and read like a teacher ready to take on the challenges and responsibilities of being an independent educational leader in the classroom. Therefore, you need to make certain your resumé distinguishes you as a teacher (not student teacher) by clearly listing all of your accomplishments and experience in the teaching profession.

If you are a second-career student (also known as licensure-only or certification-only students) and have had a very full career in a profession in no way related to teaching, tease out all your professional skills and/or accomplishments that are applicable to teaching. For example, if you worked as a sales director, list relevant expertise such as training new employees, operating your company's very complicated and sophisticated software programs, working well with colleagues, and transferable multitasking skills. It will be essential for your resumé to convince readers that you will be able to transfer your previous job skills to the classroom.

Regardless of your work experience in education, whether it's just student teaching or being a teacher's assistant for 7 years, your resumé must show you have the requisite skills necessary to be successful in the classroom. So, make certain you look at a few sample resumés of teachers and have a teacher friend or administrator give you feedback on your draft. You can never have too many eyes review this very important document. Review these additional tips on creating your resumé. Also, a sample resumé is provided in Appendix D.

Basic Resumé Tips

✓ *Choose a well-known format.* Use one of the two most widely known types: chronological (categorized by sequence of events) or functional (categorized by type).

✓ *Include the basics.* These include name and contact information, objective, summary of qualifications, education, experience and skills, awards, and professional affiliations.

✓ *Use education terminology.* Using terms such as *professional learning communities* (PLCs) will show you can participate in the greater educational discourse.

✓ *Describe all your accomplishments related to teaching.* Don't list homecoming queen, but do list President of the Service Learning Committee.

✓ *Make sure your resumé is concise.* Avoid using long narratives. Instead use bulleted lists or short summaries to convey information.

✓ *Check for errors.* Correct all grammar, pelling (oops, we meant *spelling*), and typing errors.

WHAT IS PRAXIS II, AND WHY DO I HAVE TO TAKE IT?

In addition to compiling a portfolio of your accomplishments and creating a resumé, taking and passing Praxis II is often required to obtain your teacher certification. The Praxis Series assessments provide educational tests and other services that states use as part of their teacher licensure and certification process. The **Praxis II** tests measure general and subject-specific knowledge and teaching skills (see the Praxis website, www.ets.org/praxis). In short, the test is another hurdle for you to jump over to prove you know how to teach and know the content you'll teach. We're sure you're thinking, "Isn't completing student teaching enough to show that I'm qualified to be a teacher?" Remember student teachers, once you complete this process, you'll be working in your own classroom without a cooperating teacher. Think of it this way. The bank doesn't just check to see if you have a job before they give you a loan; they also run your credit report and make you show past and current pay stubs (at a minimum). They don't want to take any chance you might not be qualified for the loan. The education profession is exactly the same. You must take and pass the courses, successfully complete the student teaching internship, and take Praxis II. It's just another way to check that you are really qualified to become a teacher.

Depending upon your content area and grade levels of certification, your state may not require the Praxis II examination for certification. So, be sure to investigate your state's requirements for certification. Your teacher education program will be able to provide you with information regarding all of your requirements for certification, including whether or not you'll need to take and pass Praxis II.

Do I Have to Study for Praxis II?

There are competing viewpoints as to whether one should study for Praxis II. Many of our colleagues believe you can't successfully complete student teaching without having the knowledge necessary to pass Praxis II. However, as your career coaches, we understand that testing of any sort can cause anxiety and a great deal of stress for many students—even extraordinarily smart students. **Test anxiety,** excessive worry that negatively affects your performance on assessments, is a very real phenomenon that strikes many student teachers struggling to handle the challenges inherent during the internship (for more information about test anxiety and how to deal with it, see www.TestingTips.com, 2009).

Whether you decide to study or not, it is important you are clear on what the test entails. At this point in your program, you want to use everything at your disposal to finish successfully. So, whether you study for 2 months or 2 days, be certain to check out what the test covers. This is a quick and easy step. It's appropriate to be confident and prepared. You can do this simply by visiting the Praxis website (www.ets.org/praxis) and reviewing the sample questions and tips they've posted for all to review.

What if I Fail Praxis II?

Unfortunately, some student teachers require more than one attempt to obtain the necessary score to pass Praxis II. If you are one of them, you are definitely not alone. Nonetheless, we know it can be disappointing when you are so close to meeting all requirements for certification, but stumble two steps from the finish line. Simply put, when you don't pass, it can be heartbreaking. Still, it's important to remember you have met all other requirements and not passing Praxis II is only a minor setback. With a few simple steps, you can get back on track. Just refer to Figure 9.3 and implement our field-tested strategies for eventual success.

Figure 9.3	Back on Track

1. *Don't panic.* Remain calm. As a teacher, you know that tests are not the only indicator of mastery. Remember the score is just a number, not the totality of you as a teacher.

2. *Study this time, or study harder.* Revisit the Praxis website (www.ets.org/praxis). Spend some extended time examining the resources offered on the site.

3. *Talk to other students who passed.* Quiz them on their strategies for success with the test. Implement those you think will work for you.

4. *Study some more.* You've taken the test at least once, so you know what to expect. Were there questions you were a bit fuzzy on? Go back and look at some of your textbooks. Review, review, and review again. Purchase a Praxis II study guide in your content area and study consistently every day.

(Continued)

(Continued)

> 5. *Implement some of the confidence strategies from Chapter 5.* Failing the test can put a strain on your confidence. Remind yourself of your awesome abilities in spite of this minor postponement.
>
> 6. *Visualize yourself acing the test and receiving passing scores.* You know it will happen sooner or later. Just see it happening now (rather than later).
>
> 7. *Figure out the best method for you (paper and pencil versus computer based).* If you hate typing, arrange to take the traditional version (with your favorite No. 2 pencil, of course).
>
> 8. *Start looking for a teaching job.* Request a letter from your teacher education program explaining that you've met all requirements except Praxis II. The reality of getting your own classroom is a great motivator.
>
> 9. *Enroll in a test preparation course.* There are educational agencies that offer courses or workshops on test-taking skills. If the issue is weak test-taking skills rather than a lack of content knowledge, a test preparation course will prove beneficial.
>
> 10. *Repeat the "back on track" process as many times as necessary.* You will ultimately pass Praxis II. Your success during student teaching is evidence you have what it takes to join the profession, so persevere. You might want to add a few additional strategies (like buying a big box of chocolate) to make this process a bit more palatable. Do what you have to do to get through.

HOW DO I GET MY LICENSE?

After you've finished the internship, created an exceptional portfolio, revised your resumé, and passed Praxis II, what's left? The next step involves additional paperwork required by your state. Because you've been teaching, you are not afraid of paperwork. Whether the paperwork involves lesson plans, notes home, report cards, permission slips, or running records—you know there are mounds and mounds of paperwork that must be completed during the school day. Surprisingly, these experiences will come in handy as this last step will require you to complete a great deal of paperwork to complete your teacher education program.

Complete Required Paperwork

First, you'll need to look into the remaining paperwork necessary for you to graduate or exit your program. For traditional students, this could mean completing your graduation application, submitting your community service logs, completing exit surveys, or submitting your senior portfolio for review. The requirements will vary by teacher education program; however, trust us, paperwork always will be involved.

Once you have completed all necessary university paperwork, you'll need to file for your teaching license. Although some universities will complete this process for you, the steps are fairly universal. You'll need to complete your state's licensure application packet. This usually includes an application, all official transcripts from every college and/or university ever attended, a license fee or copy of provisional license, and a form documenting successful completion of student teaching; official documentation of Praxis II scores may also be required.

Once your application is complete, either you or a representative from your teacher education program will submit the application to your state's department of education. There, it will join a huge stack of other applications for processing. Usually, in less than 6 weeks, your teacher's license will be mailed to the address you indicated on your application. Once you get it, show everyone you know. It's a symbol of all of your hard work and expertise. Feel free to celebrate as well because once you receive that certification (and you've verified your name is spelled correctly and they've listed your correct grade levels and content areas), you are officially done. See Figure 9.4 for a review of the process.

| Figure 9.4 | The Teaching License |

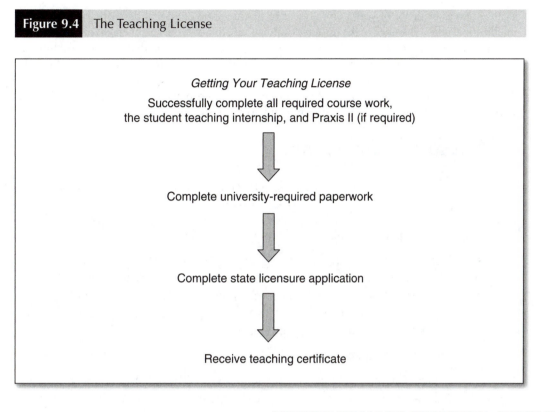

Getting Your Teaching License

Successfully complete all required course work,
the student teaching internship, and Praxis II (if required)

⬇

Complete university-required paperwork

⬇

Complete state licensure application

⬇

Receive teaching certificate

YOU'RE FINALLY CERTIFIED, NOW WHAT?

You can take a really deep breath now. All of your hard work has finally paid off. You've completed all requirements and your teacher's certificate is on its way. So, other than taking a break, cleaning your apartment, catching up on all of those movies you missed, and reacquainting yourself with your friends, family, and pets, what should you do now?

Ask for reference letters now. Make your requests while your performance is still current and clear in the memories of your cooperating teacher, university supervisor, and others who may have observed your teaching. Although many school systems' applications contain a reference form (often with a checklist and small area for comments), including a detailed reference letter along with the reference form will add depth to your application. So as not to make constant requests for letters, ask for several signed copies at once. This strategy allows you to have letters for several applications without overburdening your reference.

Begin researching school systems and individual schools. In Chapter 1, we discussed how all schools have their own distinct culture. Your goal is to obtain a teaching position in a school that is a good fit for you. Access public records and school webpages; tour schools and communities; and talk to parents, students, and teachers. If possible, volunteer or substitute teach in schools you are strongly considering. Spending prolonged and consistent time in a school will give you a clear picture of whether the school is the right match for you.

Start applying for jobs. As soon as you can, begin applying for teaching positions. Many states and school systems will allow you to apply online; however, others will require a hard copy obtained from a human resource representative. Attend employment fairs and visit career centers. The hiring process—from application, to interview, to employment offer—can take a very long time. Additionally, there are many other eager candidates searching for employment, so you'll want to begin the application process as soon as possible.

Join professional organizations and attend conferences. Professional organizations offer new teachers a wealth of information and resources. For example, many publish journals or newsletters with current research and strategies in your field. They also offer information about conferences and professional development opportunities. Some professional organizations even offer job listings or assistance in obtaining employment. Potential employers can view membership in a professional organization as evidence of your commitment to teaching and continual development. So, join an organization, take advantage of the resources, and be sure to post your membership on your resumé.

Begin the balancing act. You have firsthand experience with the demands of teaching. As you transition into a permanent position, consider how it will impact your personal life. Do you need to find care for your children? If you're commuting, do you need your car serviced? How will you budget your salary? Will you need to find a place to live? Now is the time to work on issues in your personal life important to your success as a teacher.

SPECIAL FEATURE SECTION

Resumé Tips for Special Circumstances

What if . . .

"I've never worked in education?"

- Reflect upon your work history and community experiences.
- Identify transferable skills and experiences desirable in the teaching profession.
- Write an objective that links your teaching goals to your past work history. For example, "Award winning staffing manager seeking to use training, technology, and multitasking skills in the teaching profession."

"I don't have a lot of teaching experience?"

- Fully highlight your accomplishments from your teacher education program—this includes all your volunteer and service learning activities, as well as the conferences and professional development sessions you attended.
- Describe in detail your student teaching internship. Indicate the school and duration of the internship. Also list all of your teaching assignments along with the number of students, grade levels, and content areas. Consider highlighting innovative lessons, extracurricular activities, and committee involvement.
- Express any interest you might have in supervising extracurricular activities. Your coaching skills or desire to start a recycling club will help to add to your dimension as a candidate.

"I've been out of the workforce for many years?"

- Demonstrate that you are proficient with current technology and that you have the skills to fully integrate technology into your teaching.
- Highlight your professional development activities. Describe in detail all relevant certificates, courses, conferences, and/or organizations with which you are associated.
- Carefully edit your resumé. Delete older, less relevant information. Emphasize your most recent accomplishments.

"I've been working as a teacher's assistant?"

- Demonstrate mastery over your content area. Show that you are fully prepared to implement engaging lessons.
- Spotlight your leadership abilities. Show that you have the requisite skills to lead others to accomplishing a goal.
- Explain how your teacher assistant skills translate to success as a classroom leader.
- Use teachers and administrators as references. Their endorsement will give you additional credibility.

FINAL THOUGHTS

We know you're excited about completing the student teaching internship. However, don't forget that you still have some important tasks ahead of you. Complete your teacher portfolio and resumé to show your successes and skills. If you're required to take Praxis II, review what's on the test and prepare for it. Finally, complete the mountain of paperwork required for program completion. Once you've accomplished all of these tasks, you're ready for the joys and challenges of teaching.

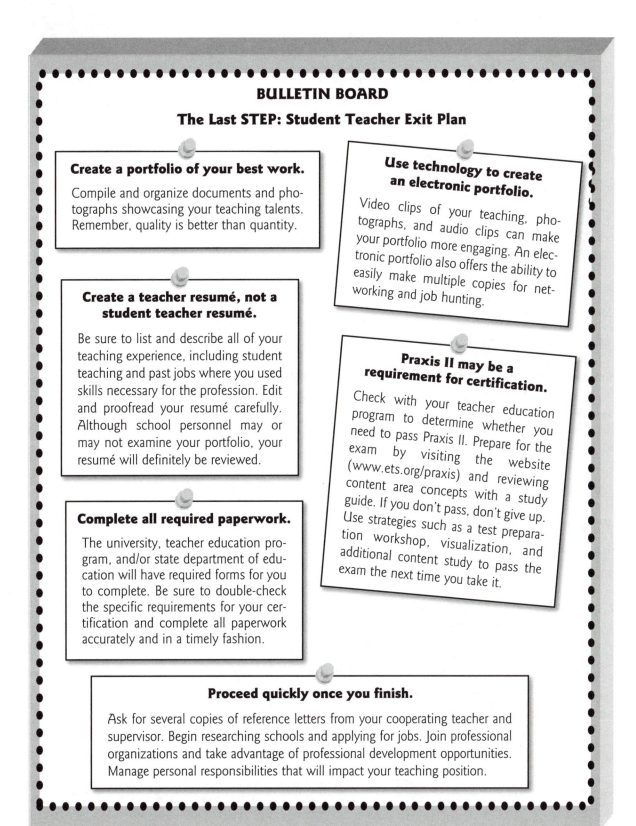

BULLETIN BOARD

The Last STEP: Student Teacher Exit Plan

Create a portfolio of your best work.

Compile and organize documents and photographs showcasing your teaching talents. Remember, quality is better than quantity.

Use technology to create an electronic portfolio.

Video clips of your teaching, photographs, and audio clips can make your portfolio more engaging. An electronic portfolio also offers the ability to easily make multiple copies for networking and job hunting.

Create a teacher resumé, not a student teacher resumé.

Be sure to list and describe all of your teaching experience, including student teaching and past jobs where you used skills necessary for the profession. Edit and proofread your resumé carefully. Although school personnel may or may not examine your portfolio, your resumé will definitely be reviewed.

Praxis II may be a requirement for certification.

Check with your teacher education program to determine whether you need to pass Praxis II. Prepare for the exam by visiting the website (www.ets.org/praxis) and reviewing content area concepts with a study guide. If you don't pass, don't give up. Use strategies such as a test preparation workshop, visualization, and additional content study to pass the exam the next time you take it.

Complete all required paperwork.

The university, teacher education program, and/or state department of education will have required forms for you to complete. Be sure to double-check the specific requirements for your certification and complete all paperwork accurately and in a timely fashion.

Proceed quickly once you finish.

Ask for several copies of reference letters from your cooperating teacher and supervisor. Begin researching schools and applying for jobs. Join professional organizations and take advantage of professional development opportunities. Manage personal responsibilities that will impact your teaching position.

EXTRA CREDIT

READ ABOUT IT

Transitioning

A+ Resumés for Teachers

http://resumes-for-teachers.com

Electronic Portfolio

http://www.electronicportfolio.org

The Praxis Series

http://www.ets.org/Praxis

Teacher Resumé

http://teacherresume.org

More on Transitioning

Campbell, D. B., Cignetti, P. B., Melenyzer, B. J., & Nettles, D. H. (2006). *How to develop a professional portfolio: A manual for teachers.* Boston: Allyn & Bacon.

Constantino, P. M., De Lorenzo, M. N., & Tirrell-Corbin, C. (2008). *Developing a professional teaching portfolio: A guide for success.* Boston: Allyn & Bacon.

Educational Testing Service. (2007). *The Praxis Series official guide.* New York: McGraw-Hill.

Grey, S., & Davis, A. P. (2008). *Praxis II elementary education: Curriculum, instruction & assessment.* Piscataway, NJ: Research & Education Association.

THINK ABOUT IT

What Do I Have to Offer?

Complete the following activity to help you to identify key information necessary to build an effective teacher resumé.

1. Describe all of your teaching experiences. Include those experiences from nontraditional settings such as camps, tutoring, and mentoring.

2. Describe all of your professional development activities.

3. Describe your accomplishments during student teaching.

4. Describe the skills and qualifications you bring to teaching.

5. What sets you apart from all the other teachers certified in your content and grade level? What makes you unique? Ask your classmates about your strengths.

TRY IT

Next Steps: What to Do Now

Directions: Now that you've completed student teaching, you still have work to do. Choose at least five activities from the next steps activity below to begin the process. Then, discuss your progress and challenges with your classmates.

Network now. Contact everyone you know in education. Let them know you've successfully completed student teaching, and you're ready for your own classroom.

Examine your personal life. Do you have everything in order so that you can be successful once you get your teaching job? Now is the time to finish those unfinished projects. Make a list of three personal projects that, left undone, might interfere with your teaching success. Now, create a list of steps to complete one of the projects within one week. Your ultimate goal is to complete as much as you can before you get your own classroom.

Xerox multiple copies of your awesome resumé and your best unit plan. You'll need them for all of your upcoming interviews.

Tweak your resumé. Take a copy of your resumé and compare it to "real" teachers' resumés. Analyze how they are different and revise yours appropriately. Then, show your resumé to as many educators as possible. Listen to their feedback and implement it.

Stay abreast of educational issues and trends. It's important you're aware of state and national trends that affect the profession. You'll be asked about them at interviews, and they will absolutely impact your teaching.

Treat yourself to a few items that make you feel like a teacher, not a student teacher, whether it's buying a new teacher wardrobe or laptop, organizing a file cabinet with ideas about activities, or something else. Believe in yourself and your abilities, and do something that is a tangible manifestation of that belief.

Examine potential schools. All schools have their own unique culture. Before accepting a teaching position, make certain that you examine the school to see if it's a good fit for you. You'll be spending a lot of time there, so make the best choice for you.

Participate in professional development. Although you are no longer required to take classes at the university, don't stop learning. Talk to teachers to discover what professional organizations they have joined and the benefits of membership. Research organizations in your field, and attend a local meeting or workshop. Take advantage of workshops, online trainings, and conferences. Go, participate, and learn.

Spend time doing the things you love. You now know firsthand how demanding teaching can be. It's important for you to have some balance in your life. Make some time each day to have a little fun.

Glossary

Assessment: Formal and informal collection, review, and use of information regarding student learning; used to determine what students know, have learned, and should learn next

Blog: An online journal where individuals post regular entries about personal experiences and opinions; readers are often allowed to comment on the entries

Brain-friendly learning (also referred to as *brain-compatible teaching and learning*): Instructional methods grounded in research and understanding of how the brain functions, in an effort to increase student engagement and retention

Change: To cause a transformation

Classroom management: A complex, yet organized, matrix of variables teachers arrange to manage behavior and classroom processes, such as instruction and social interactions

Conflict: An actual or perceived opposition of needs, values, and interests

Consequence: Something that logically or naturally follows from an action or condition

Cooperating teacher (CT): An experienced teacher selected to be a mentor, model, and guide

Cooperative learning: Small-group work that requires input from each member to complete a task or solve a problem; key factors for success include interdependence, accountability, interpersonal skills, and skills for working effectively within a group

Differentiated instruction: Instruction that is adapted so all students can reach their potential; it meets the needs of students with a variety of learning styles, those with learning disabilities or exceptionalities, academically gifted students, and English-language learners

Digital natives (also called *new millennnials* or *Generation Z*): Those who have spent all or the majority of their lives surrounded by and using technology, including computers, cell phones, video games, and digital music players; *digital natives* can be compared to *digital immigrants* (i.e., individuals who began to use such technology later in their lives, and may or may not have adapted to its routine use)

Discipline: The act of training or punishment to obtain a certain behavior or outcome

Disposition: A tendency or inclination to act or behave a certain way under given circumstances

Ethical: Concerning what is moral or right

Experiential learning: The process of learning from direct experience

Flexible grouping: Grouping that is dynamic and allows for changes in student group composition based on factors such as task, interest, learning style, and readiness

Graphic organizers: Visual tools for providing structure for information; allow students to categorize, classify, and show relationships and processes

Growth: A progression in size or from simple to more complex forms

Internet scavenger hunt (also referred to as *web-based scavenger hunt*): An electronic version of the traditional scavenger hunt, where individuals or small groups learn about and review concepts by moving through a series of prompts or questions posed by the teacher, followed by links to specific teacher-approved websites where information can be found

Learning styles: Individual strengths and preferences for taking in information

Legal: Concerning the protections that laws or regulations provide

Lesson plan: A framework for presenting instruction in a clear and cohesive manner

Mission statement: A formal, short, written statement of the purpose of a company or organization

Motivation: The intrinsic or extrinsic activation of goal-oriented behavior

Multimedia project: A method for sharing knowledge that incorporates any combination of text, graphics, animation, video, and sound

National Council for Accreditation of Teacher Education (NCATE): A council created to ensure and raise the quality of teacher preparation and teacher certification programs at U.S. colleges and universities

Organizational structure: The form of an organization or entities that collaborate and contribute to serve one common goal

Pacing guide: A suggested sequence for effective implementation and delivery of the curriculum within a particular time frame (e.g., quarter, semester, school year)

Personality theory: A branch of psychology that studies personality and individual differences

Phase: The distinguishable part of a sequence or cycle occurring over time

Podcast: A digitally recorded session (e.g., of a lecture or presentation) that can be made available electronically via download for future viewing/listening; may include any combination of audio and/or video files

Portfolio: A collection of artifacts that summarize major teaching accomplishments and strengths

Praxis II: An examination that measures general and subject specific knowledge and teaching skills; it is sometimes required for teaching licensure

Procedures: A series of steps taken to accomplish an end

Professionalism: Adhering to a set of values comprised of standards, obligations, formally agreed upon codes of conduct, and informal expectations

Race: The categorization of humans into populations or ancestral groups on the basis of various sets of heritable characteristics

Reward: The return for performance of a desired behavior; positive reinforcement

Rule: A principle or regulation governing conduct, action, procedure, or arrangement

School culture: The beliefs, attitudes, and behaviors that characterize a school

Socioeconomic status (SES): A basis or measure of a person's work experience and of an individual's or family's economic and social position relative to others, based on income, education, and occupation

Standard: A basis for comparison; a reference point against which other things can be evaluated

Standards: Uniform guidelines at the state and national level that outline the curriculum to be taught for different grades and courses; learners must master these standards in order to progress to the next grade or course

Strategic problem solving: A higher-order, cognitive process that facilitates progress toward a desired goal

Stress: The body's way of responding to different kinds of demands placed on it

Student achievement: An evaluation of performance based on a measurable standard. It may refer to academic disciplines or extracurricular activities

Student teacher (ST): A student who is teaching under the supervision of a certified teacher

Student teaching internship: A specific number of weeks spent teaching in an assigned classroom under the supervision of the classroom teacher and a university supervisor

Teacher education program (TEP): A program that provides the coursework and experiences necessary for completing requirements for teaching licensure and/or certification

Test anxiety: Excessive worry that negatively affects performance on assessments

Traits: A characteristic or property of an object or person

Transition: The act to moving from one thing to another

University supervisor (US): One who supervises or is in a leadership position and is employed by a university

Virtual field trip (VFT): A guided exploration of prescreened and thematically based web pages (including any combination of text, images, video, and audio content) that, when woven together appropriately, can create an effective online experience

WebQuest: A scaffolded learning experience using teacher-approved web resources to investigate a topic; includes an authentic, meaningful task and a structured group environment in which each member takes on a specific role and is responsible for searching for, discovering, and sharing specific information with the group

Wiki: A type of software program that allows web pages to be created and edited as a collaborative effort

Appendix A

1. I AM IN THE MIDDLE OF SEVERAL PROJECTS.

- Let people know when you have accepted other responsibilities.
- No need to make excuses if you don't have any free time.
- No one will fault you for having already filled your plate.

2. I AM NOT COMFORTABLE WITH THAT.

- You might be uncomfortable with any of a number of issues.
- It could be the people involved, the type of work, the morale implications, etc.
- This is a very respectful way to avoid a sticky situation.

3. I AM NOT TAKING ON ANY NEW RESPONSIBILITIES.

- You aren't saying that you will never help out again, just that you feel your schedule is as full as you would like now.
- Understanding your limits is a talent to be expected.

4. I AM NOT THE MOST QUALIFIED PERSON FOR THE JOB.

- If you don't feel that you have adequate skills, that's okay.
- It's better to admit your limitations up front.
- The best way to avoid feeling overwhelmed down the road.

5. I DO NOT ENJOY THAT KIND OF WORK.

- Life isn't about drudgery—If you don't enjoy it, why do it?
- Don't be afraid to let someone know you just don't want to.
- Someone else is bound to enjoy the work you don't.

6. I DO NOT HAVE ANY MORE ROOM IN MY CALENDAR.

- Be honest if your schedule is filled.
- "Filled" doesn't have to mean really filled.
- Know when you are scheduled as much as you are willing and stop.

7. I HATE TO SPLIT MY ATTENTION AMONG PROJECTS.

- Let people know that you want to do a good job for them, but you can't when your focus is too divided or splintered.
- You will be more effective if you focus on one project at a time.

8. I HAVE ANOTHER COMMITMENT.

- It doesn't matter what the commitment is.
- It can even simply be time to yourself or with friends or family.
- You don't have to justify—you simply aren't available.

9. I HAVE NO EXPERIENCE WITH THAT.

- Volunteering shouldn't mean learning an entirely new set of skills.
- Suggest that they find someone who has experience in that area.
- Offer to help out with something that you already know how to do.

10. I KNOW YOU WILL DO A WONDERFUL JOB YOURSELF.

- People often ask for help because they doubt their own abilities.
- Let them know that you have confidence they will succeed.
- You are actually doing them a favor in the long run.

11. I NEED TO FOCUS MORE ON MY PERSONAL LIFE.

- Don't be ashamed of wanting to spend time with your family.
- Having a strong family is an important priority in and of itself.
- Be willing to put your personal needs first.

12. I NEED TO FOCUS ON MY CAREER RIGHT NOW.

- Often, you have to focus your energies on a work-related task.
- You may have to give up some civic or community duties.
- If you don't do it, someone else will take on the task.

13. I NEED TO LEAVE SOME FREE TIME FOR MYSELF.

- It's okay to be selfish—in a good way.
- Treat your personal time like any other appointment.
- Block off time in your calendar and guard it with your life.

14. I WOULD RATHER DECLINE THAN DO A MEDIOCRE JOB.

- Know when you aren't going to be able to deliver a quality product.
- The reason doesn't matter—not enough time, wrong skills, etc.
- Whatever the reason is enough for turning a request down.

15. I WOULD RATHER HELP OUT WITH ANOTHER TASK.

- Saying no doesn't mean that you can't help at all.
- If someone asks you to do something you really despise, refuse.
- Then offer to help with something you find more enjoyable.

16. LET ME HOOK YOU UP WITH SOMEONE WHO CAN DO IT.

- If you aren't available to help out, offer another qualified resource.
- Helping to connect people is a valuable service to offer.
- Make sure the person you refer will represent you well.

17. NO.

- Sometimes it's okay to just say no.
- Just say it in a way that expresses respect and courtesy.
- Leave the door open for good relations.

18. NOT RIGHT NOW, BUT I CAN DO IT LATER.

- If you really want to help but don't have time, say so.
- Offer to help at a later time or date.
- If they can't wait for you, they'll find someone else.

19. SOME THINGS HAVE COME UP THAT NEED MY ATTENTION.

- Unexpected things happen that throw your schedule off.
- Accept that you may need to make a few adjustments.
- It is temporary and you will have more time when life stabilizes.

20. THIS REALLY IS NOT MY STRONG SUIT.

- It's okay to admit your limitations.
- Knowing what you can handle and what you can't is a skill.
- Your time will be more efficiently spent on something you do well.

SOURCE: Content provided by OnlineOrganizing.com—offering "a world of organizing solutions."

Visit OnlineOrganizing.com (www.onlineorganizing.com) for organizing products, free tips, a speakers bureau, and for a referral to a professional organizer near you or to get some help starting and running your own organizing business.

Appendix B

Pacing guides help teachers pace themselves so that ample time is available for addressing the required content. The following samples give you an idea of how such guides might look. As you can see, they may be presented in a variety of formats, but the purpose is consistent: to give teachers (and often parents) an idea of exactly what is to be taught and learned at specific points in the school year. The guides included here come from North Carolina (second-grade language arts and fifth-grade science curricula), Virginia (seventh-grade social studies curriculum), and California (high school algebra curriculum). Note that these are selected portions of the curriculum guides.

Pacing Guide for Second-Grade Language Arts Curriculum (Quarter 1)[1]

Unit & Week Resources		Read Aloud for Vocabulary Development NCSCOS: 3.01, 3.02, 3.03, 3.04, 3.05	Leveled Readers/ Center Introduction NCSCOS: 1.05, 3.01, 3.02, 3.03, 4.01, 4.02	Skill/Strategy NCSCOS: 2.01, 2.05, 3.02	Word Work and Spelling NCSCOS: 5.05, 5.06
Q1 WK–2	Establishing Routines and Procedures DPS Written Lesson Plans and Trade-books	*Grandpa and Bo* by: Kevin Henkes	Center Introduction and Review (Days 1–4): • Reading/ Library • Writing • Word Work/ Vocabulary Routines and Procedures to Support Independent Reading (Day 5)	Introduce, Apply, and Assess: • Predict • Author's Purpose • Draw Conclusions	High Frequency Words Word Wall Activities

(Continued)

---

[1]Accessed through Riverdeep Learning Village (http://riverdeep.dpsnc.net/lv/admin/login.jsp); specific to the school system and requires username and password.

(Continued)

Unit & Week Resources		Read Aloud for Vocabulary Development NCSCOS: 3.01, 3.02, 3.03, 3.04, 3.05	Leveled Readers/ Center Introduction NCSCOS: 1.05, 3.01, 3.02, 3.03, 4.01, 4.02	Skill/Strategy NCSCOS: 2.01, 2.05, 3.02	Word Work and Spelling NCSCOS: 5.05, 5.06
Q1 WK–3		*When I Was Little* by: Toyomi Igus	Center Introduction and Review (Days 1–4): • Science • Social Studies • Technology • Listening Routines and Procedures to Support Independent Reading (Day 5)	Introduce, Apply, and Assess: • Ask Questions • Details and Main Idea • Monitor and Fix-Up	High Frequency Words Word Wall Activities
Q1 WK–4		*Rockets and Spaceships* by: Karen Wallace	Routines and Procedures to Support Independent Reading (Days 1–5)	Introduce, Apply, and Assess: • Monitor and Fix-Up • Summarize • Author's Purpose	High Frequency Words Word Wall Activities

Pacing Guide for Fifth-Grade Science Curriculum: Landforms[2]

Day	Unit	NCSCOS Objectives	Description	Kit Resources	Additional Resources
1 2 3 4 5	5th Sci UP02	Science Strands: Nature of Science, Science in Personal and Social Perspectives	**Linking Science and Literacy** **Reading About Erosion and Landforms** Students will use informational texts to become familiar with the unique language of science		**Delta Science Reader** *Erosion*
6 7		2.01, 2.06, 2.07	**Schoolyard Models** The students will create a model of their school area	FOSS Landforms Investigation 1—Part 1 TE pgs 8–15	

[2]Accessed through Riverdeep Learning Village (http://riverdeep.dpsnc.net/lv/admin/login.jsp); specific to the school system and requires username and password.requires username and password.

Day	Unit	NCSCOS Objectives	Description	Kit Resources	Additional Resources
8		2.01, 2.06, 2.07	**A View From Above** The students make an overlay grid of their schoolyard model.	FOSS Landforms Investigation 1—Part 2 TE pgs 16–19	
9 10		2.01, 2.06, 2.07	**Mapmaking** The students make a map from their grid.	FOSS Landforms Investigation 1—Part 3 TE pgs 20–28	

Seventh-Grade Social Studies Pacing Guide[3] (August 2009)

1st Nine Weeks	2nd Nine Weeks	3rd Nine Weeks	4th Nine Weeks
Geography (USII.2c) States grouped by region *Northeast:* **Maine, Vermont, New Hampshire, Connecticut, Massachusetts, Rhode Island, New York, New Jersey, Pennsylvania** *Southeast:* **Maryland, Delaware, West Virginia, Virginia, Kentucky, Tennessee, North Carolina, South Carolina, Georgia, Florida, Alabama, Mississippi, Louisiana, Arkansas** *Midwest:* **Ohio, Indiana, Illinois, Michigan, Wisconsin, Minnesota, Iowa, Missouri, Kansas, Nebraska, South Dakota, North Dakota**	*(USII.3e)* **Negative effects of industrialization** Child labor Low wages, long hours Unsafe working conditions **Rise of organized labor** Formation of unions— Growth of American Federation of Labor Strikes—Aftermath of Homestead Strike **Progressive Movement** workplace reforms Improved safety conditions Reduced work hours Placed restrictions on child labor **Women's suffrage** Increased educational opportunities	*(USII.5d)* **Causes of the Great Depression** People overspeculated on stocks, using borrowed money that they could not repay when stock prices crashed. The Federal Reserve failed to prevent the collapse of the banking system. High tariffs strangled international trade. **Impact on Americans** A large numbers of banks and businesses failed. One-fourth of workers were without jobs. Large numbers of people were hungry and homeless.	*(USII.7c)* **Terms to know** Cold War: State of tension between the United States and the Soviet Union without actual fighting that divided the world into two camps **Origins of the Cold War** Differences in goals and ideologies between the United States and the Soviet Union (the two superpowers)—The United States was democratic and capitalist; the Soviet Union was dictatorial and communist. The Soviet Union's domination over Eastern European countries

---

[3]Accessed from http://www.pcva.us/cia/pacing_guides/Social_Studies/Middle_School/Seventh_Gradep.pdf

1st Nine Weeks	2nd Nine Weeks	3rd Nine Weeks	4th Nine Weeks
Southwest: **Texas, Oklahoma, New Mexico, Arizona**	Attained voting rights • Women gained the right to vote with passage of the 19th Amendment to the Constitution of the United States of America. • Susan B. Anthony worked for women's suffrage.	Farmers' incomes fell to low levels. **Major features of the New Deal** Social Security Federal work programs Environmental improvement programs Farm assistance programs Increased rights for labor	American policy of containment (to stop the spread of communism) North Atlantic Treaty Organization (NATO) versus Warsaw Pact **Major conflicts in the post–World War II era** South Korea and the United States resisted Chinese and North Korean aggression. The conflict ended in a stalemate.

Suggested Pacing Guide for High School Algebra I 2008–09[4]

Textbook: *Algebra I, Prentice Hall California Edition*

Time	Topics: Content & Assessment	CA Standard
14 days	***Chapter 1& 2—Introduction to Algebra/Integers and Rational Numbers***	
	Review of Fractions *(simplification and operations)* (1 day)	1.0
	Decimals/Fractions/Percents (1 day)	1.0
	Order of Operations & 1.1 vocabulary (1 day)	1.0
	1.2 & 1.4 The Commutative, Identity and Associative Properties (1 day)	1.0
	2.1 & 2.2 Integers and the Number Line & Rational Numbers (1 day)	1.0, 2.0
	2.3 Addition of Rational Numbers (1 day)	1.0
	2.4 Subtraction of Rational Numbers (1 day)	1.0
	2.5 & 2.6 Multiplication and Division of Rational Numbers (1 day)	1.0, 2.0
	2.3–2.6 Operations with Integers (1 day)	1.0, 2.0
	1.5/2.7 Using the Distributive Property *(over + and -)* (1 day)	1.0, 4.0, 10.0
	2.7 Using the Distributive Property *(factoring & combining like terms)* (1 day)	1.0, 4.0, 10.0
	2.8 Inverse of a Sum and Simplifying (1 day)	1.0,2.0,4.0,10.0
	Review/Assessment (2 days)	

[4]Accessed from http://www.acoe.org/acoe/files/EdServices/AUSDHSAlgPacingGuide200809.pdf

Time	Topics: Content & Assessment	CA Standard
15 days	***Chapter 3—Equations***	
	3.1 The Addition Property of Equality *(1-step add/subt.)* (1 day)	5.0
	3.2 The Multiplication Property of Equality *(1-step mult./div. with focus on fractions)* (1 day)	5.0
	3.3 Using the Properties together *(2-step equations)* (1 day)	5.0, 25.0
	3.3 Using the properties *(Focus on multiple ways to solve)* (1 day)	5.0, 25.0
	3.5 More on Solving Equations *(variables on both sides & combining like terms as a first step)* (1 day)	5.0
	3.5 More on Solving Equations *(0, 1, infinite solutions)* (1 day)	5.0
	3.6 Clearing an Equation of Fractions or Decimals (1 day)	5.0
	3.7 Formulas *(Solving for y in an equation with 2 variables—needs supplement)* (1 day)	5.0, 25.0
	3.7 Formulas *(Solving for various variables in a formula)* (1 day)	5.0, 25.0
	1.6 Writing Expressions (1 day)	5.0
	3.4 Expressions and Equations (1 day)	5.0
	3.10 Using Percents (1 day)	5.0
	3.11 More Expressions and Equations (1 day)	5.0
	Review/Assessment (2 days)	

Appendix C

DETAILED LESSON PLAN TEMPLATE—*GENERAL*

Your Name **Lesson Date(s)**	
Subject Area:	Grade Level:
Lesson Topic:	Duration of Lesson:

OBJECTIVES FROM NC STANDARD COURSE OF STUDY

Competency:	
Obj. #:	Objective:
Obj. #:	Objective:

Key Vocabulary	**Key Questions (at least 3)**

Materials, Resources, Technology Needed

Procedure (Madeline Hunter's 6 or 7 steps)

Anticipatory Set

What will students learn or do—based on your objective? How does this relate to what they already know? Why do they need to know it? Focus on the objective. Write exactly what you will say.

Teacher Input/Modeling

You must model the concept or skill from your objective with at least three (3) examples for a new skill, and one clear example for a skill in review. Model exactly what you will have students doing in guided practice and independent practice. This section must be described in detail. Enough detail should be given such that another teacher can walk in and teach this lesson based upon your description.

Example 1:

Example 2:

Example 3:

Guided Practice

Provide several opportunities for students to attempt the task with your guidance. This can be oral, board work, hands-on, small-group or paired work, or other active learning—but refrain from individual worksheets.

Check for Understanding

Write what you will do as students are attempting the task, in order to determine if they understand what they are supposed to do.

Independent Practice

Students are practicing the same skill or concept you taught during teacher input and that they practiced under guided practice. Students must exhibit the new skill or concept by themselves so you can see if they have mastered the criteria that you have set in your lesson objective. Limited worksheets may be used at this time.

Check for Understanding

Write what you will do as students are attempting the task, in order to determine if they understand what they are supposed to do.

Closure

Summarization of the key points of the lesson **facilitated** by the teacher. Three (3) to five (5) explicitly designed questions must be written and asked of the students to check for understanding of key concepts and content taught in the lesson. Must link back to your objective and modeling.

Assessment

How will you measure your lesson objective? This can be formal or informal.

Additional Required Components

Meeting the Needs of All Learners

Include modifications and or differentiation strategies of the designed lesson plan for other students in the classroom.

Fast-Finisher Activity

Provide another opportunity for those students who complete independent practice quickly to try the skill in a new or different way. This should be directly related to the original objective, but should not be another worksheet.

Infuse Cultural Diversity

State how you can infuse cultural diversity into the lesson plan (i.e., culturally responsive instruction, materials, and/or curricula). Go beyond the 3 F's: Food, Fun, & Family. Consider what is socially and culturally important to your students and how it can be connected to the lesson.

Infuse Technology

Cite websites used to design the lesson and infuse technology into the lesson presentation. Provide URLs for appropriate sites children can visit to practice the skill or to learn more about the concept.

Post-Teaching Reflection

After teaching this lesson, reflect on the following: What part of this lesson went really well? What might you change about this lesson if you use it again? What have you learned about teaching, learning, and children? How does this experience match with what you have been reading in the textbook and learning in class?

LESSON PLAN TEMPLATE—SMALL- OR WHOLE-GROUP READING

Book Title: **Page or Chapter:**

Group: **Level:**

Before Reading

Review/Preview

Help students call up important information using a picture walk, book preview, or summary/review of previous reading.

Challenging Content

Introduce concepts, vocabulary, language, and text features that may be unfamiliar. Pre-teach vocabulary that cannot be determined using context clues.

Focus Question

Help students focus their reading by providing a question that they will be able to answer upon completion.

During Reading

Type of Reading

[ ] Shared [ ] Echo [ ] Choral [ ] Paired [ ] Independent [ ] Flexible

Check-In (Individual)

Tune into each student's reading skills and strategies such as fluency, decoding, and comprehension. Ask questions that reflect reading comprehension. Take notes.

After Reading

Post-Reading Task (Individual)

Students will finish reading at different times, so have related and meaningful early finisher tasks ready. These should **not** be worksheets, but should relate to the use of strategies during real reading.

Post-Reading Discussion (Group)

Facilitate discussion about the main points from the selection. Be sure to use (and encourage the use of) vocabulary that was used in the text. Help students make connections to the text, themselves, and their world. Let the students do most of the talking.

Strategies (Group)

Focus on strategies good readers use. This may be a review of a strategy, or explicit teaching of a new strategy. You may also want to point out strategies that you saw students using well during the reading.

Reflection

What worked well? What will you need to remember for the next time you meet with this group or use this text?

LESSON PLAN TEMPLATE: GUIDED DISCOVERY

Your Name Lesson Date(s)	
Subject Area:	Grade Level:
Lesson Topic:	Duration of Lesson:

OBJECTIVES FROM NC STANDARD COURSE OF STUDY

Competency:	
Obj. #:	Objective:
Obj. #:	Objective:

Key Vocabulary	**Key Questions (at least 3)**

Materials, Resources, Technology Needed

Procedure (Guided Discovery Steps)
Set the Stage—But Don't State Objectives Yet!
Begin by providing just enough background information (tap into students' own prior knowledge) to provide a context for the upcoming task.

Provide Instructions

Tell students exactly what they are to do—without revealing what they will learn, discover, or observe. Be very clear. It may be helpful to have instructions displayed. Be prepared to repeat them as needed.

Guided Practice (e.g., a lab experiment)

Students attempt the task. Write what you will do during this time, in order to determine if they understand what they are to do and to see if they are reaching the expected outcomes.

Regrouping for Instruction

Stop the activity briefly. As a class, talk about what was learned or observed. Take time to clear up any misunderstandings.

State the Objectives

Tell students (or clarify) the purpose for the task. What were they supposed to learn? Why is it important? Allow opportunities for students to share their own insights, but always steer them back to the intended objective.

Independent Practice

Allow opportunities for students to reflect on their learning in their journals or small-group discussions. As you listen to or read about their learning, be sure to clear up any remaining misunderstandings.

Closure

Students should assist with summarization of the key points of the lesson. Three (3) to five (5) explicitly designed questions should be written and asked of the students to check for understanding of key concepts and content presented in the lesson. This must link back to your objective, guided practice, and regrouping for instruction.

Assessment

How will you measure your lesson objective(s)? This can be formal or informal.

UNIT PLAN ESSENTIALS

An effective unit of instruction can last from a few days to several weeks. Regardless of the time frame, or the content covered, there are several components that should be included in any unit:

- a *rationale* that justifies teaching the unit. It should argue the merits of your unit's theme and include a list of anticipated student learning outcomes, key course activities, and culminating project(s).
- a *professional resource list* compiling all sources used to create the unit (e.g., methods textbooks, teacher manuals, web-based sources, journal articles, etc.)
- a list of *materials* to be read (fiction and nonfiction books, poems, plays, student-produced texts), viewed (art, sculpture, films, PowerPoint presentations), and heard (music, audio tapes, podcasts) by students during the unit as they explore the unit's key ideas and problems
- an *introductory activity* that engages students in the unit, taps prior knowledge, and serves as a scaffold for students before they begin exploring the instructional materials

- a series of *lesson plans* arranged in an appropriate sequence to prepare students to take increasing responsibility for their own learning. The unit's lessons should feature brain-friendly teaching strategies or other research-based methods of differentiated instruction, diversity components/extension activities, and re-teaching elements. Lessons should be constructivist and include student choice, opportunities for collaboration, and technology components. They should be written thoroughly enough that someone else could teach the lesson from the plan. Each lesson should include clear student learning outcomes and link to the state standards.

- a set of formative and summative *assessments* (and accompanying *assessment rubrics*) that allow students to demonstrate the new knowledge they have constructed regarding the unit's key concepts. Prompts and formative/summative assessments must be authentic, varied, and culturally responsive. When possible, they should incorporate collaboration and problem solving.

Appendix D

Sample Resumé

_____ DIANA M. WESLEY

Telephone: (H) 555-234-6789 or (C) 555-333-1360 **E-mail:** dmw@gmail.com

Address: 123 Elm Street, Small Town, NC 27789

_____ QUALIFICATIONS

NC Elementary Education Teaching License, May 2010, North Carolina Central University (GPA 4.0)

Bachelor of Arts (Education), June 1998, University of the Free State, South Africa (GPA 3.86)

_____ RELATED EXPERIENCE

1st-Grade Student Teacher, Ridge Road Elementary School, Durham, NC
(January 2010–May 2010)

- Plan and implement developmentally appropriate lessons and learning experiences, aligned with the NC Standard Course of Study, for 1st-grade students.
- Guide students in classroom discussions in order to scaffold their learning.
- Design and facilitate cooperative learning groups focused on specific learning outcomes.
- Provide small group instruction in literacy and math to meet diverse educational needs.
- Provide classroom management to enhance the learning experience of a cohesive classroom community.

3rd-Grade Teacher Assistant, Penny Road Elementary School, Cary, NC
(August 2007–December 2009)

- Gave small group instruction and tutoring in literacy and math for ethnically and economically diverse 3rd-grade students.
- Implement lesson plans in the absence of lead teachers in Grades 3 through 5.
- Provide administrative assistance for three 3rd-grade teachers.

Substitute Teacher, Wake County, NC Grades 2–7
(April 2007–August 2007)

- Implement lesson plans in the absence of classroom teachers in Grades 2 *to* 7.

Kindergarten Literacy Center Volunteer, Baucom Elementary School, Apex, NC
(August 2006–June 2007)

- Lead literacy and reading centers two days per week for kindergarten students.
- Lead math or thematic centers one to two days per week, as requested by the lead teacher.

Self-Employed Home Daycare Provider, Apex, NC
(January 2001–April 2005)

- Provide care for two children ages 4 months through 3 years.
- Provide developmentally appropriate educational experiences for infants through preschoolers, including read aloud activities, prereading and premath skills, arts and crafts, and weekly field trips.

4th-Grade Sunday School Teacher, Bloemfontein, South Africa
(1996–1998)

Volunteer Music Teacher, St. Boniface Primary School, Kimberley, Republic of South Africa
(1994)

- Plan and implement lessons in basic music theory and soprano recorder technique for disadvantaged children ages 7 to 12 years.

Volunteer Drum Majorette Trainer, St. Boniface High School, Kimberley, Republic of South Africa (1994)

- Design and teach choreographed team drills to a squad of 50 girls in Grades 8 through 12.
- Teach baton and flag handling skills, in addition to proper posture, self-confidence, and music interpretation.

OTHER WORK EXPERIENCE

- *Armed Nuclear Security Officer*, Harris Nuclear Plant, New Hill, NC (April 2004–April 2005)
- *Armed Nuclear Security Officer*, Harris Nuclear Plant, New Hill, NC (September 1999–July 2000)
- *Office Assistant III*, Division of Prisons, Program Services, Raleigh, NC (1999)
- *Waitress* in Family Restaurants, Kimberley and Bloemfontein, South Africa (1993–1996)

I appreciate your time in considering my application for a teaching position.

Further Readings

CHAPTER 1

Cheng, Y. C. (1993). Profiles of organizational culture and effective schools. *School Effectiveness and School Improvement, 4*(2), 85–110.

Cherubini, L. (2008). Teacher-candidates' perceptions of school culture: A mixed methods investigation. *The Journal of Teaching and Learning, 5*(2), 39–54.

Deal, T. E. (1993). The culture of schools. In M. Sashkin & H. J. Walberg (Eds.), *Educational leadership and school culture* (pp. 3–18). Berkeley, CA: McCutchan.

Fyans, L. J., Jr., & Maehr, M. L. (1990). *School culture, student ethnicity, and motivation.* Urbana, IL: National Center for School Leadership.

Geertz, C. (1973). *The interpretation of cultures.* New York: Basic Books.

Hazard, W. R. (1976). *Student teaching and the law.* Washington, DC: American Association of Colleges for Teacher Education. (ERIC Document Reproduction Service No. SP009739)

Phillips, G., & Wagner, C. (2003). *School culture assessment.* Vancouver, British Columbia: Agent 5 Design.

Raywid, M. A. (2001). *Small by design: Resizing America's high schools.* Naperville, IL: North Central Regional Educational Laboratory.

Strike, K. A., & Ternasky, P. L. (Eds.). (1993). *Ethics for professionals in education: Perspectives for preparation and practices.* New York: Teachers College Press. (ERIC Document Reproduction Service No. ED 377 589)

Thacker, J. L., & McInerney, W. D. (1992). Changing academic culture to improve student achievement in the elementary schools. *ERS Spectrum, 10*(4), 18–23.

Wolk, R. (2010, April). Education: The case for making it personal. *Educational Leadership, 67*(7), 16–17.

CHAPTER 2

Johnson, S. (1998). *Who moved my cheese? An amazing way to deal with change in your work and in your life.* New York: Putnam.

Kitchel, T., & White, C. C. (2007). Barriers and benefits to the student teacher–cooperating teacher relationship. *Proceedings of the 2007 AAAE Research Conference, 34,* 710–712.

National Council for Accreditation of Teacher Education. (2008). NCATE Professional Standards. Retrieved from http://www.ncate.org/ . . . /stanards/NCATE%20Standards%202008.pdf

Rando, R. A. (2000). *Adaptive supervision in counselor training.* Retrieved from http://ccvillage.buffalo.edu/Village/ElecProj/Rando.htm

Weasmer, J., & Woods, A. M. (2003). The role of the host teacher in the student teaching experience. *The Clearing House, 76*(4), 174–177.

CHAPTER 3

Allport, G. W., & Odbert, H. S. (1936). Trait names: A psycholexical study. *Psychological Monographs, 47,* 211.

Carver, C. S., & Scheier, M. F. (2000). *Perspectives on personality* (4th ed.). Needham Heights, MA: Simon & Schuster.

Cattell, R. B. (1965). *The scientific analysis of personality.* Baltimore: Penguin.

Cattell, R. B. (1990). Advances in Cattellian personality theory. In L. A. Pervin (Ed.), *Handbook of personality: Theory and research* (pp. 101–110). New York: Guilford Press.

Conn, S. R., & Rieke, M. L. (1994). *The 16PF fifth edition technical manual.* Champagne, IL: Institute for Personality and Ability Testing.

Fairweather, A. (2005, January 29). *Dealing with difficult people.* Retrieved May 19, 2010, from http://ezinearticles.com/?Dealing-with-Difficult-People&id=12110

Funder, D. C. (2001). *The personality puzzle* (2nd ed.). New York: Norton.

CHAPTER 4

Dunham, J., & Varna, V. P. (2002). *Stress in teachers: Past, present, and future.* London: Whurr.

Joseph, R. (2000). *Stress-free teaching: A practical guide to tackling stress in teaching, lecturing, and tutoring.* London: Routledge.

CHAPTER 5

Kounin, J. (1970). *Discipline and group management in classrooms.* New York: Holt, Rinehart & Winston Inc.

Marzano, R., Pickering, D., & Pollock, J. (2003). *Classroom instruction that works: Research-based strategies for every teacher.* Alexandria, VA: Association for Supervision & Curriculum Development.

Tate, M. (2006). *Shouting won't grow dendrites: 20 techniques for managing a brain-compatible classroom.* Thousand Oaks, CA: Corwin Press.

Wong, H., & Wong, R. (2004). *The first days of school: How to be an effective teacher.* Mountain View, CA: Harry K. Wong.

Albert, L. (1996). *Cooperative discipline.* Circle Pines, MN: American Guidance Service.

Apple, M. (1995). *Education and power.* New York: Routledge.

Berliner, D. C. (1988). Effective classroom management and instruction: A knowledge base for consultation. In J. L. Graden, J. E. Zins, & M. J. Curtis (Eds.), *Alternative educational delivery systems: Enhancing instructional options for all students* (pp. 309–325). Washington, DC: National Association of School Psychologists.

Brophy, J. E., & Good, T. L. (1986). Teacher behavior and student achievement. In M. C. Wittrock (Ed.), *Handbook of research on teaching* (3rd ed., pp. 328–375). New York: Macmillan.

Byrne, R. (2006). *The secret.* Hillsboro, OR: Artria Books/Beyond Words.

Canter, L., & Canter, M. (1976). *Assertive discipline.* Santa Monica, CA: Canter & Associates.

Doyle, W. (1986). Classroom organization and management. In M. C. Wittrock (Ed.), *Handbook of research on teaching* (3rd ed, pp. 392–431). New York: Macmillan.

Glasser, W. (1999). *Choice theory.* New York: HarperCollins.

Jones, F. (1987). *Positive classroom discipline.* Santa Cruz, CA: Jones & Associates.

Jones, F. (2000). *Tools for teaching.* Santa Cruz, CA: Jones & Associates.

Kohn, A. (1993). *Punished by rewards: The trouble with gold stars, incentive plans, A's, praise, and other bribes.* New York: Houghton Mifflin.

Kohn, A., & Kohn, A. (1999). *Punished by rewards: The trouble with gold stars, incentive plans, As, praise, and other bribes.* New York: Mariner Books.

Kounin, J. S. (1970). *Discipline and group management in classrooms.* New York: Holt, Rinehart & Winston.

Marzano, R. J., Pickering, D. J., & Marzano, J. S. (2003). *Classroom management that works: Research-based strategies for every teacher.* Alexandria, VA: Association for Supervision and Curriculum Development.

Moskowitz, G., & Hayman, J. L., Jr. (1976). Success strategies of inner-city teachers: A year-long study. *Journal of Educational Research, 69,* 283–289.

Tate, M. L. (2006). *Shouting won't grow dendrites: 20 techniques for managing a brain-compatible classroom.* Thousand Oaks, CA: Corwin Press.

Wong, H. K., & Wong, R. T. (2009). *The first days of school: How to be an effective teacher.* Mountain View, CA: Harry K. Wong.

CHAPTER 6

Anderson, R. C. (1977). The notion of schemata and the educational enterprise: General discussion of the conference. In R. C. Anderson, R. J. Spiro, & W. E. Montague (Eds.), *Schooling and the acquisition of knowledge* (pp. 415–431). Hillsdale, NJ: Erlbaum.

Bodkin, R. (2006, November 5). *How to make your students WANT to pay attention in class.* Associated Content. Retrieved from http://www.associatedcontent.com/article/80395/how_to_make_your_students_want_to_pay.html?cat=4

Bowman, S. (2008). *Preventing death by lecture.* Glenbrook, NV: Bowperson.

Bush, G. (1990, July 18). Presidential Proclamation 6158. Retrieved from http://www.loc.gov/loc/brain/proclaim.html.

Dunn, R., & Dunn, K. (1978). *Teaching students through their individual learning styles: A practical approach.* Reston, VA: Reston Publishing.

Dunn, R. S., & DeBello, T. C. (1999). *Improved test scores, attitudes, and behaviors in America's schools: Supervisor's success stories.* Santa Barbara, CA: Greenwood.

Elias, M. (2005, March 30). So much media, so little attention span. USA Today. Retrieved from http://www.usatoday.com/news/education/2005-03-30-kids-attention_x.htm

Guthrie, J. T. (2001, March). Contexts for engagement and motivation in reading. *Reading Online, 4*(8). Retrieved from http://www.readingonline.org/articles/art_index.asp?HREF=/articles/handbook/guthrie/index.html

Hootstein, E. W. (1995). Motivational strategies of middle school social studies teachers. *Social Education, 59*(1), 23–26.

Jensen, E. (1995). *Super teaching.* San Diego, CA: The Brain Store.

Jensen, E. (2000). *Brain-based learning.* San Diego, CA: The Brain Store.

Johnson, L. (2005). *Teaching outside the box: How to grab your students by their brains.* San Francisco: Jossey-Bass.

Nolen, S. B., & Nicholls, J. G. (1994). A place to begin (again) in research on student motivation: Teachers' beliefs. *Teaching & Teacher Education, 10*(1), 57–69.

Nunley, K. F. (2003). *A student's brain: The parent/teacher manual.* Kearney, NE: Morris.

OECD. (2008). *New millennium learners: Initial findings on the effects of digital technologies on school-age learners.* Paper presented at the OECD/CERI International Conference, "Learning in the 21st Century: Research, Innovation and Policy," Paris

Prensky, M. (2001). *Digital natives, digital immigrants.* Retrieved from http://www.marcprensky.com/writing/Prensky%20-%20Digital%20Natives,%20Digital%20Immigrants%20-%20Part1.pdf

Sousa, D. A. (2001). *How the brain learns* (2nd ed.). Thousand Oaks, CA: Corwin Press.

Sylvester, R. (1995). *A celebration of neurons: An educator's guide to the human brain.* Alexandria, VA: Association for Supervision and Curriculum Development.

Zahorik, J. A. (1996). Elementary and secondary teachers' reports of how they make learning interesting. *Elementary School Journal, 96,* 551–565.

CHAPTER 7

Elksmin, L. K. (2001). Implementing case method of instruction in special education teacher preparation programs. *Teacher Education and Special Education, 24,* 95–107.

Sands, D. I., & Barker, H. B. (2004, Fall). Differentiating instruction in teacher education. *Teaching and Learning, 19*(1), 26–49.

Whitaker, S. D. (2001). Supporting beginning special education teachers. *Focus on Exceptional Children, 34,* 1–18.

CHAPTER 8

Boreen, J., Johnson, M., Niday, D., & Potts, J. (2000). *Mentoring beginning teachers: Guiding, reflecting, coaching.* York, ME: Stenhouse.

Bray, J. (1995). *A comparison of teacher concerns for the non-traditional student teacher and the traditional student teacher.* East Lansing, MI: National Center for Research on Teacher Learning.

Bridges to success. (2002). *Developmental phases of beginning educators.* Retrieved from http://www.tr.wou.edu/bridges/contact.htm

Bullough, R., & Gitlin, A. (1995). *Becoming a student of teaching: Methodologies for exploring self and school context.* New York: Garland.

Defino, M. E. (1983). *The evaluation of student teachers* (ERIC Document Reproduction Service No. ED240103). Washington, DC: ERIC Clearinghouse on Teacher Education.

Dewey, J. (1933). *The question of certainty.* New York: Capricorn.

Kolb D. A. (1984). *Experiential learning: Experience as the source of learning and development.* Englewood Cliffs, NJ: Prentice Hall.

Lewin, K. (1951). *Field theory in social science: Selected theoretical papers* (D. Cartwright, Ed.). New York: Harper & Row.

Lowman, J. (1984). *Mastering the techniques of teaching.* San Francisco: Jossey-Bass.

Moir, E. (1990). Teaching phases. Unpublished article originally written for publication in the newsletter for the California New Teacher Project, California Department of Education (CDE).

National Center for Education Information (NCEI). (2005). *Alternative routes to teacher certification.* Retrieved from http://www.ncei.com/Alt-Teacher-Cert.htm

National Center for Education Statistics (NCES). (2002). *Special analysis: Non-traditional undergraduates.* Washington, DC: Institute of Educational Sciences, U.S. Department of Education.

CHAPTER 9

Darling-Hammond, L. (2006). *Powerful teacher education: Lessons from exemplary programs.* San Francisco: Jossey-Bass.

Delandshere, G., & Arens, S. A. (2003). Examining the quality of evidence in preservice teacher portfolios. *Journal of Teacher Education, 54*(1), 57–72.

Goodson, F. T. (2007). The electronic portfolio: Shaping an emerging genre. *Journal of Adolescent & Adult Literacy, 50*(6), 432–434.

Knapper, C. K. (1995). The origins of teaching portfolios. *Journal on Excellence in College Teaching, 6*(1), 45–56.

Shore, B., Foster, S., Knapper, C., Nadeau, G., Neill, N., & Sim, V. (1986). *The teaching dossier: A guide to its preparation and use.* Ottawa, Ontario: Canadian Association of University Teachers.

TestTakingTips.com. (2009). *Reducing test-taking anxiety.* Retrieved September 11, 2009, from http://www.testtakingtips.com/anxiety/index.htm

Zeichner, K., & Wray, S. (2001). The teaching portfolio in US teacher education programs: What we know and what we need to know. *Teaching and Teacher Education, 17,* 613–621.

Index

About the Authors

Kisha N. Daniels has worked extensively in the areas of teaching and learning with children, public school teachers, administrators, and university students for 20 years. She holds a BA in elementary education, an MEd in school counseling, an MSA in school administration, a specialist certification in curriculum and instruction, and a EdD in educational leadership from the University of North Carolina at Chapel Hill. As a teacher and administrator in large, urban school districts, Kisha has devoted her work to utilizing engaging curriculum to support diverse learning styles. She is currently an Assistant Professor at North Carolina Central University in the Department of Curriculum and Instruction, where she teaches courses in literacy, foundations of education, and professional studies. She also supervises teacher candidates and administrative interns. Kisha is actively involved with building and sustaining community partnerships in an effort to extend the scholarship of teaching through service learning. This focus has guided her research and writings on teacher quality and the impact of collaborative teaching and community engagement to which she is credited with many journal articles.

Gerrelyn C. Patterson earned a BA in English Literature from North Carolina Central University, an MEd in English Education from the University of Virginia, and a PhD in Curriculum, Culture and Change with an emphasis on teacher education and race, class, and gender issues from the University of North Carolina at Chapel Hill. She has more than 15 years of P–12 and university teaching experience as a teacher educator and literature and composition instructor. Gerrelyn has worked as a consultant and researcher with the Comer School Development Program at Yale University, taught in the Master's in Teaching Program (MAT) at the University of North Carolina at Chapel Hill, and added to the body of work documenting school desegregation in North Carolina as a researcher with the Southern Oral History Program at the University of North Carolina at Chapel Hill. Currently, she is an Assistant Professor at North Carolina Central University where she teaches undergraduate and graduate courses in lesson planning, classroom management, and middle school philosophy. As the Middle Grades Education Coordinator, she has the opportunity to supervise student teachers in urban and rural middle schools and build service-learning partnerships between university faculty and P–12 teachers. Her passion involves training P–12 and university faculty in the areas of effective and practical classroom management, engaging instructional strategies, and service learning.

Yolanda L. Dunston has 18 years of experience in P–12 and higher education in the state of North Carolina. She earned a BA in Elementary Education, a MEd in Special Education—Literacy Studies, and a PhD in Literacy all from the University of North Carolina at Chapel Hill. Her focus is on effective teaching for both pre-service and practicing teachers, particularly in the area of literacy. She has been a teacher at the pre-school and elementary level, a private consultant for struggling middle and high school students, and an Adjunct Instructor at UNC–Chapel Hill teaching undergraduate emergent and early literacy courses. Yolanda has prepared instructional materials for Pearson Prentice Hall and is a contributing author for the text *Aftermath of Hurricane Katrina: Educating Traumatized Children Pre-K through College* with a chapter dedicated to using literacy and language strategies to help children cope and progress academically after a tragedy. Currently, she is a tenured Assistant Professor at North Carolina Central University in the Department of Curriculum, Instruction and Professional Studies in the School of Education, where she coordinates the Elementary Education program, teaches undergraduate and graduate methods courses in literacy, facilitates the student teaching seminar, and supervises student teachers in the field.

SAGE Research Methods Online

The essential tool for researchers

Sign up now at www.sagepub.com/srmo for more information.

An expert research tool

- An **expertly designed taxonomy** with more than 1,400 unique terms for social and behavioral science research methods

- **Visual and hierarchical search tools** to help you discover material and link to related methods

- Easy-to-use navigation tools

- Content organized by complexity

- Tools for citing, printing, and downloading content with ease

- Regularly updated content and features

A wealth of essential content

- The most comprehensive picture of quantitative, qualitative, and mixed methods available today

- More than **100,000 pages of SAGE book and reference material** on research methods as well as editorially selected material from SAGE journals

- More than **600 books** available in their entirety online

Launching 2011!

⑤SAGE research methods online